MW00769479

Taking the Salute

My Life

BY

ALHAJI SIR AHMADU BELLO

K.B.E., M.H.A.

SARDAUNA OF SOKOTO

Premier of the Northern Region of Nigeria

CAMBRIDGE
AT THE UNIVERSITY PRESS
1962

CAMBRIDGE UNIVERSITY PRESS
Cambridge, New York, Melbourne, Madrid, Cape Town, Singapore, São Paulo, Delhi

Cambridge University Press
The Edinburgh Building, Cambridge CB2 8RU, UK

Published in the United States of America by Cambridge University Press, New York

www.cambridge.org
Information on this title: www.cambridge.org/9780521041508

First published 1962
Re-issued in this digitally printed version 2008

A catalogue record for this publication is available from the British Library

ISBN 978-0-521-04150-8 hardback
ISBN 978-0-521-09268-5 paperback

CONTENTS

LIST OF ILLUSTRATIONS

Plates vi*a*, xiv*b*, xv*a* and xvi*a* are reproduced by kind permission
of the Northern Region of Nigeria Ministry of Information, Plate
xvi*b* by kind permission of Francis Uher

PREFACE

I HAVE not written this book through any wish to obtain further publicity, or because I like writing about myself, but because I have been persuaded to write the story of my life as it may throw some light on the development of my country during a time of change and progress in Nigeria and Africa as a whole.

I have lived through practically the whole period of the British Colonial occupation of Northern Nigeria and the final achievement of self-government and independence.

I have been called upon to play a part in this fascinating development of an independent nation, and the account of what I have done in my life may be of assistance to students and others who are interested in the differing patterns of the newly independent nations of Africa.

I have never sought the political limelight or a leading position in my country. But I could not avoid the obligation of my birth and destiny. My great-great-grandfather built an Empire in the Western Sudan. It has fallen to my lot to play a not inconsiderable part in building a new nation. My ancestor was chosen to lead the Holy War which set up his Empire. I have been chosen by a free electorate to help build a modern State.

I am not unaware that I have often been a controversial figure. I have been accused of lack of nationalism and political awareness because I considered that independence must wait until a country has the resources to support and make a success of independence. I have been accused of conservatism because I believe in retaining all that is good in our old traditions and customs and refusing to copy all aspects of other alien civilisations. I have been accused of many other things, but the views of others have never made me deviate from the path which I am certain is the one which will benefit my people and country. I have always based my actions on my inward convictions, on my conscience and on the dictates of my religion.

Many people have assisted me in different ways in the preparation of this book. They cannot all be mentioned by name, but I am most grateful to them. I must, however, mention my old friend Sir Rex Niven, whose advice and help in the preparation of this book have been invaluable—I am indeed grateful to him.

This, then, is the story of my life. The attempt of a Northern Nigerian to do his duty by his people and the principles of his religion. As is written in the Holy Koran, Chapter XI, Verse 88, 'I only desire reform as far as I can. There is no power in me save through Allah. In Him do I trust and to Him do I turn.'

AHMADU BELLO

KADUNA
9 August 1961

THE HOUSE OF FODIO

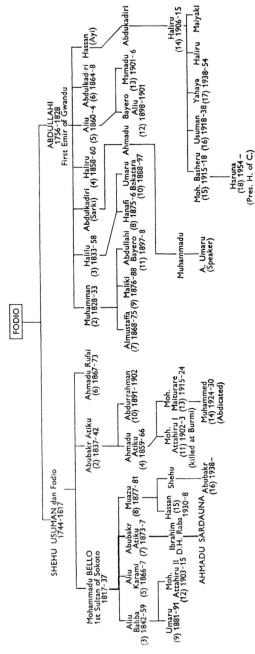

(Numbers indicate order in succession)

CHAPTER 1

MY FIRST HOME

IN THE NAME OF GOD THE COMPASSIONATE,
THE MERCIFUL, I BEGIN THE STORY OF MY LIFE
AND OF THE POLITICAL DEVELOPMENT OF
NORTHERN NIGERIA THUS—

ACROSS the northwest corner of Nigeria the Sokoto River describes a vast semicircle of nearly four hundred miles, from its source near Zaria to its junction with the River Niger; a point on that mighty waterway about six hundred miles from the sea. About half-way along this flashing arc, in its green farm land and swamps, is the modern town of Sokoto. Here the river is about a quarter of a mile wide in the rains and even in the dry season carries quite a substantial volume of water. Sokoto was founded in 1809 by my distinguished great-grandfather, Sultan Bello. I will tell you about him and the circumstances of its founding later on.

About twenty miles upstream of Sokoto and on the north bank—that is, on the opposite side of the river from Sokoto—is the little town of Rabah. It was here that I was born in 1910. My father was the District Head. There are forty-eight District Heads in Sokoto Emirate and he was one of them. Only seven years had passed since the British drove out the Sultan Atahiru from his own capital, chased him across Nigeria and eventually caught up with him and his devoted followers on the borders of Bornu. Here he made a last stand, on a deserted hillside, and died fighting, far from his people and his home.

His standard was found near his body. It was folded up and taken to England. Only this year, after Independence,

I

was it brought back and formally restored to the present Sultan at a distinguished ceremony. It had been very well preserved and was given back in a large and handsome frame.

Native administration in its present form was, of course, in its infancy and my father and the other District Heads were feeling their way. The handful of British officers were in full control. Rabah, being so near to Sokoto, and my father being regarded as heir to the throne of Sokoto, was constantly visited by them. I do not think that there was any particular antipathy against them. It was the will of Allah that they should be there; they were not evil men and their administration was not harsh; in fact, we gained much from contact with them though, of course, the real gains were to come in later years. In those early days there were hardly any technical officers, and those available seldom left headquarters—there was so much to do there.

My father was responsible for some sixty villages in eight village areas, containing about thirty thousand people. In those days there was not very much paper work. There were lists of taxpayers for each village, for the District Heads were responsible for counting the people and for the collection of their tax, though this was in practice in the hands of the Village Heads. He was responsible to the Sultan for the suppression and prevention of crime and here again he worked through the Village Heads. There were no police in these rustic places, any more than there are now. He had to use his followers and servants to arrest criminals, and so did the Village Heads.

On the other hand there was an Alkali, a native judge, in the village. It was he who heard all cases and to him my father would hand over wrongdoers. He was a good old man and very wise in the law, but we children were frightened of him and kept out of his way. The women of the house always threatened to send us to him if we misbehaved. The court was just across the little square from our house. It was a mud building; it had great thick walls and a flat mud roof; inside it was quite plain except for a little raised dais on which the old man sat to hear his cases and to give judgement. It was possible to appeal to the

2

Sultan in Sokoto if you didn't like the result of the case, but most people were content and didn't appeal. Anyhow, what poor man wanted to go into Sokoto and face a lot of haughty strangers round the Sultan's gateway?

Down a little lane to the left of our big entrance was the river. There were sheets of still water here; backwaters of the main river they were. On them grew pink and blue water-lilies. They were full of fish and that was very useful to us. But they were also full of mosquitoes and that was a bad thing, though we didn't realise it at the time. We thought that they were just a nuisance. We did not realise that they brought malaria in their sting.

There were canoes on the river and we used to go out whenever we could. We would swim there and play in the water when it was hot. In the rains the river came up and up, and sometimes would lap the walls of the lowest houses. It could be quite frightening then and the roar of the water was heard a long way away.

Our farms were up the valley behind the village. They were not far from where the motor road comes in now. We spent a lot of time on the farm. My father, being an important man, had many acres of land, very fertile land it was too. He wanted all the help he could get when the corn was ripening. I mean by this, guinea corn of course, and millet: we used to get wonderful crops of corn, for the ground was rich and not far above water. Even in the terrible years before 1914, when hundreds of thousands of people died of starvation, we didn't do too badly. I was too young to remember this, but I was told that for three years there had been little rain and the ground was parched and barren.

What we children really liked was the harvest. Then we cut off the heavy heads of corn—and each head could weigh a pound—and tied them in bundles to be pounded to separate the grain from the stalks; then they were winnowed and put into big leather sacks and taken back to the house to be poured into the huge granaries there. These were about ten feet high,

3

with a round hole in the shoulder through which a man could slip—they used to scare us by dropping us in on to the slippery corn until we screamed to be pulled out. These granaries were about six feet across at the shoulders, and when they were filled the hole was sealed with a clay plug and a little thatched roof was popped on top, just like a funny hat. By the way, they were built on big stones clear of the ground so that the white ants couldn't get into them. The grain would keep a long time in these granaries.

Then back on the farms we started cutting the thick reeds on which the corn grows. These were stacked until they were wanted; we always admired the skill of the craftsmen in the many uses they had for these reeds, making, for example, doors and beds and excellent fencing—it would even keep a goat out —and dye was made from a pigment in its skin and the leaves were used for wrapping food and so on.

The mat-makers with their sweet-smelling grass fascinated us and so did the carpenter with his simple tools. But the best of all was the blacksmith turning the cold black iron into such useful things with a few hammer blows here and there—or so it seemed to us.

When the great moon rose over the wide valley we danced, in imitation of our elders, through the nights. There were drummers and a few pipers from the village, but sometimes we got real experts from Sokoto: they were expensive but well worth it. And the men with the tame hyenas used to come and put their ugly charges through their tricks.

You must remember that all round us in the bush were many wild animals. Big hyenas came near the villages and would steal the sheep and goats if they could do so, but they never touched human beings, unless they were frightened or cornered. There were plenty of antelope of all kinds; we used to go out with the hunters to kill them. Their meat was very good. It was fun to do this, but rather a strain since we had to be so very quiet when we got near the animals, or they would run away and the hunters would say that they would never take us with

4

them again. But of course they did, for they were kind-hearted people. Some of them were very brave.

The hunters used to say: if you met a lion when you were alone in the bush, do this—stand quite still and then put down your weapons; move two or three paces slowly towards the lion and make obeisance on your knees. After all, he is the King of the Bush. Then you can go back and pick up your arms and the lion will take no notice of you.

They used bows and arrows and spears, and carried long knives in their belts. They had strange charms sewn up in leather to protect them from the dangers of the chase. There were other dangers than those from the animals, for they believed that the bush, or certain parts of it, was haunted by spirits, most of them evil. We were frightened of them too, but much more so of the great wind-devils that you could see sweeping across the plains, lifting great clouds of dust and even small animals and household stuff in their track.

We had to make our own amusements. There were, of course, no toys or games, so we loved the times when the story-tellers would come and sit in the dusk and tell us stories that I shall never forget.

As I have said, our house stood at the lower end of the town by the river. It had a big square entrance, with a domed roof. My father used to sit here with the elders and his personal servants. Here the affairs of the District were settled, and here the messengers from the Sultan were received.

Behind this was an irregular open compound with the horses tethered by the foot to wooden pegs driven into the ground. Beyond that again was another entrance passage, stacked with fodder for the horses, and beyond that my father's own house. Round this, and shut off from the front part of the house, were the women's quarters where my mother and the other wives lived with their children. Through all this wandered many clucking chickens, as they do to this day in many houses. My grandmother was a daughter of Dabo, Emir of Kano, and my mother was a Sokoto woman.

5

By the time I went to school—that is, when I was ten—there were ten half-brothers and fifteen half-sisters of mine in the house. My nearest half-brother, Shehu Malami, was six weeks older than I. On the whole we kept fairly well, but if one fell sick there was nothing that could be done about it, beyond the offering of prayers and drinking of water in which the correct charms had been washed. Some of the children died, but though I was sick from time to time God's destiny lay before me and I was brought through it. Of us all I now have only three half-brothers and seven half-sisters alive, mostly living in Sokoto or Rabah, or in Kaduna with me.

Just outside the town to the north was a round rest-house in its own compound with boys' houses behind it. It was here that the white officers used to stay when they came on tour. My father and his people used to go out along the road to meet the District Officer or sometimes the Resident, and to escort them in, in a fine cloud of dust raised by the many horses. Then he would come down to the house to greet my father and the villagers, and often they would go up to the rest-house and sit under the trees and discuss things.

The District Officers varied a great deal and some of them were very helpful, but some thought too much of their own position to think properly of others. They were always very keen on the tax being collected properly and, of course, the villagers thought that the reason for this was that they took a good deal of it, if not all, for themselves when it got to Sokoto. It wasn't till quite recently that the ordinary people really understood that the tax money went into the Native Treasury and was spent on the people of the area. Sometimes the District Officer would become ill and we were sorry for them, but there wasn't much that we could do. We children used to hang around in the bush outside the rest-house compound and watch everything that went on.

Complaints to the District Officer were the really funny things. In any village there are always a number of people who are dissatisfied about something or who feel they have been badly

6

treated, though it may have been many years ago. These people think nothing of going to the D.O. and spending the whole day waiting for an interview and, indeed, in spending quite a lot of money on bribing the messengers to let them in. We naturally knew them all very well and also knew that they went every time a new D.O. came round.

Some received petitioners very courteously, but others drove them off with blows and curses. Whatever it was, they seldom got what they wanted, but that never stopped them going up again and trying it on. Mind you, sometimes there were genuine grievances and they got a fair hearing; sometimes they were taken in to Sokoto to see the Sultan. This caused a good deal of perturbation in my father's household, as you could never be quite sure what sort of view of things would be taken in headquarters.

In those days there was no school on Western lines in the village. When we were old enough (about five years old), my half-brother and I with three sisters were sent to Mallam Garba, the Liman of Rabah. He sat under a tree or in his porch surrounded by about forty children. He taught us what he knew of Arabic: it probably wasn't very much but it proved helpful later on. We learnt the Holy Koran by heart with his guidance: he did his best to explain the Arabic to us, but sometimes it was far too deep for our young minds, and sometimes we felt that it was rather too deep even for his.

We wrote on wooden 'slates' with reed pens dipped in ink we had made ourselves. When the slates were filled with our youthful Arabic writing, we washed them off and started again.

We never saw a printed book until we went to school; there were no newspapers or magazines: the Europeans had them and sometimes they would show us the pictures but usually of the King and Queen or of soldiers and we really didn't think very much of soldiers. I believe that there were small local papers printed in Lagos, but I know they never reached us.

Our Mallam's fees were paid in kind—in grain, or meat or

7

cooked foodstuffs, and sometimes someone would give him a piece of cloth or a nearly new mat. He tried to keep discipline and on the whole he succeeded, but when he got angry and tried to beat us, everyone ran away except the one he managed to catch. We were always frightened that he would report us to our fathers, but he was a kind old man and seldom stayed angry for long.

My father died when I was six years old. He was followed as District Head by my uncle. He only survived eighteen months before he was dismissed. Then my half-brother became District Head, but my mother and I continued to live in the house through all these changes.

After two years with the old Mallam, my brother decided to send me to school—that is, to the strange new-fangled school in Sokoto, very different from the one I knew sitting under the tree. Here I was among friends, there I would be among strangers from all over the Province. I was excited at the prospect and my friends were envious and sad. The British had asked my father to send one son before, but I was too young at the time.

At last the day came. My loads were packed up and put on the carriers' heads. We mounted our horses—my mother, the District Head, my half-brother and I—and with my attendants we set off weeping on the twenty-mile journey to Sokoto. We were escorted for a mile or more by the wailing family and villagers, and could hear their lamentations long after we were out of sight. The path followed the foot of the rising ground beside the river, and Rabah was soon lost to sight behind a low spur. We always went on horseback, for the river has, oddly enough, never been used for transport: in the rains it is too wide and swift, and in the dry season it is too shallow. It was infested with crocodiles during flood, and was considered very dangerous in general.

When I reached Sokoto late in the evening I found that I was not the only sad one, but I was not lonely as were so many of the new boys, who had come from great distances: not only

8

were there many people whom I had seen in Rabah, but also there were numerous relatives—indeed, far more than I had dreamed of. I must now go back a bit and in the next chapter will tell you about these relatives and about Sokoto itself.

A village street

CHAPTER 2

MY FAMILY

My father was a son of Abubakar, known as Atiku na Rabah, who was the seventh Sultan of Sokoto and reigned for four years from 1873. During his reign there was no particular incident and life went on much as usual. All Atiku's brothers—that is, my great-uncles—were Sultans: five of them were the Sultans preceding him and the youngest followed him on the throne. Their father was Sultan Bello, the son of the famous and revered Shehu Usuman dan Fodio, the Great Reformer, as we call him. Bello, who took the title of Sultan on his father's death, was my great-grandfather.

To those who are not fully aware of the history of this part of Nigeria, I must explain a little at this point. The Shehu Usuman was a Fulani leader born about 1744 in the country then called Gobir, north of the Sokoto River—an ancient kingdom. He was not only a leader but a great preacher and a man of the utmost piety. To quote a British parallel, he was a combination of John Wesley and Oliver Cromwell. He was among a people who were nominally Muhammadan: I say nominally, for the religion had become very corrupt and many pagan practices had crept in and had taken a firm hold even in the highest quarters.

The Shehu Usuman declared a Holy War against the polluters of the faith. In 1804 he started by attacking the Chief of Gobir, one of the worst offenders, in whose territory he was living. This local war went on for some time, and it was not until 1808 that the capital of Gobir was taken and destroyed; the kingdom of Gobir then disintegrated but by no means did it die. Meanwhile, to cleanse the religion, the Shehu had organised revolts in all the great Hausa states: the Fulani living in them rose and overthrew the Hausa kings. The Shehu appointed new rulers either from among the victorious generals or from among other important Fulani. Thus two-thirds of the present Northern Region came directly under the control of the Shehu and his son Bello, to whom he delegated more and more authority until he himself finally went into retirement.

The countries which did not come under the Fulani rule were the area now known as the Bornu Province, the Plateau Province (less Wase), the Jukon, Tiv and Idoma peoples south of the Benue, and small parts of Kabba and Ilorin Provinces. Thus it extended far west of the present Nigerian borders (into modern Ghana) and deep into what is now the Cameroon Republic.

This was too much for one man to deal with and so the Shehu divided it into two portions. One was based on the ancient town of Gwandu, a hundred miles southwest of Sokoto, but still in the Sokoto valley. This was given to Abdullahi, the Shehu's brother, as first Emir of Gwandu. The capital has since been changed to Birnin Kebbi, but the same family are still on the throne and the present Emir, Alhaji Haruna, C.M.G., C.B.E., the President of the House of Chiefs, who is a distant cousin of my own, is a direct descendant of Abdullahi.

This Western Empire, as it was called, extended down the Niger and included the Nupe Kingdom, then based on Raba (not to be confused with my birthplace) and Ilorin. It was this section of the Fulani government that came up against the Yorubas, when the Emir of Ilorin was engaged in the endless wars of the last half of the nineteenth century.

The other Empire, the Eastern Empire, was based on Sokoto and included all the great Hausa states down to the Benue at Nasarawa, Muri, and Yola. This never came in physical contact with the people of the present Eastern Region, with whom our relations have usually been amicable in the last few years. Both Empires were liquidated when the British entered Sokoto, and the Emirates of Sokoto and Gwandu were confined to their home territories. The Hausa Emirates have continued to this day as they were founded by the Shehu.

It was in 1808 that Bello, not yet the ruler but his father's lieutenant, decided to build a capital at Sokoto on neutral ground. The site is a good one. The town is built on a low ridge which ends in an abrupt bluff above the Sokoto River. Though still wide here, the channel is confined between low hills and is thus narrowed, the swampy edges are not so extensive as elsewhere, and it is obviously a good site for a ford. On the other hand, the steep slopes give a strong defensive position from the north and it was from the north that the young kingdom had most reason to expect attack. On each side there are low valleys which gave added protection. Only from the south is it vulnerable and in this direction it was safely covered by their friends and relatives at Gwandu. There was an ample water supply all the year round—a very important point in that area—and good fertile ground down by the river. The fact that this valley now comfortably supports close on two million people is evidence of its fertility.

The British traveller, Clapperton, who visited Sokoto in 1824 and 1826, described it as a clean and tidy place.

The city is surrounded by a wall about 24 feet high, and a dry ditch [he wrote]. The wall is kept in good repair and there are eleven gates. The clay walls, which surround all African towns, compounds and even individual huts, give a dull appearance. . . . Animation is given by the great number of slaves and others moving to and fro or lounging or lying in the shade at the doors of great men.

By that time Shehu Usuman was dead and his tomb, inside his own house, was already an object of pilgrimage and was visited by Clapperton. He went on,

the House of the Sultan is surrounded by a clay wall, about twenty feet high, having two low tower-like entrances, one on the east, the other on the west. The eastern one is entirely guarded by eunuchs, of whom he has a great number, I suppose because the harem is on the eastern side. The whole of his house forms, as it were, a little town of itself; for in it there are five square towers, a small mosque, a great number of huts, and a garden, besides a house, which consists of one single room, used as the place for his receiving

12

and hearing complaints, receiving visitors and giving audiences to strangers. . . .

Within a few yards of it stands a large square clay tower, with an entrance in the west side. The interior of this is common in most of the great men's houses in Houssa. It is the shape of a dome, formed of eight arches springing from the ground; in the centre of which is a large bright brass basin, acting as it were in the place of a keystone to the arches, which are turned by branches plastered over with clay. From the arches, about one-third up, runs a gallery quite round the interior building, having a railing with pillars of wood, covered and ornamented with clay. There are three steps leading up to this gallery, from which everything in the dome may be seen or heard. Passages also lead from it into small rooms, having each one small window, or square hole, some appearing to be used as store-rooms, and others as sleeping-rooms. The floor of the dome was covered with clean white sand. The height might be, from the floor to the brass basin in the centre of the arches, from thirty-five to forty feet. The air inside of this dome was cool and pleasant; and Bello told me he often used it as a place to read in during the heat of the day.[1]

Clapperton on his second journey presented to Sultan Bello a large number of remarkably assorted presents, including many yards of damask, weapons, stockings, a ream of foolscap paper and two bundles of black lead pencils, a fine chronometer and, at his special request on the earlier visit, a number of books in Arabic. Among these was a copy of Euclid's *Elements*. Two days later he wrote,

saw the Sultan this morning, who was sitting in the inner apartment of his house with the Arabic copy of Euclid before him. He said that his family had a copy of Euclid brought by one of their relations who had procured it in Mecca: that it had been destroyed when part of his house was burnt down last year; and that he could not but feel very much obliged to the King of England for sending him so valuable a present.

Bello was a good scholar and read anything he could find in Arabic. He wrote a number of books, of which the most important, *Im Fakul Maisuri*, is a history of the Fulani, and *Raulat al Afkari* is about local government. Unfortunately, the fighting

[1] Extracts from *Journal of a Second Expedition into the Interior of Africa* (Commander Clapperton).

13

in various parts of Hausaland at this time, being for the most part under direction of men without Bello's understanding of the value of learning, brought about the destruction of ancient Hausa records then existing in other capitals.

Sultan Bello must have been a remarkable man, for he lived through twenty years of very testing time. The countries of Gobir and Zamfara, whose kingdoms had been destroyed by his father, revolted against him, but he subdued them finally after several campaigns. At the same time he had to control his vast empire and to advise and direct the Emirs of very distant places. It is difficult to describe how remote these places are from each other, even in these days of good roads and fast cars.

Then there were no roads at all. However important a man might be, the fastest way he could get about would be on horseback. By this method of transport it would take him nearly *forty* days to do the journey from Yola to Sokoto, travelling every day, and that takes no account of the difficulties and dangers of the route, the swollen rivers, hostile people and bandits, savage animals, sickness and accident to man and horse. And yet that is how it had to be done. Even Kano, the most important centre of the Empire then, as it is now, was twelve days' march away, and that lay across great waterless areas. The Sultan's control could not have been close or intimate, but it must have been effective.

Even at the start things were not at all easy. When the Shehu died in Sokoto in 1817 he expressed the wish that Bello should succeed him as Sarkin Musulmi, or Commander of the Faithful for the Western Sudan, while remaining as ruler of Sokoto in charge of the Eastern Empire. However, this was not known to the Shehu's brother Abdullahi, who was at Gwandu at the time and who thought he would succeed his brother as a matter of course. No sooner had he heard the startling news that the Shehu had willed otherwise than a rising broke out at Kalam Baina, near Gwandu, whose people had gone over to a rival. Things looked pretty bad, but Bello with generosity and promptitude sent men to his assistance and the revolt was crushed.

The two rulers met after the victory. Bello was on his great war-horse, Abdullahi on a mare, as befitted his position as a learned Mallam. Bello, being the younger man, made ready to dismount to salute his uncle, following strict etiquette; his uncle waved him to stay where he was and then bowed in his saddle and greeted Bello as Commander of the Faithful.

Thus by mutual tact the rift was closed. What might have been a disastrous breach was healed, and ever since then our two families have lived in perfect friendship and amity. This was just as well, as they both had their hands full in their own territories and mutual rivalry would have had serious consequences.

One of the Gwandu difficulties I have already touched on in passing. This was the state of affairs between the Ilorin Emirate and its neighbours. Though the actual ruler of Gwandu kept out of it as much as he could, the problem remained a nagging difficulty during six reigns and must have been constantly at the back of their thoughts.

In 1817 a man called Afonja was Governor of Ilorin, then an important Yoruba town and part of the domains of the Alafin of Oyo. He broke away from his master and declared himself independent. Feeling a little insecure, he made friends with a Sokoto Mallam, one Alimi; the latter called together numbers of Muslims, including Yoruba Muslims, to form an army to defend Ilorin from the inevitable attack. They say that Alimi, who was in many ways similar to the Shehu, a man of piety and learning, only lent his name and his great influence to this force. Others say that he was an ambitious adventurer only interested in carving out a kingdom for himself. However that may be, attacks were beaten off successfully. Then the Muslim auxiliaries became out of hand: Afonja enlisted Yoruba help to drive them out, but not only did they fail to do so, but Afonja himself was killed and his body was burnt in Ilorin market.

Alimi died and his son, Abdulsalami, followed him in power. But he was a very different kind of man and he asserted himself at once. He was given a flag from Gwandu and his new Emirate took its place in the Western Empire (under Gwandu).

15

From that time an almost continuous state of war existed between the Emirs of Ilorin and the Chiefs of the Yorubas, especially those of the new town of Ibadan which grew up at this time and completely overshadowed Oyo. These wars went on with varying success and at one time it appeared as though the ancient prophecy, that the Fulani would dip the Holy Koran in the sea, would come to pass. A Fulani column penetrated south of Ibadan, but the fortune of war turned against them and the chance never came back.

In the end the fighting was stopped by British intervention from the coast and Colonel Lugard's activities on the Niger at the end of the last century. These wars had reached no conclusion or proper settlement when they were interrupted, and have always caused soreness between the two races. This is still not cured and much of the difficulties of the past few years must be regarded in this light, however much it may be denied in some quarters.

The main difficulties of the Eastern Empire were revolts by the suppressed peoples of Gobir and Zamfara who had been brought under Sokoto, but other revolts broke out at intervals all over the Empire. All these took much time and energy and patience to suppress and in spite of all efforts were constantly breaking out again and again. Much trouble came from the old Hausa rulers who had taken refuge in Damagaram which is now part of the Republic of the Niger.

Sultan Bello became attached to the town of Wurno, and lived there later on rather than in Sokoto. It lies over the hills from my Rabah and in the next valley, that of the River Rima. It was here that he died in 1837, just as Queen Victoria came to the throne, so far away from us and yet destined to have so much effect on our own lives and fortunes. And it is here that he lies buried. With him are my grandfather and his two brothers, the two Alius who were both Sultans.

It is a pretty place as one descends from the hills. The river winds through a wide valley and the gentle foothills run down to it: they are covered, but not densely, with low trees, and the houses and compounds are scattered about them. It has been my privilege and pleasure, while I have been Premier, to restore this tomb of my ancestors and to surround it with a new and permanent wall.

Between the time of Sultan Bello and the present day there have been sixteen Sultans, of whom nine have been on my side of the family, that is, in the descent from Bello himself. It is not usually the custom in Nigeria, certainly not in any part of the North, for the succession to be automatically from father to son, though at times it may so happen. On the death of the ruler the small council of 'king-makers' meet and go through the extended family. They then pick the most *suitable* candidate for the appointment: he may be from the late ruler's family, or may be from a parallel family having a common ancestry. In Sokoto, for example, the succession has varied between Sultan Bello's family and that of his younger brother Abubakar Atiku (who was Sultan from 1837 to 1842). I have included a genealogical table to illustrate this. (See p. x.)

Until recently the Governor had the legal right to approve the selection of the 'king-makers' at his discretion, but before Independence a Council of Chiefs was set up who go into the whole matter and whose advice must now be accepted by the Governor. They also concern themselves with the conduct and 'discipline' of all grades of chiefs.

On the 15th March, 1903, a British column reached Sokoto from Kano under General Kembal and Colonel Morland: there was only a little fighting at Sokoto and there were no casualties on either side. The heaviest engagement was between the Kano people under their Waziri and the British advance guard near the great rocks of Kwatarkwashi, 140 miles from Sokoto. Today the railway runs a few miles to the west of this place and there is a good all-weather airfield just beyond it. It lay on the direct route from Kano which the British were following; some of it runs through difficult country.

The Emir of Kano had in fact been on a visit to Sokoto and Wurno at the time of the march on his capital and was returning with the escort he had with him when they fell in with the British column. He had not 'fled' from Kano as the High Commissioner said in his report. This was due to a confusion with some of the Emir's Councillors who had got away just before the attack.

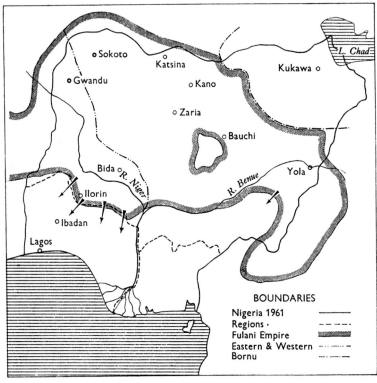

BOUNDARIES

Nigeria 1961	————
Regions ·	– – –·– ·
Fulani Empire	▓▓▓▓
Eastern & Western	–··–··–
Bornu	–·–·–

Looking at it all now with all my present knowledge I see that the constant fighting bore heavily on the people: that the Courts were just and carried out the law faithfully within their rights; that the taxation, though not unjust in principle, was sometimes unfair in its incidence, and, as has happened so often in all parts of the world at various epochs, the lowest class, being the least influential and unvocal, suffered more than it should have. Changes were bound, in the nature of things, to come; we could not have resisted external influences much

18

longer and, even if some had wished to do so, the effect of education, which too must have come to us before very long, would have forced a general tidying up.

Whatever the rights and wrongs of the attack on Kano and Sokoto may be, the British were the instrument of destiny and were fulfilling the will of God. In their way they did it well. Even at the actual time there was no ill-will after the occupation. We were used to conquerors and these were different: they were polite and obviously out to help us rather than themselves. We soon realised the difference between Lugard's government and the ambitions of the Royal Niger Company. Though they chased the Sultan across the country and killed him, they supported the new Sultan Muhammadu Atahiru, my father's first cousin, who was ruler when I was born, and his Councillors.

They made no drastic changes, and what was done came into effect only after consultation. Everything went on more or less as it had done, for what could one Resident, an assistant and a few soldiers in Sokoto do to change so vast an area as Sokoto Emirate? The new position was so generally respected that when the unfortunate outbreak took place at Satiru the Sultan was among the first to go to the help of the British in Sokoto.

Another matter which caught the imagination was that the incident which actually started the Shehu Usuman dan Fodio on the Fulani wars took place in 1803. A prophecy was made known that the Fulani Empire would last for one hundred years. No one then was greatly surprised when its end came on the grazing ground outside Sokoto almost exactly one hundred years later. Exactly fifty-six years later, to the very day, the Northern Region was granted self-government when the British Governor handed over power to me and my government on the balcony of gleaming Lugard Hall in Kaduna.

CHAPTER 3

SCHOOL AND COLLEGE

WHEN I went to Sokoto to school, Muhammadu Maiturare was the Sultan (1915-24): he belonged to the Atiku branch but was, of course, one of our relatives. In fact, there were literally hundreds of relations in and near Sokoto and I cannot say that I knew them all: some were very distant indeed, but they were all kind to me.

Among my friends at school were Maigari Gwamba, Alhaji Ibrahim of Gwandu and others, who have done well in local affairs. The first of these is still with us, a trusted friend and assistant, a Gwamba Fulani of Gwamba who is not as old as he looks. At present he is my Chief of Protocol.

We used to go to the Sultan's house every Friday and he would give us Kola nuts to encourage us in our work. This was, of course, after the general gathering for prayer; a large number of the family used to be present every week and everyone took their places in strict precedence although the schoolboys used to keep together.

The school was over to the south of the town quite close to the old town wall, more or less where the ECN power station is now. It was known as the Sokoto Provincial School and was maintained by Government and not by the Native Authority. There were no other modern schools in the whole of the vast province. The buildings were, of course, all made of mud—everything was in those days, even the Resident lived in a mud house, and very good they were too. In many ways they were preferable to concrete houses and far more preferable to those of modern design. They were very cheap, and quick and easy to build and just as easy to alter. Our craftsmen were excellent and brought in new techniques shown them by the Europeans.

The classrooms were long narrow rooms with lofty mud vaults in the classic style: there were shutters over the window openings and the floor was of hard beaten earth. This kept them cool and pleasant to work in. Only in the rains when the shutters had to be lowered were they awkward, for they became very dark and it was almost impossible to see our books.

We were not given books at first; we had to learn how to form the letters and we copied them on to slates. This stage did not last long and we were soon promoted to writing in ink and reading from books. We were taught in Hausa and the books were, of course, in that language. By the time I went to school there were a number of these available, but they do not compare with the variety that is now obtainable even in small shops in the towns.

After two years, when we had mastered the principles of reading and writing, we were put on to English and after a while we were taught some subjects in English, without any Hausa aids. Arithmetic and geography and history were taught, together with readings of the Holy Koran. The history, oddly enough, was that of England so far as detail went, though we had a good deal of world history as background, hard as it was for us to take in. Meanwhile we went on with our Arabic.

I was a very keen student: indeed, most of my school fellows were, and I cannot remember an idle boy. Learning was so important to us that we gave every minute to it. I remember I used to work into the night (as I do to this day) studying my books and learning my lessons. Of course, we had no proper lamps in those days and I used raw cotton as a wick in an earthenware bowl full of groundnut oil. It gave a smoky light, but it was better than nothing.

There used to be a good many interruptions, for often some of the other boys would come into my hut and discuss what we had learnt or had heard the teachers talking about. Then I would be expected to give them some food. Things were, however, very cheap then and for sixpence I could get enough from the market to entertain quite a number of boys.

There were two of us to a little round hut with a thatched roof. There was nothing in the hut except a sleeping-mat and a box for each one's clothes. It could be very cold round Christmas and at the height of the rains.

We were fed by the school kitchen and ate the food in wooden dishes in our huts. The food was very plain but quite good, and we thrived on it. I was very thin when I first went to school, but grew steadily. A dish of gruel and a bowl of mashed guinea corn or rice twice a day was what we got. Sometimes there was fish—there was plenty of fish in the great river—and sometimes meat, mutton or beef. We didn't have the sweets and cakes that they have in British schools and on the whole our teeth were the better for it. But that is not to say that we didn't have sweet things, all growing people must have them. There are excellent confections made out of honey and wheat or grain flour that are obtainable everywhere in the North. We had a little money to spend on this kind of thing; my pocket money was not more than £1 4s. 0d. a month. It does not sound very much, but it seemed plenty to us.

Talking of teeth, if anything went wrong with one's teeth, there was little that could be done about it except to have them taken out, and that was a painful process. I remember to this day when I had my first tooth extracted by a barber mercilessly with nothing to relieve the pain.

In the same way if we fell sick it had to be pretty bad before the doctor would come and see us. His real job was to look after the soldiers and the government servants, black and white, and he had little time for anyone else. Besides, some of them were very lazy and did not bother much.

Some of the Europeans used to come to the school and talk to us and explain things, but even at that early age we realised that there were vast differences between the various Europeans we came across. Quite apart from national characteristics, such as accents and funny ways of talking, they differed in their natures to an extent out of our experience.

Within sight of the school across the open grazing grounds south of the town we could see the square fort with its mud walls and big gates and the sentries behind the parapets, pacing eternally. There were a few houses inside the walls, but most Europeans lived in mud houses outside in a little group. We did not like the soldiers: they were our own people and had conquered us for strangers and had defeated our people on the plain just before us.

This feeling was very common all over the North. It is only recently that we have accepted the idea that soldiers are a necessary body of men and that they are the ultimate sanction for the maintenance of the peace and that they are doing the duties of the profession they have taken as their own for their lifetime. Fortunately we have never been bossed about by white soldiers. Do people realise that Nigeria is one of the very few countries in the world in which white regiments have never played any part? Indeed, I don't suppose many people realise how tiny a force there is here at present to keep the peace among so very many millions. It may well be that there are not enough of them.

However, the officers were quite good people, and so long as they had plenty of polo and could go out shooting game or birds they were well content. We envied them this life to some extent, for we never had the chance of following these pastimes.

We played games, football, rounders, and fives. These did us a lot of good and were not hard to learn. We had one teacher who was responsible for all this.

Our headmaster was a man from Jema'are. He had been taught in the Kano Nassarawa School. The other teachers were all of Hausa and Fulani extraction, local men. We certainly owe them a real debt: they put our feet on the way of education and gave us a really good start. Little did they know how far some of us would be going and how useful to the country their early efforts were going to be.

There was one Education Officer for the whole province and so we didn't see much of him except in the distance, for all that his office was in the school compound. He had to get round all the six Emirates that then made up the province, and try to get people interested in education. This was harder than you might have thought. There was a good deal of conservatism and feeling against modern education and teaching of new subjects. Many people did not want to lose their children's help just when they were starting to be useful on the farm. This applied even more to girls' education.

These factors are still to be found and have to be fought against: very different is the position in the South where there is great competition to get into the schools, and that in spite of the fees that have to be paid. In the North education has always been free. There was a small nominal fee for the Middle School, but in practice hardly anyone paid it and every conceivable excuse was presented for not doing so. Where there was no chance of getting the fee paid, the pupil was held to be a Native Administration 'scholar'. In spite of this very generous treatment, it was difficult to get pupils for the schools until recently.

Now things are beginning to change, and people even in remote villages are beginning to see that there is an advantage in this new development. In some ways the North was fortunate in its slow start, for we have been able to absorb almost all our educated people and there has been no unemployed class of intelligentsia.

Naturally there were boys who never made the grade, who were dismissed before they had completed the course, a process described by the educationists, rather heartlessly, as 'wastage'. Most of these went back to their families and did not create a problem. Some of them did useful work in minor Native Authority posts.

On the other hand the 'slow start' went on too long and it would have been much better if the pace had been increased much faster in the last twenty years than was the case. For now demand has increased far beyond supply. As is well known we are suffering severely from lack of sufficient educated people to fill the available posts, whether in Government or in Native Administration or in commerce. And yet it would be intolerable for us to be forced to take into our service otherwise unsuitable people just because they have attained a reasonable educational standard; we must also insist on good character and genuine merit and a capacity for hard work if we are to make full use of the great resources at hand here.

I said just now that the teachers in Sokoto produced many men of merit and of eventual service to the country; but, as in other schools and colleges, there were a number of pupils who passed the full course very successfully and never achieved much success in later life, honourable though their careers undoubtedly were. This applies, I imagine, to schools anywhere in the world: scrutiny of lists of old boys of most distinguished schools and colleges will, I am sure, show that only quite a small proportion achieve success in adult life and very much fewer reach the top of the ladder they set out to climb.

But to go back to my days at school. We had two holidays a year and it was with the greatest delight that we got on to our horses and rode back across the plains or the swamps, according to the time of year, to our homes and respective families. I used to take my school books home with me and do what I could to get on with my studies, but there were many distractions at home and it was not at all easy to do so.

At the end of each term we sat for examinations and I am glad to say that I did quite well at these tests and even to some extent enjoyed them. In the last examinations I passed out, after five years, as top in the class. We also had essays to write and general knowledge papers. Here we were rather handicapped, as we had few books of reference or books on general subjects. There were few people to talk to us about anything even outside our own province, but we did our best. Our favourite subjects were history and arithmetic.

I hope we do not sound rather a prim lot, perhaps even bookworms, for we were really just like other boys and enjoyed our

25

games and jokes and tricks. I remember the time when we used to go on paper-chases in the winter whilst the cold harmattan wind was blowing—bitingly cold it was.

On the other hand there was never any suggestion of indiscipline or failure to keep the rules; northern boys on the whole are very well-behaved and questions of discipline rarely a bother to the headmaster. The rules were simple and reasonable and not likely to cause friction. It is the petty restrictions that make people annoyed, I find: major matters do not have the same effect. The only one that bore hardly on us was that we were not allowed out in the town; the townspeople, however, used to come to the school and sell us small things for use or for food. The teachers were kind and patient and rarely lost their tempers with us; in fact, they were seldom even indignant.

In 1926 the time came to set out on the next step in my education. At this period the most advanced training to be had in the north was at Katsina College, which was, in effect, for the training of teachers. There was such a general shortage of good teachers that all promising boys were entered here for the five-year course. And a very good course it was; much of the teaching was in the hands of Europeans. Katsina boys have always been distinguished by the excellence of their English and especially of its pronunciation.

This was entirely due to the care that was given to the teaching, for all subjects were taught in English from the start and any slipshod speech by the students was immediately jumped on. We had to go on saying the offending word until we got it perfectly, then we never forgot it. The result was well worth while. British visitors have frequently commented on the excellent English spoken by the educated Northerner: this was due to the careful teaching in the first place and to the way in which it was passed on to generations of pupils.

Katsina is about 170 miles from Sokoto by the most direct route. We walked it with our carriers bearing our loads. It took us seven days without any rest, except at nights. It was hard going, for much of it was sandy and bushy and the weather was

26

very hot indeed. We could not use horses because part of the route was infested with tsetse fly.

When we reached the jungle area known as the Dajin Rubu, I was going lame and could only walk with very great difficulty. Eventually, we reached a place called Dumburum, right in the centre of this country and there we stopped for a rest.

While we were resting we heard the roaring of lions. I had never heard it near by before and thought that it was the sound of cattle mooing—the sounds are not dissimilar. I thought to myself, as the District Head's son, what a lot of cattle tax they must be able to collect even in such a lonely place. Then a passing hunter shouted, 'Don't you hear the lions roaring? If you want to get away safely, you had better get moving quickly.'

You have never seen anyone move as fast as we did. My lameness vanished like magic and we never halted until we had reached the nearest large town fifteen miles away.

On one of these journeys it was very cold in the harmattan wind. Our master, Mallam Nagwamatse, was with us with his family. We lay on the bare ground: we hadn't enough blankets and, though we got out of the wind as much as we could, it was bitterly cold.

I know that Europeans laugh at us when we talk about it being cold here, so I feel perhaps that I should justify this a bit. During the height of the rains—that is, in August—and during a mild harmattan—that is, January—the lowest temperature may be about 50° F.—a modest figure for Europe. But in a bad harmattan, when the wind has been blowing for several weeks and the dust brings visibility down to four or five telegraph poles—about 300 yards—then it can fall below 40°, and that is cold anywhere out of the Arctic. Further, the temperature round 3 p.m. may be in the 80s and that gives you a drop of 40° in a few hours. Such a severe change is rarely experienced in Europe.

In 1958 Tim Johnson, who was then Resident Kano, found ice on the fire buckets at the airport, and you can also find it in a severe season in swampy depressions of the high

Plateau. To us who are used to heat and who do not normally wear anything thicker than cotton, this cold can be very trying; it seems to paralyse some people's minds as well as their bodies.

We did this trek on foot for the first two years and it was not until 1928 that we were lucky enough to get ourselves taken there by motor lorry over the new roads—rather a long trip it was but how much more comfortable and sensible than stumbling through the bush. Even by lorry it took two days.

Katsina College was officially opened in 1922 by Sir Hugh Clifford, the Governor of Nigeria, with considerable ceremony. It was a matter to which he attached great importance and his opening speech was formally published in the official *Gazette*. This is part of what he said:

This College is designed to serve all the Muhammadan Emirates in Nigeria, and, as you are aware, the young men who will receive in it their training are drawn from every part of the Muhammadan States. It was necessary, however, to select some place at which to establish this College; and it was for two reasons that I selected Katsina as the most appropriate place for the purpose.

The first of these reasons is that Katsina in ancient days was held in high repute throughout the Muhammadan Emirates as a seat of learning and of piety; and it is good, I think, that this tradition should be perpetuated. My second reason was that Katsina, though it is an important town and the administrative capital of an important Emirate, is not as yet so close to the railway and to the commercial centres of Nigeria as to make it unsuitable for that quiet and tranquillity and that freedom from distractions which are so necessary for young men who are devoting their lives to study.

It is very necessary that the youths who will receive their training in this College, and who will thereafter carry the torch of learning and knowledge to all parts of the Muhammadan Emirates in order thereby to enlighten the ignorance of their countrymen, should concentrate all their energies and all their attention upon the task that is set them during their period of training. That they should cherish no other desire or ambition than that of fitting themselves by a long course of training for the great work of teaching others the things which they here will learn. And that while living in this College the ordinary lives of young Muhammadan men of birth and standing, they should be subjected to no influences which might tend to make them careless about the observances of their religious duties, forgetful of the customs and traditions of their fellow countrymen or lack-

28

ing in the respect and courtesy which they owe to their parents, to all who occupy positions of authority and to all old people.

For to these young men will hereafter be entrusted the duty of training and instructing the boys who attend the Provincial Schools in which they will later be employed. And it will fall to them to teach those boys, not only the lessons learned from books which they will here acquire, but the way that good Muhammadans should live, the good manners, good behaviour and the courteous deportment without which mere booklearning is of little worth.[1]

These principles were faithfully carried out and the exhortations were always in our minds.

The College lies just inside Katsina town: though it is now known by another name the site is still used for higher education and some of the original buildings still exist. They were much the same as those of the Sokoto school, being made of mud with vaulted roofs. But here the students lived in 'Houses' on the British public school principle: the idea was to give a corporate team spirit and teach the boys to work as one unit and in competition with other units.

In 1930 there were six Houses in the College and I was the head of the one called Illela. This won the banner for cleanliness, but perhaps we were rather more pleased by winning the prize for cricket. I was very fond of this game and did so well in it that I was given my College colours in my last year, 1930. We used to play against each other's Houses and sometimes against European teams.

My favourite game, however, was fives. This had been introduced by Mr S. J. Hogben who had been at Eton. He brought to us the Eton variety of the game—among other differences it has a little spur wall on one side which adds a great deal to the complexities of playing. It is a first-class game and is the quickest way of getting exercise if you haven't much time. We now want to persuade people to play it all over the North.

I was captain of this game at Katsina, and taught a lot of men who have now reached positions of prominence in the

[1] Extract from speech by Sir Hugh Clifford, G.C.M.G., on the Opening of the Training College for Muhammadan Teachers at Katsina on Sunday, the 5th March, 1922.

service of Nigeria. I, and some of my colleagues, still put in half an hour or so of an evening, whenever we get the chance: and we are teaching young people to play it. I felt greatly honoured when, on one of my visits to Great Britain, I was invited to play the game at Eton. As a result of this a fives team from that college came out here in 1961 to give us a run for our money. It is a simple game since it does not require any equipment once you have got the court. Though it is 'simple' in one sense, it is quite difficult to play.

We were well taught at all games, and even at sports, though most of the events were quite natural to us, we found that proper coaching and training improved our performances a great deal. I was best at fives and cricket, but competed in all events.

At Katsina they played polo. The teams of Europeans and Africans were well worth watching, and though I was never very excited about polo myself, I am always glad to see a game. After all, we were practically brought up on horseback and anything to do with horses comes as second nature to us.

My classmates included a number of people who are now in prominent positions in this Region. There was, for example, Alhaji Shehu, the Madaki (Master of the Horse) of Kano and Deputy Speaker of the House of Assembly; the ex-Emir of Dikwa, Mustapha; Alhaji Muhammadu Ngileruma, Permanent Representative of Nigeria at the United Nations in New York; Alhaji Maigari Gwamba, who was at school with me as I have mentioned; Mallam Hassan, Makama of Abuja, a member of the House of Assembly, and Alhaji Ibrahim Demsa, who is now working in the NRDC offices.

Apart from these, there were others who were there either just before me or just after me; among them were the Prime Minister of the Federation, Alhaji Sir Abubakar Tafawa Balewa, Alhaji Aliu, the Makama of Bida (now Northern Finance Minister), and Alhaji Isa Kaita, Minister of Education. In fact, the list is quite extensive, for at least three-quarters of those who coming from the Northern Region have held office as Minister of the Federation, or of the Region, or as chairmen, or members of Boards of various kinds have been ex-students of Katsina College.

You will see by this list of names that my friends came from widely different places, as did those whom I have not named. We had to adjust ourselves to living with strangers and people of different ways of life and thought. In fact, my House was mostly made up of Kanuri and they ragged me a great deal, especially the man who became Shettima Kashim, now Waziri of Bornu. He was a year senior to me and is one of my lifelong friends.

We soon got used to mixing with these strangers and we got on well in spite of these differences; the friendships we made then have gone on through the years unbroken and indeed unchanged, and there has been quite an unusual solidarity between us. Except for Kanuri we had the common link of the Hausa language, but we were all Muslims. There were no people from non-Muslim areas among us. I see now that this was perhaps a fault; it might have been better to have had more varieties of men in the College. Anyhow, a similar College should have been established for non-Muslims, but that was not part of Sir Hugh Clifford's plan. He had in mind the special colleges for princes, I think, which they had in India.

As he said, Katsina has always had a considerable local reputation for learning, taking its place after Timbuktu in this respect. For centuries people have come from all over West Africa to sit at the feet of the learned Mallams of Katsina to improve their knowledge and to enlarge their experience. It has been claimed that there was in effect a University there, but in these days of specialised meanings it would probably be unwise to use so definite a name for this rather casual and flexible arrangement. It was, however, probably not unlike the Universities of the Middle Ages in a general way.

To this day there are different quarters in Katsina town named after the people who came and lodged there, e.g. the Ward of the Songhai, or of the Melle, or of the Asben from the north. Though there are no longer the unorganised learned

Mallamai, there are still plenty of very intelligent and well-informed people there.

The Katsina people, since they speak the same language, are among those known collectively as Hausas; but there are considerable differences in custom, habit, and way of thought between them and my own people in Sokoto, and indeed between them and the people of Kano who are only a hundred miles away. To that extent we felt that we were among strangers, but they were very kind to us and did all they could to help us.

The old Emir Mohammadu Dikko was a remarkable man and one greatly respected; in many ways he was very like his son, the present Emir, especially in intellectual curiosity, which is so strongly marked in both of them. We used to see him from time to time and sometimes he would come round on an unofficial visit to the College; this we appreciated very much, and not only for the honour he did us but also for the presents he left behind.

The Head of the College was G. A. J. Bienemann, and among the staff the most conspicuous were Gerald Power, C. R. Butler and C. E. J. Whitting, but they were all very kind and helpful to us.

Here I made my first acquaintance with a good library, and here I found for the first time the variety of subjects and interests that lay before those who could read and understand their contents.

While I worked for all I was worth and learnt everything that came my way, and, as at school, read far into the night, I found here for the first time the relaxation and excitement of adventure stories. I was absorbed by tales of courage and endurance and determination, whether they were fiction or fact, and so were my friends. For this reason we have always had a respect for the European explorers and for those who through their own personalities have overcome difficulties and survived tribulation.

We had a very full curriculum and we worked hard; again I was most proficient at mathematics, but passed out very well in all subjects. Our teaching staff did the best they could for us and we are very grateful to them for their patience and care.

Probably the most valuable, however, were the unofficial, out-of-school contacts, when all sorts of subjects were discussed and we learned about the outside world. There were, at that time, only a few administrative officers and hardly any technical people—a doctor, an engineer, an inspector of works—but quite a number of education officers. There were no soldiers. Until the previous year Katsina and Daura had been part of Kano Province; then they came under Zaria, which was not at all a good arrangement.

You must remember that we were still very much cut off from the rest of the world. The main line of the railway, it is true, reached Kano as early as 1913 and a new branch had been built to Kaura Namoda in 1929, via Gusau, but we had never seen a train, much less had we travelled in one. We had not even been to Kano, and Lagos was just the name of a remote town where that mysterious body called the 'Government' resided and from which occasionally—very occasionally—high officials would venture out to visit places as remote as Katsina.

Nigeria in those days was practically unknown to the outside world, just as much as it was unknown to us. Visitors were very few and far between: those who came had to come by sea. That meant a month on the two voyages and naturally busy people were not able to come unless there were very strong reasons. The Gold Coast, as it was then, might have been as far away as the United Kingdom and its people as foreign. This was a great pity: we would have gained a lot from mutual intercourse. But it was impossible and it was no one's fault. Now it is so easy to get here by air that one tends to forget how utterly remote we were until the first Air Mail services: these came to us from Khartoum once a week by the old Imperial Airways.

We didn't know much about aeroplanes, though we knew that they had been seen at Kano, where they had landed on the polo ground, and at Kaduna, where they had landed on the race-course. We never imagined for a moment that we should not only use these wonderful appliances, but do so with pleasure; and not only use them as passengers, but be in a position to hire them, great or small, whenever we wanted to; still less that we would actually have several of our own entirely at our disposal.

We never dreamed that people of every degree of importance would come out of the skies to visit us or that a British Royal Princess would fly from Kaduna to Sokoto or Maiduguri, as happened in October 1960. Still less did we expect the Queen herself to come among us from the sky in her grace and majesty.

Anyhow, we were very cut off. Naturally it never occurred to us at the time that we were so isolated, any more than it does now to a family in the mountains of Adamawa, but, in fact, we were, as we now appreciate.

We kept pretty well, all things considered, apart from colds and fevers. The doctors in Katsina took rather more interest in us than those at Sokoto; we were a more important institution than a 'mere school'. But in spite of that we still suffered from toothache and there was no dentist. The doctor had equipment for pulling teeth, but naturally we didn't want that to happen if it could possibly be avoided.

There were few cases of serious illness, the worst were guinea-worm and malaria; outside the college walls there were great epidemics in the dry season of cerebro-spinal meningitis; at that time there was no cure for this dreadful disease and even if there had been there were no doctors to administer any treatment.

CHAPTER 4

SOKOTO AND RABAH

AFTER the five years' course at Katsina we dispersed to our respective Provinces. The real purpose of that course had been to train us as teachers, and so when we got back home we naturally became teachers. Advanced education in the North was then devoted to teacher training, and this is the reason why the large majority of those from the North, who at present hold positions of importance in Nigeria, started their working lives as teachers. Some of them continued for years in this profession— as, for example, Sir Abubakar, the Federal Prime Minister—but others switched into other activities, mostly in branches of the Native Administration.

I was appointed by the Sultan to be a teacher, or, as we say, Mallam, in the Sokoto Middle School, and so I became a Native Administration employee. This was, in fact, my old school, rather transformed and under a new name. The old Provincial School had been expanded upwards, to take in a higher level of education, and a crafts school had been added to it. There was a Sokoto man, M. Sani Dingyadi, as headmaster; he became a prominent member of the NPC, and later a Nigerian Senator. The British Education Officer took a keen interest in what was going on. He was supposed to let the headmaster have a free hand: in this, some were better than others. The one I remember best in this respect was Mr Norwood.

There was also a Crafts officer, a Mr Nicholson, who was personally in charge of the crafts side. Here the boys were taught practical work in the wood-working shop and the blacksmith's forge and so on. Those who had a natural bent for this kind of work sometimes specialised in it and did good work after they left school in this particular sphere. Many boys did not like it at all, and the sons of important people used to despise it and think that it was beneath their dignity. We persuaded them out of this attitude in the end. This side was scrapped as an economy during the great 'slump' of the early 'thirties: it was an unfortunate and short-sighted decision and a lot of ground was lost.

So far there was no girls' education. Some years were to go by before the first attempts in this direction were made: the same difficulties arose here as had arisen about boys' education. These are still not yet fully overcome and the position is further confused by the early age for marriage, just before the school-leaving age, that the parents are accustomed to. It is not often realised that to make drastic changes in the way of life of communities, to alter customs that have continued since the beginning of memory, presents not only grave spiritual difficulties but may well provoke a danger to the peace that might affect great numbers of innocent people. So we have had to be careful.

I was appointed at a salary of £60 per annum, and was responsible for teaching the top and bottom forms English and geometry. This did not worry me particularly, but I must admit that I was dismayed when I was told that I was to teach Arabic as well. While I knew that I was well-grounded in the language, I also knew its difficulties and the difficulties that lie in trying to teach it. However, I had to tackle it and did the best I could.

In those days I was still known by my school name of M. Ahmadu Rabah, from my birthplace, or as Daudu Rabah, i.e. heir presumptive to the throne of Rabah.

My report from Katsina said that I was athletic and good at dealing with people, and so I was given charge of games and sports. This, I must say, I enjoyed very much, though it made a long day of it and I was usually very tired by evening. I had sometimes as many as 300 exercises to correct in an evening. I tried not to let this sort of thing interfere with conversa-

36

tion and, especially, with my reading times, but it was difficult to avoid it and I had little chance of going into the town or to the canteens, as some of my colleagues did.

I had those days in mind when in the course of a speech in the old House of Assembly—in July 1951 it was—I said, 'I think that teachers deserve the greatest respect. Teachers are confined mostly to school premises. Those who are not on the school premises are in their houses trying to prepare lessons. What leisure are they enjoying?'

Among the boys I dealt with there were some very intelligent characters: most of them were pretty good, but some were outstanding. Among these were the present Magajin Gari, a leading Councillor of Sokoto, and Alhaji Umaru Gwandu, a distant cousin of my own, who is now Speaker of the Northern House of Assembly. There were also the Waziri of Gwandu, M. Umaru, M. Usuman Madawakin Gwandu, and many others.

My fellow teachers, who were, of course, older than I was, were good men and my relations with all of them were very friendly.

The three years during which I was teaching in the Middle School were those of the slump. Looking back on that time, I doubt whether we were really conscious of what was happening. The fact is that, though the Government of Nigeria as a whole suffered severely owing to the terrible fall in world prices for primary products—that is, for the oil seeds, groundnuts, palm kernels and the like—the effect on the individual in, say, Sokoto was comparatively slight. The price of groundnuts dropped from £6 a ton to £2 10s. which is 2s. 6d. a donkey load; but this was not as overwhelming individually as it would be now.

As it was, the people of the old Southern Provinces suffered more severely, since palm oil played a greater share in their lives. You see, in those days the export of groundnuts was small —200,000 tons was a good crop; nowadays 500,000 tons is considered to be on the low side. The price was very meagre and the amount that any individual brought to market was much smaller than it is now. He used the money so earned for

37

paying his taxes and for buying imported goods, mostly a little cloth and hardware for his household. The slump stopped the importation of these things and so he could not buy them; enough money still remained for his taxes.

Taxes were reduced in some places, but the Native Authorities, though they had to insist on the severest economies, were able to maintain their staffs. The Government were not able to do so and large numbers of experienced men were 'axed': some departments were reduced, not merely to skeletons but to ghosts of their former selves. The remaining government staff lost a tenth of their pay. Government revenue fell from over £6,000,000 to under £4,000,000.

The whole thing was completely disastrous. Nigeria was a new country. It had already gone through the shock of the First World War, when most non-military activities came to a standstill. It was just beginning to develop. Roads were being built and the country was being opened up: there were plans for schools and hospitals and dispensaries. Everything was put aside. Development could not be considered again until the outside world began to recover and until we replaced some of our staff losses.

We came into the slump later than in Europe and we came out of it later: it was not until 1934 or 1935 that we had regained the point at which we had been cut off. We see now that it was a mistake to have acted as we had done. No doubt any nervous government would have taken this line, and an occupying administration was more likely to be forced into this course than any other.

We should, I think, have bought all the material we could find money for; the prices of commodities, especially iron and steel and building materials, had fallen steeply; we still had reserves and we could have used a reasonable part of them in laying in supplies cheaply. Transport rates had fallen and we could have had cheap deliveries. We should have retained all the people we could possibly afford in order to keep the machine running.

We should have put in all we had to ensure this; the slump could not go on for ever and, even if it had done so, our economies could have been brought in gradually, while we kept up our development steadily. But as I have said, an occupying power could not do this: they could not afford to take the risks involved, and the Colonial Office would never have departed from its crippling, though well-intentioned, principle of clear annual balances. A responsible government would have looked at the problem in a different light and from a different point of view.

Four years after we had started to recover we became involved in the Second World War: our third disaster in thirty years.

All the time I was working at the school I went on trying to learn and to read anything I could find of interest. I enjoyed my service there and I think I played a useful part. I certainly got on well with the boys and my colleagues, and, of course, my numerous relatives in the town.

A big change came in 1934 when the Sultan appointed me to be District Head of Rabah in succession to my cousin who had just died. Thus at the age of 24 I became one of the youngest District Heads appointed. At that time there were forty-eight District Heads in the Sokoto Emirate—we still refer to it as the 'Emirate' though it is under the Sultan—of varying size and importance. These made up the historic kingdom deliminated by Sultan Bello and virtually unchanged since then.

The District Head was, under the Sultan, in absolute control of his District and was virtually responsible for everything that went on in it. It was naturally a position of great responsibility and trust, and usually the posts were reserved for older and more experienced men: most of the appointments were hereditary, but a few were unrestricted. Rabah was one of the former, and I was the most suitable candidate in the family. The Sultan was further impressed by the modern learning and knowledge that I had managed to acquire and felt that the sooner I got experience in administration, the sooner I would be ripe for

39

other and higher posts. For this I am very grateful to him. I certainly profited greatly by this early responsibility.

Rabah District then covered three hundred square miles, with a population of some thirty thousand people. It lay between the Sokoto and Rima Rivers, and therefore was partially in the river plains and partially on the high ground above them. The people were agriculturalists, living in scattered villages of between, say, 500 and 1,000 people. They tilled their farms and grew their corn for domestic use, and a few groundnuts and small crops of tobacco and hemp. The villages were pretty well self-contained and the local craftsmen met the village needs in mats, pots, iron-work, and wood-work. They all kept livestock—goats and sheep, and chickens—and had interests in economic trees in the bush. The cattle were mostly owned and cared for by the nomad Fulani, as they are to this day.

Though the Fulani were very poor by general standards, they were not poor in their own lights. Their needs were simple and were simply met. They had weatherproof houses, which they made themselves, and no man went hungry; the aged, the cripple, and the infirm were provided for by the village; their amusements were simply and traditional; they had little contact with the outside world, though traders and musicians wandered round and in the dry season many of the men went off to the south trading or carrying loads.

The villagers' only serious handicap was water. Those who lived in the river valleys could draw from shallow wells, but it was a different story for those who lived on higher ground. There they had to be very careful of water in the dry weather—that is, the seven months from November to May. If they were lucky they had wells, but they were deep and drawing water was not easy; if they were unlucky they had to go for some miles to bring back a pot of it. Nevertheless I was always surprised that none of these people ever moved their villages on account of water shortage.

Water is still the great headache for this Government. We have succeeded remarkably in the provision of wells in out-of-the-way places, but the problem still remains of how to get the water out of a deep well without elaborate machinery and how to produce sufficient supplies for an ever-increasing demand. For availability inevitably creates demand.

Their other worry was sickness, but this was not so serious a worry as we might think since they had no knowledge of the effects of modern methods and treatment. They therefore treated illness with time-honoured medicines and had surprisingly good results. There were, however, dreadful epidemics which carried away thousands, and against these nothing could be done.

The District Head was, as I have said, responsible for all that went on in his District. This responsibility was naturally simpler in some ways than it is at present, but it was nevertheless very real. The two most important things were the collection of taxes and the keeping of the peace.

In both these the Village Heads had an important part to play. Indeed, primarily the peace was in their hands: it was their duty, as it still is, to apprehend wrongdoers and bring them to the District Head; to suppress any public disorder; and to keep careful note of the movements of strangers in their areas, often a source of crime and trouble. To achieve this they relied on their friends, their households, and their followers. They had no paid assistance, any more than they have now. They had no judicial powers, and have none now, but they were expected to use their influence to sort out minor rows, especially domestic ones, to avoid them developing into public scandals or disturbances.

Wrongdoers were brought in to the District Head, and, since he too had no judicial powers, he handed them over for trial to the District Alkali. Once they were sentenced it was the District Head's duty to send them under escort to Sokoto for imprisonment; they could appeal to the Sultan if they wished to do so, but there were no legal 'avenues of appeal' as there are now.

If serious troubles were threatened, the District Head went with his people to help the village. On the whole I was always surprised at the small amount of crime or disturbance. There is no doubt that the small self-contained village unit was the reason for this. Everyone knew what was going on in this kind of community and only the most foolhardy would risk doing anything to upset it.

Sudden excitement, a quarrel over probably a trivial cause, violent words and a violent blow might end in wounding, or even in murder, but it was astonishingly rare. Mind you, our people, being strict Muslims, never drank anything intoxicating and thus one primary cause of trouble did not exist. Incidentally, they did not waste vast quantities of valuable farm products on making fermented liquor as did people farther south.

The Village Heads and the District Head were responsible for the collection of taxes. This started with the annual count of the whole population. It was quite an accurate count, so far as the men were concerned, but women were always more difficult to count and children only appeared in many cases as token figures. It was thought that as neither of the latter were taxed, they did not matter very much. The Village Head had lists of all householders and of all adult men in the house. These were checked and revised each year.

The incidences of taxation were worked out by a rather complicated process. I will not go into it here, save to say that it was as fair as could be expected and very much more fair and, of course, infinitely cheaper than the complicated scientific methods of today, and much fairer than the 'head tax' so usually employed elsewhere in Africa. The tax of the whole village was worked out in Sokoto and announced to the Village Head and Elders, and it was their job to divide it fairly over the population, so that the richer paid more than average and the poorer less and the very poor practically nothing.

It was the District Head's duty to see that all this was carried out and that the tax, so soon as it was announced, was paid in as quickly as possible. The Village Head did the actual collection and much depended on his personality. Touring District Officers used to implore the people to save up their money for the inevitable tax and I was very glad about the response during the latter part of my time there.

When the time for collection came, there was often a fearful fuss to get the actual coins required for the tax—it was only a matter of six or seven shillings per tax-payer in those days—and the people rushed to the markets with produce and livestock for sale. Naturally the markets were glutted and prices fell sharply; the rich trader came in and bought at ridiculous prices and did very well out of it. There was nothing wrong with all this, it was just that the people would not take heed of the warnings or think for themselves. And so it happens every year, even now, in many places.

The total tax for Rabah District was about £3,000 when I took over. The District Head tends to be judged at headquarters by his ability to bring in his tax early and bring it in complete. My first efforts were disastrous and I was most mortified to find that I was the last of all the District Heads to complete my tax collection. There was a good deal of quiet sneering at the bright young District Head who couldn't do what the old uneducated men could do so easily.

I was determined to do better next time and, by God's help, I was successful. The following year I was about half-way up the Districts, being the twentieth to complete; but the next season saw us as the third, and in the fourth year I was the first of all the forty-eight to complete.

When I went to Rabah I had been away from it for fourteen years. I had been there, of course, on holidays, but they were less than a month at a time and can scarcely be said to count. In spite of this absence, things had not changed very much: many of my relatives were still there and my childhood friends had grown up. I moved into my father's house. It was almost the same as when I was born and I felt myself very much at home.

I was, of course, very young, but I had all the confidence of youth and was strong in my grip on the new learning. I don't think that I felt nervous, and was sure of support from relatives and friends. A few, of course, were jealous of what I had done, but when all was said and done I was my father's son and no one disputed my right to the post, or, if they did, it never came to my ears.

I have said that there was no hardship in the District, but it was far from being a rich one. In fact it was really quite poor, but I could see that there were assets if the people would put their backs into it. After all, it was only a day's march from Sokoto, then a large and growing town with a big market, with European trading firms and a considerable demand for produce. But there was much waste of energy and effort, for many of my people went off in the dry season on long journeys to the south, either as petty traders or mere labourers, when they should have been at home.

I found a popular appeal. I used to say to gatherings of villagers, 'Do you know that there is great wealth in our soil? Why is that? Where are our dead relatives and friends? Where are the great ones of the past? Where is the Blessed Shehu himself?' They would answer, 'Of a truth they are all in the ground.' And I would say, 'Do they not give the ground its blessing and richness? Will they not help us now? Let us then till the soil and bring out its wealth for our benefit and profit.'

I first used this method in Rabah and, after I got the agreement of the people, we held a *gayya* (a gathering together to help) and everyone came round and dug up a huge field on the hillside, which I planted with cassava, till then a little-known crop in that area. It flourished, and when it was ready, at the end of the year, I threw it open to all and announced that anyone was welcome to come and take cuttings from it for their own use. This they did, for they saw the use of the crop, and they planted it themselves. Now this is a dry-season crop, and so they were discouraged from going off and wasting their time in long and exhausting journeys when they would be better employed at home looking after their wives and families and livestock.

Another possibility lay at hand obvious for all to see. That was the swampy ground and lakes that lay for miles on either side of Rabah. I persuaded the people to tackle these swamps and drain them so that they could plant rice, and later sweet-potatoes, on this inundated ground. This was another dry-season occupation and proved to be popular and lucrative.

Later we tried wheat and that too did well. I found that if you spoke to the people and explained carefully what was wanted and its objects and the assistance it would bring to the home, there was little difficulty in getting them to co-operate. I was pleased when I found that people who had left the district began to trickle back again, persuaded by rumours of its new prosperity. All this, of course, was one of the reasons why we were able to collect tax so easily.

Irrigation was obviously needed—and it still is—but it was too difficult for us and we were wary, for we had once been bitten. An enthusiastic but inexperienced District Officer, when I was a child, built a dam across an arm of the river below Rabah, without considering too closely the consequences. The rains came and the dam filled up, and the first thing we knew about it in my father's house—near the water-side it is, as I have said—was when the water trickled in over the thresholds of our huts and houses. That evening the villagers went out with their hoes and breached the dam, and that was the last we heard of it.

I tried to interest the young men in something better than sitting about and gossiping like old women. I too was a young man and could share with them. So of an afternoon, when I was in Rabah, I would go out and find many of them in the square in front of the great doorway. Then we would discuss what we should do, and then all of us, without regard to rank or position, would take part in, say, running or wrestling, or riding races on horseback. Thus we got exercise and plenty of companionship.

We had no school in Rabah or indeed in any place in the District, and that worried me a great deal. I was determined to end the ignorance and illiteracy I found everywhere. I built a thatched hut myself and I got together the elder children of my relatives. I taught them myself how to read and write—there was no one else to do it. When they had learnt enough they became the scribes of the Village Heads and did their best to teach others as they had been taught. Thus was started the 'war against ignorance' which has in recent years developed into a huge adult education scheme with far-reaching effects. In due course I was successful in getting a formal elementary school established in Rabah.

I also set up an office for myself where the affairs of the District could be attended to and the books and records could be properly kept. This was the first one in Sokoto Emirate, and the other Districts saw its value and in the end all of them had such offices; they have been developed a good deal since then but that was the origin of them.

Roads and trade routes were matters of great importance and I set to work on improving them and opening them up. One of these led across the ford to a big town called Rara on the south bank of the Sokoto River. This place had lost a lot of its houses, as the river had eaten away the land on which they stood. I managed to persuade the people to dig a new channel for the river, and the old one, which had caused all the trouble, became fine arable land from which the village derived much benefit.

It was at Rara that I had a genuine failure. In my endeavours to improve the wealth of the District I managed, after a great deal of effort, to persuade a trading company to take up a plot there at Rara and build a little store. This town was more accessible from Sokoto than was Rabah and so was more suitable as a trading station, and I had hopes of starting a good trade there. But for once I received no support from the people: they were quite lukewarm about the scheme and said it was better to take their cotton to market than to this canteen. I took along two bags of my cotton as a start, but the thing would not go and, a year after I left, the plot was abandoned.

At that time there were few real motor roads, though some were 'motorable' with preparation and precaution. On these there were no bridges or culverts and they could only be used in

46

the dry season: but, anyhow, there were very few motor cars or lorries. The routes between most places were trade routes cleared back of grass and shrubs to a width of seven or eight feet by communal labour. They were comparatively straight and went as directly as possible between villages.

On one of these roads near Rabah I planted a farm of sweet-potato. It did very well and flourished, but I got nothing out of it myself. As the sweet-potatoes ripened, the passers-by would stop and say, 'Wait a moment, I must see how the District Head's potatoes are getting on.' So they would dig them up to sample them. In the end there were none left when I came to lift them. But I did not mind since it was cultivating a taste for a new crop, and that was a good thing to do as it increased the prosperity of the country.

While I was in Rabah I found the greatest difficulty in keeping up my English. There was no one who spoke it locally, and visiting Government staff tended to polish up *their* Hausa and were reluctant to speak English. I found the greatest help was in reading from cover to cover the *Illustrated London News*. I was sent copies of this every month, as they reached him, by a young officer called L. T. Stevenson, who was on his first tour as an Assistant District Officer in Sokoto. He retired recently as Resident, Sokoto, and I have always been grateful to him for this thoughtful kindness. These papers were not only very useful from the point of view of learning English, but also enabled me to acquire a great deal of general knowledge which has stood me in good stead ever since.

There was an interesting situation at a place called Tofa: quite a small place it was, lying at the foot of a steep and rocky hillside. In the rains the water used to rush off these slopes and it looked as though the villagers would have to abandon the site and move elsewhere. It is odd that in so dry a neighbourhood water should cause such trouble, but that is the fact. I went and examined the place and persuaded the people to dig a deep trench at the foot of the hillside to catch the water and deviate it in a safe direction. We watched the result in the first rains

47

with interest and anxiety, for water is tricky stuff to deal with. We were greatly relieved when we found that it worked perfectly and the village was saved.

By hard work and devotion to detail and availability to all, so that all could come to me and lay their complaints, I gained the confidence and respect of my people and, indeed, I might go so far as to say their love and affection. So much was this so that even to this day people from that District still chase me in Kaduna and come into my house at all hours.

On the other side of the picture I can say my relations with the Administrative Officers with whom I came into contact were on the whole amicable: they varied greatly each to each, and so naturally did one's own reactions towards them.

CHAPTER 5

GUSAU

In 1938 there came a big change in my life and I left Rabah for Gusau. It was in this year that the Sultan Hassan died and was succeeded by Abubakar, who was his nephew and who is the present Sultan, now Sir Abubakar, G.B.E. He is my third cousin, Sultan Bello being our common great-grandfather.

Sir Abubakar had been the Sardauna of Sokoto in the lifetime of Sultan Hassan, and when he became Sultan this title became vacant. It is peculiar to Sokoto and restricted to men of the ruling house. Like other similar titles it is greatly sought after, and the holding of it is a great honour. It is difficult to describe its exact significance nowadays: titles such as Waziri, which is 'Prime Minister', or Madaki, 'Master of the Horse', are easy to understand; the title 'Sardauna' is not so simple but its original meaning was probably 'Captain of the Bodyguard'.

Its insignia are an ancient sword and baldric which are handed in by the last holder on laying down his office and presented to the new holder personally by the ruler. Traditionally in battle he went before the ruler, as leader of the princes, to clear the way for him; he, of course, also protected him should the fighting draw unpleasantly close. He was known as the 'Brave One with the Sword' or the 'Brave Road-Opener'.

One of the new Sultan's early acts was to promote me to a new post at Gusau. This transfer was superficially very pleasant and encouraging, but there were not lacking dark undertones and hidden motives, as is so common with official appointments of all races. For me personally, however, the darkest side of the picture was that I was instructed to leave Rabah forthwith. I had always been very attached to Rabah and was still more

49

attached to it when I was District Head; it is still to me my home-town and I go back to it whenever I get the opportunity.

Huge crowds assembled to say good-bye when I left and they shouted, 'Good luck to the big man with the wrist-watch' and 'God be with you' and 'God give you a pleasant place'. I was always known as the 'man with the wrist-watch', for they were unknown in Rabah before my time: sometimes it was 'son of tall man with the book', for my father was learned and used to go about carrying Arabic books to read whenever he could do so.

Gusau is some 135 miles from Sokoto, or about half-way along the Zaria road, which is now the main way into the Province. It used to be a small town until the railway reached it and since then it has grown continuously. When I went there first, there were about 10,000 people, but the population is now well over the 70,000 mark and is still growing. It is a considerable trading centre for a large and populated area. There were numerous canteens, as we call them here—the stores of the trading firms—some of them European (British or French), some Lebanese, a few Nigerian.

The railway goes on to Kaura Namoda to the north. That is not a very important place now, though it was sufficiently important in the 1920s to justify the construction of the railway to it. They say that there was once a proposal to move the Sultan and his administration from Sokoto to Kaura Namoda, where he had a country house and estates. I imagine that it was a 'British' scheme, logically correct but politically unsound. It would obviously have been convenient to have the capital of an important Province nearer the centre of things, but it would have been out of the question to abandon Sultan Bello's town, his own creation. Anyhow, the idea was dropped.

To the east of Gusau and in clear sight are the great Kwatar-kwashi rocks; a thousand feet and more they rise above the plain, sheer on one side but broken into foothills and valleys on the north. It was near here that the small British column in 1903 very nearly met disaster at the hands of the Waziri of Kano.

Here, too, live the great vultures, which are said to be the largest in Africa.

I was sent to Gusau, not as a District Head, but in an entirely novel capacity. I was to supervise the work of fourteen District Heads—their Districts lay along the eastern boundary from the French border to the present Niger boundary. This was promotion indeed. There were also, at Gusau, branches of Native Administration departments from Sokoto which came under my control, especially the sub-treasury, which received all money collected locally on behalf of the Sokoto Native Administration and made all local payments. This was a great saving on the former system whereby everything was centred in Sokoto and every transaction, however small or big, had to take place there.

There was also a District Officer posted here permanently: he came under the Senior District Officer at Sokoto, for it was part of the Sokoto Division. There are dozens of Europeans of all sorts in Gusau now, but at that time the District Officer had only three others with him. There was an Engineer, an Agricultural Officer and a Medical Officer. The latter was the most outstanding. He was Dr Thomson, a man whose devotion to duty and friendly nature made him much liked, and his departure was much regretted. His profound knowledge of chest diseases was a great help to our people.

Indeed, in the whole Province we had very little technical staff. There was a doctor and a sister at Sokoto for the fine Native Administration Hospital there—apart from Sokoto and Gusau, there was no other medical work in the whole of the vast Province—with a Forestry Officer, an Agricultural Officer, an Engineer and some assistants, and, of course, an Education Officer. My own relationship with all of them has been good because my education made me understand them better than others were able to do.

My appointment to Gusau was accompanied by promotion to be a member of the Sultan's Council in Sokoto. I am proud to continue to be a Councillor in spite of holding office as Premier of the North. I still attend the meetings when I am in

51

the neighbourhood and always receive copies of the minutes wherever I may be. Council meetings were, and are, held in Sokoto on Thursday each week. I would go to Sokoto early on Thursday morning in time for the meeting. I would then stay there for a week until the following Thursday and I would leave on Friday morning and get back to Gusau in time for the afternoon prayers. Of course, by that time we had motor cars, and though the road was only an earth one there was little traffic and you could travel almost as quickly as you can now.

In the week I was in Sokoto I would go round the departments whose representatives were with me in Gusau and clear up their difficulties for them. I also inspected the police and prison there, as they both fell within my portfolio as a Councillor. So the time was not wasted; actually there was a good deal of gain in being there, for interviews were so much more satisfactory than trying to get things done by letter.

In the year after my appointment, as all the world knows, Hitler made war on the United Kingdom and we were naturally drawn into it with all other territories of the British Crown. It never occurred to us that there was anything odd about this and we took the position as being quite natural.

What did strike us as being very peculiar was the fact that civilised nations, and there is no denying that both sides were civilised, should plunge into a war, apparently in a light-hearted manner, and thus do exactly what they spent so much time and energy in preventing us from doing. After all, I was a war chief of Sokoto: had I moved out against, say, Argungu, our neighbours and traditional enemies, at the head of an army, I should soon have been rounded up by the WAFF and would have received a stiff sentence for such conduct, if I was lucky enough to get off without being hanged. And yet here was Europe doing just that.

We were glad to help, but at first there did not seem to be very much that we could do. Reservists were mobilised and troops were ready for action. They couldn't do very much until Italy declared war, and that was not until 1940; then the Nigeria

Regiment went to East Africa and helped, very materially, to drive out the Italians and restore the Emperor of Ethiopia to his throne. Recruiting was pushed as much as possible, but no pressure was employed: all the men were volunteers. The North produced something like one hundred thousand men for the army, quite apart from those for other activities later on.

The great Chiefs—the Sultan, the Shehu of Bornu, the Emir of Kano, and the Emir of Katsina—each raised from their immediate people a company of infantry. It was quite a good idea, but it didn't work very well in practice and there was a good deal of friction and difficulty behind the scenes. I don't suppose the Generals had any idea of what was really happening and it doesn't matter now as it is all past and forgotten.

The Government decided to establish big reserves of grain for use in case of disaster and for feeding of troops and labour on the mines and on military works. One Friday in 1942 I got back to Gusau as usual, and on the Sunday I went on to Chafe, twenty-seven miles away. I had only been there two hours when a messenger arrived from the sub-treasurer at Gusau—he was M. Haruna Gwandu, who is now Emir of Gwandu and the President of the House of Chiefs—saying that a telegram had come from Sokoto instructing me to go back there as soon as possible. I left at once and reached Sokoto on Monday morning.

On the Tuesday there was a Council Meeting and the Sultan said:

I have called you in because I have a very heavy responsibility for you and your Districts. I think that it is within your powers but it will involve a lot of work, and we are sending to you, to help you, a Senior District Officer. We want you to collect as soon as possible, 3,000 tons of millet and 3,000 tons of guinea corn. At the same time we want 3,000 men collected, and they must be volunteers, to go to the Plateau as labour for the tin mines. The grain will all be paid for and the collection must be fair and reasonable.

This same duty was placed by the Government on all Provinces at this time and these figures were the Sokoto Emirate share of the Provincial total. But I had to make all the collections for the Emirate—other Districts were not involved.

53

The Senior District Officer posted to Gusau was Sharwood-Smith, who ten years later appointed me to be first Premier of the Region. He was of great assistance to us in this work and his guidance was most valuable. He gave me all the moral support I required.

These figures at first sight seemed to be alarming, but when they were divided up among the villages in proportion to their tax-payers, the individual results were not excessive; they came out at about 100 lbs. of grain per tax-payer, and that was not a great deal. The payments, however, for this supply, which were in cash, to many thousands of individuals at considerable distances away, and its collection and transport, presented great difficulties. The corn was bought by firms at the scale and railed as soon as bagged. Thus we did not have the added difficulty of storage which worried other places. The storage of corn is always a difficult business and one that calls for great care.

The assembly of the men was even more difficult. The number of spare and unattached men available at any given time is comparatively small and it cannot be more than a matter of a few hundreds in quite a large area. Besides this we were building the Gusau airfield—it was one of the outer ring defences of Kano, had we had any fighter aircraft to man it. We were also supplying labour for road construction and improvement and railway maintenance, and, of course, there was a constant call for recruits for the army.

Further, the farmers were encouraged to produce as much as they could from their farms. This is, of course, a family matter and hardly any labour is employed, but the pressure made it difficult for anyone to leave their own farms. And the greatest difficulty was that the people were naturally reluctant to leave their own neighbourhood and no one wanted to go on to the cold and windy high Plateau to dig for tin in pits ninety or a hundred feet deep.

We had to allocate quotas to each village and hope for the best. Force was not to be used and I don't think that it was, but no doubt some form of moral pressure was involved. Anyhow, we got the required numbers in the end and they were sent off by train loads to Jos. They were quite well paid and most of them did pretty well. They were encouraged to send back money to their families, but this by itself was far from easy and became yet another burden on the hard-pressed administration. All this took a great deal of very hard touring and much exhortation on my part, but God was kind to us and we managed to collect all the grain and the men in very good time and well ahead of schedule.

The Sultan was an enthusiastic supporter of the British Red Cross—we then had no Red Cross of our own—and of the Win-the-War Fund, by which money was raised for buying fighters for the R.A.F. I could never really see the force of this one, for the British would have had to find the money anyway, and did the £5,000, that fighters were said to cost *each*, really represent the price?—if it did, then they have gone up a great deal in recent years.

Meanwhile we put up with serious cuts in imports and did our best to live on local produce. Here locally produced salt and wheat came into their own and so did rice. Naturally Europeans suffered more than we did in this respect.

Our serious difficulty arose to the north and west of the Province. When the Germans occupied part of France, the colonial territories remained under the control of the unoccupied part, which was called Vichy France. We assumed that these, though theoretically independent, were in practice under the control of Germany. Therefore the areas I have mentioned, being still under Vichy, were potentially hostile and might be used as a base for possible German attacks on Nigeria and also for probable espionage.

We had no troops to spare for frontier protection and were asked to raise mounted levies for the purpose. I was greatly concerned with this, both in raising them and in directing their operations. The fourteen Districts that came under me at Gusau had about a hundred miles of frontier with the French territories to the north of the town of Sabon Birni. This was of course a 'European' frontier, the one originally demarcated at the beginning of the century. It was quite arbitrary and followed no natural features, for there were no natural features for it to follow. It ran in straight lines from point to point and was marked by iron telegraph poles.

These straight lines cut through tribal areas, and even severed family farms, but the most awkward place was where they actually cut through a market. It did not interfere with ordinary daily activities in peace time. Fortunately, we had no nonsense about passports or other 'travel documents' or life would have been quite intolerable in those parts. There were no permanent frontier guards or customs posts, any more than there are any now, in most of these places. But in war it was quite a different matter. The British side (our side) of this market was evacuated every night and everything was cleared away into the village. The French raided it for anything they could pick up, but didn't get much.

One day the frontier levies thought they would put a stop to this. It was the day of the landings in North Africa. We had been warned that they were going to happen and ordered to stand-by in case of trouble. Not very far away from this market was a group of buildings the French used as a barracks for their soldiers. Our people drew up on the frontier and fired at these buildings. We hoped that the French would come out and have a fight, but they never showed a sign of life.

It was here that later on we caught a French-African soldier fully armed: it did not present much difficulty for he had crossed the frontier and he was very frightened. In fact we caught several when they strayed across the frontier from time to time —we were scrupulous on our part in not crossing it in force, as we did not want to give Vichy any form of excuse to take their own action. Our military command wanted to have a French rifle and a set of equipment for their own information and thus we were able to supply them.

The French were naturally very angry about this and issued orders that I was to be captured and taken to them. But I don't

56

think they made any serious attempt to carry out these orders, certainly nothing that I knew about. This did not prevent my travelling along the frontier frequently and sleeping in this very market town on the border.

We used to send across the frontier, it is true, sometimes, to distribute the propaganda leaflets written in French and printed in Kaduna. They were called, I think, the *Red Quill* and were intended to give our side of the picture, with accurate war news, and so to bring people over to us. I do not think that in practice they had any noticeable effect. The people who took the pamphlets over were people who were constantly travelling about and no one took any interest in them. They were, of course, quite unarmed.

We were surprised that the French did not make any attempts on us. They were much stronger than we were in men and our airfields were very exposed. We could not have done much to keep them out had they made an attack in strength.

Looking back at all this I think that they thought that we were much better armed than they were; indeed, there is now evidence to support this view. But they did not seem to have much idea of what was going on in Nigeria: had they realised the immensity of the air traffic to the Middle East, I think they must have done something to interfere with it, but they did not, which was just as well. Against air attack, of course, we should have been quite helpless. I do not think that there were any anti-aircraft guns available and the troops guarding the airports were raw and only partially trained. No one was guarding the Gusau airfield except perhaps an NA policemen on patrol: and it was not more than a hundred miles from the frontier.

I did much of my touring by motor, for there were motorable roads northwards to Kaura Namoda and Isa, and eastwards into the Zamfara Valley, apart from the main road itself. There were also some rather poor side roads which could be used in the dry season. A great many places, however, were not on a road, any more than they are now, and these I had to visit on horseback. Sometimes I had to go on foot. These were slow ways of getting about, but infinitely more rewarding than rushing about in a motor.

On much of this touring I used to accompany the District Officer stationed at Gusau. As I have said, they varied in value and calibre to a surprising extent. From some one could learn a great deal, and not only about administration, but from others there was little gain. Who goes to a dry well for water? I used to send in reports of my touring to the Sultan, and the British officer reported to the Resident at Sokoto. Nothing much came of these. If one wanted anything one had to go and fight for it! They replied soon enough if *they* wanted anything.

It was while I was at Gusau that an incident took place which very nearly put an end to my career in the administration: it shows you that, however well and virtuously you may live, things do not always go as one would like them to.

One afternoon a friend came to me in my house in Gusau and said, 'Look, a plot is being arranged against you, so that you will fall into an unescapable trap.' When I asked what sort of plot, he said that people were being organised to lay complaints against me so that I would be involved in a court case. I replied, 'Tawakkaltu Alal Haiyil Lazi Layamutu' (I depend on the Soul that never dies). A week later I heard that some Fulani (nomadic cow-men) were being told to say that they paid cattle tax to me which never went into the Treasury.

After necessary investigations by an instigated administrative officer who was specially sent for the purpose, I was summoned to appear before the Sultan's Court. I was tried and sentenced to one year's imprisonment. Knowing my own reputation and standards and the way the case was tried, I appealed to the Supreme Court. The learned Judge (Mr Ames), with two Muslim jurists, allowed my appeal and I was therefore acquitted. My dependence on 'the Soul that never dies' proved right. Some people now think that I might have drunk a certain Koranic verse connected with Prophet Yusuf which led to his imprisonment in Egypt and later his prominence. How true this is is left to you to judge.

There were more than two thousand people outside the Court in Zaria; they went mad with excitement when the result was announced. My return through Gusau was a triumphal procession.

But, in fact, nothing can be quite the same after such an experience and I was glad to be recalled to work in Sokoto. There I threw myself into my duties as Councillor and did all I could to improve the police and prison and lock-ups and the other departments put in my charge from time to time. War was coming to an end; our troops were in Burma in the two West African Divisions; the pressure on our frontier was at first slackened and then disappeared completely. Little did we know it, but the dawn of a very new kind of day was dawning.

All this time I used to read anything I could get my hands on; whenever I had time and when others were resting or sleeping I would read. I found that three or four hours' sleep at night was all I needed, and in the day I never rested of an afternoon as is so common a practice here. I know that it does help a lot of people, but I know quite well that I only feel ill if I give way to it.

I was still very inexperienced about matters outside Sokoto Province and was anxious to extend my knowledge as soon and as far as possible. Fortunately I was able in 1949 to go on a trip to Lagos with the Wali of Bornu, my old friend of Katsina days, as you will see below. Here we found a lot of things that surprised me greatly.

I saw Lagos Harbour and went down to the beach and saw the ocean for the first time and was taken on board a big ocean-going ship. I visited public offices and many buildings and saw many different kinds of people in the teeming streets of Lagos. I began to realise what a complicated thing it must be to run a country of the size and complexity of Nigeria. Before long I was to have better means of judging this. I found myself in the thick of it.

CHAPTER 6

THE DAWN OF POLITICS

DURING 1946 discussions were going on about a new Constitution for Nigeria. The Constitution at that time had been in existence since 1922: it had never been really satisfactory, even when it was first published, but no particular public interest had been taken in the matter until just before the war; then agitation was started against it. Oddly enough this was by Southern people, who were to some extent represented, though not at all adequately. Strong opposition should really have come from us Northerners, for we were not represented at all.

It seems inconceivable nowadays that this vast area and population had absolutely no say in the legislation or finances of the country for a quarter of a century. And yet that is the simple truth. In fact, the position was odder still, for even the Legislative Council could not enact legislation affecting the North, though they could pass a budget which affected it. They could ask questions about it, but they could not interfere in its organisation or policy. The fact that they did not want to do so probably permitted the system to continue for the length of time it survived.

The Governor personally, without advice or recommendation, could, and did, enact legislation affecting the Northern Provinces, as the Region was then called—that is, of course, the Governor of Nigeria; the Regions had Chief Commissioners until recently. To make it all fair and reasonable there were on the Legislative Council 'the ten senior officers for the time being lawfully discharging the functions of Senior Residents in Nigeria', of whom some would inevitably be Northern officers. It was their duty and privilege to represent the Northern Provinces in Council; their intellectual ascendancy was apparently so great that they managed this without opening their mouths, save on the most formal motions. The Chief Commissioners were also members and they, it is true, were a little more vocal, but on the whole officials, apart from the Attorney-General, the Chief Secretary and the Treasurer, were not encouraged to break silence.

The small number of unofficial members did their best and spoke whenever they could on a variety of subjects. These men were mostly nominated and represented 'areas', in much the same way as another member might represent, say, 'shipping' or 'mining'. In spite of this, huge areas of even the Southern Provinces were left unrepresented. Needless to say, there was a very solid and substantial majority on the official side in the Council: this followed ordinary 'Crown Colony' practice at that time.

It is a curious reflection that the salaries of officials, whether of Government or NA, and consequently of trading firms, remained unchanged during this period of legislative stagnation. There was, I imagine, no connection between the two, but between the salaries' revision of 1920 and that of 1945/46 (Harrigan) there was no alteration.

Sir Bernard Bourdillon started an enquiry asking officials for proposals for a revised Constitution. So far as the North was concerned the matter was wrapped in deep secrecy and no one but senior officials were consulted. It is indicative of the general outlook of those days that when a Resident ventured to suggest the possibility of elections, say at village level, he was abruptly told that he was two hundred years ahead of his time.

Sir Arthur Richards (now Lord Milverton) continued the enquiries and discussions and carried them through to the conclusion known, after him, as the 'Richards Constitution'. This came into effect towards the end of 1946. The result, though odd in many ways and undemocratic almost throughout, was an improvement on what had gone before: is not something going the right way better than nothing stationary?

61

For the first time Provinces were represented on a legislative body. Further, for the first time there was a selection of Members by Africans. For the first time there was an unofficial majority in all the areas, thereafter called Regions, and in the Legislative Council itself. For the first time, and this was important to us, the North was represented at Lagos and the Regions met on common ground. For the first time the Legislative Council was purged of its solid phalanx of mute officials, and African representatives of the Regions were permitted to have their say. There were, of course, a number of officials: that was inevitable, but they were not cyphers.

The new Regional Council of the North—a House of Assembly and a House of Chiefs—could discuss Bills likely to affect the Region: they could recommend amendments—the fact that no one in Lagos was compelled to take any notice of their recommendations, though it might have been embarrassing, did not really affect the issue. They could discuss these matters in the open and possibly some day something more would come of it. They could also vote on the small sums of money available for expenditure in the Region; and so were sown the seeds of the future, extended and complicated debates on, and control over, a substantial budget.

Their most important function, however, was one which took less than half an hour to cover. They were entitled to elect from among their fellow Members representatives to go to Lagos to the new Legislative Council. The North elected five unofficial Members of the Assembly and the Chiefs four of their number. Thus there was representation from, it is true, rather a narrow field, but none the less made up of men selected by their fellows without any suggestion of official inspiration.

The new Legislative Council had fourteen Regional Members plus six Chiefs (two from the West), four elected Members (Lagos and Calabar), and four nominated (one for the 'Colony')—that is, twenty-eight unofficial Members. There were sixteen officials, including the Governor and three Chief Commissioners. Thus there was a clear 'unofficial' majority of twelve, should they all join together in opposition to the Government. In practice this was not a very likely situation and I don't think it ever happened. The Government may have been narrowly defeated on a few occasions but, being an 'official government', it could not very well resign.

The House of Assembly in Kaduna was elected by the Native Authority Councils of each Province. Most Provinces sent in one single Member, but Kano sent three and Sokoto two. We elected the Waziri of Sokoto and the Magajin Rafi of Gwandu as our Members.

At that time I was not concerned with politics: I was getting on with my job in Sokoto and in the Sokoto Council and there was plenty to do. The Native Administration had not been seriously interfered with by the war. In fact, we had gained to some extent. We had actually made a little extra money by supplying labour and by the demand for certain products. We had been more on our own and had been allowed to use our own initiative. There was a dearth of administrative officers and we could get on with what lay before us at our own discretion; we no longer had to listen to a stream of advice and exhortation from the variety of administrative officers who had moved across our vision before the war. Some of these people could never realise that we had been administering our units with more or less success long before they were thought of in the country. Some, of course, were very good and really helpful.

These elections, however, gave me something to think about. Obviously the Waziri was the senior councillor and so was the right man to go to Kaduna; equally obviously there had to be a man from Gwandu, and the Magajin Rafi was the right choice there. I knew that I had been considered, but had been turned down. The more I thought of it, the more I felt that I ought to make an attempt at being elected, some time before long, but owing to the way in which I had been treated I suppose I must have lost interest to some extent.

There did not seem to be any immediate chance of a new election occurring, so there was time for me to improve myself.

63

I knew little about Nigeria and nothing about the world outside. I wanted to improve my English still further, though it was not bad, and to extend my knowledge of the theory and practice of Government. Eighteen months later the chance to do all this came and I was offered a visit to the United Kingdom under the British Council to study local government. I jumped at this as it was exactly what I had in mind.

I arrived in England by air on the 10th January, 1948, and had the usual round of visits in London. Then we went on to the town of Richmond in Yorkshire. We were to study local government there and also British methods of farming, dealing with livestock and the like. I was fortunate enough to be accommodated by a Mr J. Fletcher and his family. He worked for an insurance corporation. I stayed with them for a month in great comfort.

I was delighted to live with an English family as part of their life; I learned a great deal about the English and the way they lived and thought, and it has been of the greatest service to me ever since. I shall always look back in gratitude to these people. They were not rich and their house was a small one, but I was made to feel at home in it and I appreciated the trouble they took over me and admired the way that they took trouble over each other in everyday affairs.

I profited greatly from all I had seen and from the many people of all walks of life whom I met and talked to on this visit. British farming was very interesting, but had hardly any relation to our problems at home. It was, however, worth while to see how others dealt with their problems, and I was impressed with the knowledge that was possessed even by the small and apparently untrained farmer.

Soon after I came back from England the opportunity I sought arose. The then Waziri of Sokoto died and a vacancy was created. By now things had changed and there was a desire that I should stand for election. I resisted this for a time, but after a long discussion with Sharwood-Smith, who was then Resident, and Michie, who was the SDO, I agreed to put the country's interests first. In due course I was elected and became the second Sokoto Member.

At that time there were no formal political parties in the North and we voted as we thought fit. As a matter of fact, most unofficial members were preoccupied with the affairs of their own Province and paid little heed to the affairs of the Region, still less to the country as a whole. Indeed, in the first speech I ever delivered in the House I drew attention to this and begged members to take a wider view of things.

The present Lugard Hall was being built to accommodate the Regional Council as it was called at that time: there was difficulty over the delivery of steel for the roof, especially the curved members required for the dome, and the building stood open to the skies. It was an achievement that it had got as far as it had, and that speaks a good deal for the foresight of Sir John Patterson, the Chief Commissioner at that time.

In the meanwhile, until it was finished, we held our meetings in the hall of the Trade Centre, as it was called then—that group of buildings devoted to technical education west of the railway at Kaduna North station. This was the best building available in Kaduna though it was not by any means ideal. It was long and rather narrow, and the public had to be cramped together, like cattle, at one end, where they could neither see well nor hear.

Each Member had a tiny desk in front of his chair: they were specially made and were completely unsuitable as they were much too small for the papers that are inevitable in any legislature. We sat with our Residents—one Member, one Resident alternately, except for us and Kano. We sat on each side of the Resident, who was Sharwood-Smith. There were two rows of Provincial Members facing each other and across the end were the nominated Members and the four technical Members for Education, Medicine, Works and Agriculture. The two Secretaries and the Senior Crown Counsel sat together at the end of one line.

The Resident sat with his Provincial Member to give him help and confidence. Some of them did and some did not:

65

some knew much less about what was going on than we did ourselves. Some people said that this was done to overawe the Members, but this was patent nonsense. Some Residents really understood what was required and gave valuable assistance to their Member and put him in the right way. The President was the senior Resident in the North at the time. In consequence it was not always the same man who presided. An unsatisfactory arrangement though officially understandable. Apart from Prayers there was no ceremony beyond that followed in any ordinary committee, and the proceedings were very simple.

The other Provincial Members included future Ministers such as Abubakar Tafawa Balewa, the present Federal Prime Minister, and the Makaman Bida, our present Minister of Finance. The proceedings were in Hausa and English, as they are now, and the four interpreters had interesting futures before them. Two were Northerners: one of them is now the Speaker of the Assembly and the other is the Minister of Education for the North. One of the Europeans finished as Deputy Governor and the other as Financial Secretary.

When I went to Lagos in 1949 I met for the first time, and saw in action, Nigerian politicians of the calibre of Dr Azikiwe. I began to see that we in the North would have to take politics seriously before very long. If we did not do so we should be left far behind in the future governmental development of Nigeria.

We were lucky in that we had time to think things out. It was God's will that the next elections were not to be 'direct' and that politics had only a small place in them. I will explain about this in due course.

In the meantime I went on with my duties. I had left Gusau and was now living and working in Sokoto. There were two meetings of the House of Assembly each year. I paid attention to what others were doing and saying, but did not feel urged to join in debates to any great extent. In fact, I think I only spoke four or five times. The next time I spoke it was as Minister of Works.

By 1949, the year in which I entered the House of Assembly, Sir John Macpherson, who had become Governor of Nigeria about twelve months before, decided that the time had come to reconsider the Constitution, though it had then been running for less than three years.

Lord Milverton had contemplated revision only after a far longer period than this, but it was typical of Sir John to get in first and to anticipate agitation for a change. There had been a certain amount of grumbling in Lagos and along the Coast, but it was sharply limited in extent and in volume. The great bulk of the people had no particular opinion either way. By no stretch of the imagination could it be said that there was any strong, still less universal, feeling in the matter. On the whole the Northern opinion was against any change at that time.

Nigeria is so large and the people are so varied that no person of any real intellectual integrity would be so foolish as to pretend that he speaks for the country as a whole, and yet there are plenty of people who have no hesitation in making sweeping statements of a general nature (pretending that it has general agreement) which could represent the opinions of only a very small section of the community in a particular area.

It is only when the feeling of the Legislatures has been taken after free debate, or where a large and dominant political party has been consulted, that it is possible for the leader to offer what may be taken as an opinion widely held: even then it cannot be of universal acceptance. I want to make this clear, since the position here is quite different from that in smaller and more homogeneous countries and great caution must be exercised in accepting general statements. Even I, who have a pretty general knowledge of the Northern Region, would hesitate before I made a statement without prior consultation involving opinion in, say, Benue or Bornu Province.

Anyhow, Sir John issued a questionnaire on suggested improvements in the Constitution which went down to village level for discussion. A series of meetings continued the discussion, each on a higher level (representing lower groups), until the feelings of Provinces became clear. Then there were meetings in Regional Headquarters.

67

In Kaduna we met, chiefs and representatives, in the dining-hall of the Police College, as we had no proper meeting-place, and thrashed the matter out. Here we agreed on a general policy for the Region, and selected people to go to the Nigerian meeting to be held at Lagos to prepare drafts for a meeting to be held at Ibadan. I was fortunate enough to be one of those chosen.

With me went Abubakar Tafawa Balewa and the Wali of Bornu. We were armed with the unanimous decisions taken at the Kaduna meeting and we were expected to put them through this final stage, if it were reasonably possible to do so.

At Ibadan we met the people from the other Regions and Lagos. It says a lot for Sir John that he would not attend these meetings himself, neither would he permit any European, except the Attorney-General, to be present. The matters were of the highest importance to the country and to the future of British Administration, and yet he left them entirely in our hands. The Attorney-General (later Sir Gerald Howe) presided and did it extremely well. He kept the business moving but in no wise did he try to use his position to influence the discussions.

The major point of divergence was in the creation of Ministers. We in the North had decided that the time was not yet ripe for this: we felt that, if any other Region wanted to have them, there would be no objections, but we thought that for ourselves and for Lagos we could afford to delay for a while. The reasons for this were a natural caution on our part and a feeling that perhaps our people were not, so far, sufficiently experienced to fill the posts. In the end, however, we swallowed our feelings and agreed to bring it in during 1952.

There was a good deal of arguing about our boundary with the Western Region, which was decided in our favour on the status quo. The Presidency of the House of Representatives also provoked discussion. We were adamant that it should not be a Southerner and gained our point on a compromise.

And there was the vital matter of representation in the House of Representatives. In the Legislative Council there had been

68

equal numbers of Members from each Region with some additions for Lagos, etc. There was therefore a strong body of opinion in favour of the same arrangement in the new House. Naturally this feeling was strongest in the two southern regions: equally naturally we were greatly opposed to it and felt that our future chances of survival depended on some other system being employed. The fairest way all round, and, of course, the one which favoured us the most, was to go by population. At that time we had had no census since 1931 and depended on annual estimates of population, but it was generally conceded that the North had at least as many people within its boundaries as had the other two together. For this reason we were determined to secure for ourselves at least as many representatives as those for the other two regions together.

We were so worried before the Ibadan meeting about these points that we raised a 'fighting fund' to pay for a special delegation to go to London should we be forced into a position leaving no alternative to this drastic course. We collected many thousands of pounds. In the end we did not need it as we had largely succeeded in attaining our desires and we turned it into a scholarship fund for Northern boys. So far twelve men have gone to British Universities with this support and I am glad to say that only one of these has failed.

The Constitution was made more democratic and an electoral principle was brought in. Executive Councils were set up in the Regions and a Council of Ministers in Lagos. The 'subjects' normally dealt with by a Government were divided up. Some of these, which were of 'local application' and of a local significance, were given exclusively to the Regions, provided that no Regional law would be effective if it conflicted with a Central Ordinance: the balance of 'subjects' remained in the hands of the Centre.

The numbers of Members of the three Assemblies were substantially increased—in the North from 15 to 90 elected Members and the others likewise; the new House of Representatives, which replaced the Legislative Council, received 136 elected

Members. The important principle of representation by population was then accepted by all, so that the North should return as many elected Members as the East and West together. Naturally, there was a good deal of argument before this was agreed.

The proposed system for the elections was important and I must explain it for a moment. As I have said, the Members at that time, including of course myself, were chosen rather than elected by a very small and socially restricted body of privileged people. The one member per Province (at most three) was now to be enlarged suddenly to between five and twenty Members each, according to their total population. A new system had to be found to choose the Members and, after a great deal of discussion, it was agreed that the electoral college method would be the best for the time being.

Every adult male in a village—in the East and West women also could vote—gathered together on a certain day and at a certain time, and they proceeded to elect about one-tenth of their number as their representatives. These then met at a common centre and did the same thing. The people thus chosen met with others at the next level and so on.

In the end a Provincial College thus chosen met and elected the number of men required to go to the House of Assembly for that Province. In the North there were in some places as many as five electoral steps, but, in the other Regions, there was usually one step only, and the final elections were at Divisional and not at Provincial level as with us.

There was still a difficulty to be met. We realised that this system might produce a crop of quite inexperienced, possibly illiterate, and even possibly otherwise unsuitable Members from whom it might well prove to be almost impossible to build up a ministerial system of government. It was essential that our first steps in this direction should not fail for lack of the right people at the top, and our solution was to put into the final college in each Province, up to one-tenth of its number, Members chosen by Native Authorities or groups of Native

1(a). Rabah village with modern improvements

1(b). The Sokoto River behind my father's house

II(*a*). The Tomb of Sultan Bello at Wurno

II(*b*). Outside my house in Sokoto today

III(*a*). The Governor visited Sokoto Middle School in 1931

Front row: Daniel (Resident), Alexander (Lieutenant-Governor), Sir D. Cameron (Governor of Nigeria), the Sultan Hassan, the Waziri Abbas; *Back row:* Sardauna, Shehu Salame (deceased), Mohammadu Wakilin Doka (deceased), A. Abubakr (Madakin Sokoto), Sani Dingyadi (Makama and Senator, then Headmaster), M. Umoru Liman.

III(*b*). The Local Government Course in England

Front row: Madakin Bauchi, Shettima Kashim (Waziri of Bornu), Sardauna, Ahmadu Waziri (Ambassador in Khartoum), A. Sa'adu Alanamu (Agent-General in London); *Back row:* Al. Sanusi (Waziri of Zaria), Umaru Faruk (Kano), Miss Sasfield (British Council), Sambo Chiroman Hadejia (deceased), Al. Haruna (Emir of Gwandu), Abdu Anace (Madakin Kontagora, M.H.A.).

IV. H.M. the Queen leaving Kaduna

v(*a*). With H.R.H. the Duke of Gloucester at Kaduna

v(*b*). With H.R.H. Princess Alexandra

vi(a). The Sultan of Sokoto in Council

vi(b). With Sir James Robertson, when Governor-General

vii(*a*). With Sir Bryan Sharwood-Smith; K. P. Maddocks is facing the camera

vii(*b*). With Sir Gawain Bell and Mr Speaker, Alhaji Umoru Gwandu

VIII(*a*). With the Emir of Kano, Sir Muhammadu Sanusi

VIII(*b*). Leaving for the first London Conference, with Ibrahim Imam (then on our side) and the Makama of Bida

Authorities from senior Native Administration staff and Councillors. This came to be known as the 'NA injection'. In the end quite a number of these men were returned to the Assembly as well as other suitable men and the danger was over. Ministries could be formed with adequate popular support.

All these proposals were thoroughly discussed at Ibadan and received unanimous support at the meeting. I would like to stress this. Nevertheless, after these elections were successfully held, Southern politicians started a considerable attack on the system, which they called undemocratic, and on the 'NA injections' which they called much worse.

It was true that the electoral college system tends to restrict the part that political parties can play. For example, it is obviously difficult, indeed nearly impossible, for a man to set out from the lowest step on the ladder determined to fight his way into the Assembly, unless he was quite exceptional or had prearranged support in *each one* of the higher colleges. This would be difficult since it was by no means clear who would be elected to the higher colleges or in what numbers the supporters might find themselves on each rung. It was equally obvious that the NA Official 'injected' into the Final College had a much better chance of getting elected than those who came up from below. We were fully aware of this and so were the other Regions, and that is why the West adopted the same plan. It meant, however, that the existing political parties were not able to take much part except in the lowest level of all.

The real point, however, is that everyone at that meeting agreed on all these proposals and everyone faithfully carried them out and that on the whole they worked quite well. It was also clear that the system could only be a temporary expedient, a 'practice run' as it were, to assist those who had never organised, and those who had never taken part in, an election on the ballot box principle, or indeed in any other kind. It must be remembered that at this time the whole conception of electing representatives for any purpose whatever was quite foreign and unknown to the people in general. The political grumbling about the system did not start till some time afterwards.

For the election of Members to the New House of Representatives, replacing the old Legislative Council, we retained the former system of choosing from among the Members of the Houses of Assembly and Chiefs. We felt that it would be unwise to impose a second set of elections, those to the House of Representatives, on top of those to the Assemblies, on a totally inexperienced public. It was, of course, not a satisfactory solution and was one that might in the end have led to disaster had the Constitution run on much longer than it did.

A serious difficulty was, for example, the presence of Members of the Council of Ministers in Lagos as backbenchers in their own House of Assembly and vice versa. You could thus have two Ministers, say, of Education in the same House, one for the Region and the other for the Centre (as it was then), and in the House of Representatives you could have four Ministers of Education (or other subjects, dealt with by the Regions).

CHAPTER 7

NATIVE AUTHORITIES AND REFORM

BEFORE we leave the old House of Assembly, I must mention an important debate that took place in it. In August 1950 Abubakar Tafawa Balewa moved that an independent commission be set up 'to investigate the system of Native Administration in the Northern Provinces and to make recommendations for its modernisation and reform', adding that full discussion at all levels should be permitted on any report produced.

Abubakar made what was for him a long speech: it was also an important speech but, then, many of his speeches are. It was certainly the most dramatic speech made in the old House and as dramatic as any made in subsequent Houses. He based his remarks on a passage in Lord Lugard's Political Memoranda— 'There are not two sets of rulers—British and Native—working either separately or in co-operation, but a single Government in which native Chiefs have well-defined duties and an acknowledged status equally with the British Officers. Their duties should never conflict and should overlap as little as possible....'

This, though eminently sound, had never been implemented. The Chiefs had, he thought, no well-defined place and no one in the hierarchy knew his rights, obligations or powers. The people, on the other hand, were still ruled by might and little effort was made to win their confidence either by the black superiors or white officials. The Chief's Councillors were often too frightened to give him unpalatable advice or to take a line which did not agree with his. They had no popular backing. Those with the new Western learning were not accorded their proper place, where they could use their knowledge to the general advantage.

73

Some of this seemed to him to be due to the change in character of the Administrative Officer. The earlier ones were friends and teachers: the later ones—many of them, but by no means all—were not. Admittedly they were snowed under with paper work, but that could perhaps be overcome. The NA staff wanted far more detailed training—for example, there was hardly a District Head who could write a comprehensive report on his District. Native Treasury systems and procedure wanted overhauling and straightening out. He proposed that a special commission be appointed made up of two Members from outside West Africa, two Administrative Officers (retired and current), and one unofficial old friend of the country. He did not like the idea of a wholly alien commission.

No one had hitherto ventured to comment publicly about, much less criticise, the Native Authorities and the Administration. The schoolmaster from Bauchi was on dangerous ground, but that did not worry him at all. He was the apostle of truth and quite fearless. In some quarters heads were wagged and eyebrows lifted, and it looked very much, they thought, as though the North was not going to be spared 'those crazy nationalists'—indeed, he might well be a revolutionary. However, the House did not think so and warmly applauded his speech.

He was supported by Yahaya Ilorin, the Wali of Bornu, and Muhammadu Ribadu of Adamawa, and Shettima Kashim from Bornu: between them they covered much of the Northern Provinces. They welcomed his courageous speech—and it was a courageous speech—and added some contributions of their own in support. The Government could not, however, accept the motion, as the form of Commission suggested was not agreeable to them, but it was made very clear that the Government accepted the principle of the motion. It was put to the vote: all the officials voted 'NO' as they had to by instruction; all the unofficial voters, except for Ribadu who apparently was not there at that moment, voted 'AYE'. The motion was carried by one vote.

The result of this motion was that the Government appointed two senior Administrative Officers, K. P. Maddocks (who is now Sir Kenneth Maddocks, Governor of Fiji) and D. A. Pott (now Permanent Secretary to Local Government), to hold an enquiry. They travelled to every Native Authority area in the Region and enquired into the details of the administration in each and their proposals for the future.

Their report, province by province, was printed and published towards the end of 1950 and circulated for discussion. It seems to have missed the Budget Session of 1951, and it was not until the July meeting of that year that I moved that a Select Committee of the House meet another from the House of Chiefs, who had already agreed to establish a similar Select Committee, to discuss the Report. During the course of my speech on this motion I said:

Northern Native Administration systems have always been accused as being a poor, autocratic, and Fulani Government. I just want to assure the House, and not the few extremists, that the Fulani Government was based on a democratic and a religious footing. Nothing was done without consultative bodies and, if at all, there is any deterioration in the system, that has been brought about by modern times. . . . When the British came to this country they found that we had our Chiefs, Schools, Judges and all that was necessary for civilisation. They made some slight changes which were accepted by all the people. It can also be said today that changes would be welcomed but not drastic ones that might bring the country to a state of chaos. I am now appealing to the House for this Committee to be appointed in order to get down to work and prepare something praiseworthy that will help for generations to come. . . .

At that particular time M. Abubakar was in England on a course and so was not able to take part in the debate. I had, however, been over the matter with him before his departure and we had agreed on the general line to be followed.

The Select Committee numbered twelve from each House—that is, one Member and one Chief from each Province. Among the Chiefs were the Sarkin Musulmi, the Shehu of Bornu, and the Emir of Kano. The present Emir of Kano was among the

75

Assembly members, I represented Sokoto, and among others were Abubakar from Bauchi, Ribadu from Adamawa, and the Wali of Bornu. There were two Residents, those of Plateau and Kano, and H. H. Marshall, who is now Attorney-General of the Region, then Acting Senior Crown Counsel. The chair was taken by the late A. J. Knott, who was acting as Secretary, Northern Provinces, and was normally Financial Secretary. We met several times between the 17th July and 9th August, 1951, in the Lugard Hall.

There was considerable discussion, but the proceedings were marked by amiability and a desire to produce a progressive solution in the shortest time. It was realised by all that this in fact was a turning-point in the history of the North and would be a new charter, not only for the Native Authorities, but also for the people as a whole.

The functions of Village and District Councils and the methods of electing people to them were discussed and it was agreed that they should receive annual grants from their Native Treasury, if possible, against expenditure estimates. The District Councils would approve the appointment of Hamlet Heads and would recommend that of Village Heads.

The new Chief's Advisory Councils, as established in Sokoto and Bornu and known as 'Outer Councils' to differentiate them from the Chief's own traditional Council, should be partly elected by the Districts and partly nominated, with certain ex-officio members. This Outer Council would consider matters put up by Districts or those sent to it by the Native Authority, and especially proposed legislation. It would also scrutinise the annual Estimates and development schemes.

The Select Committee was addressed (in a rather curious interlude) by R. S. Hudson on the use of Local Government Committees. He was (and still is) an expert in the Colonial Office, and later on he came out to advise us on the formation of Provincial Councils, as will be mentioned in its place. After this digression the discussion resumed and it was agreed to recommend further delegations of financial powers to increase a sense

76

of responsibility in the Native Treasuries. Attention was paid to the necessity for Native Administration staff training and the introduction of general conditions of service, and the discouragement of bribery.

The two most pressing and difficult subjects were the double relationships of the Native Authorities, firstly to their respective Councils—that is, the traditional councils—and secondly to the Administrative staff. These were of such importance that I have no hesitation in quoting in full the pertinent portions of the report on the relationship of the Chief to his Council:

It became apparent in the course of these discussions that the traditional authority of a Chief in the Northern Provinces prior to British occupation was exercised with the advice and support of an equally traditional Council. In the years immediately following the British occupation, Government policy had tended to place undue emphasis on the authority of the Chief and this was reflected in the appointment, under the Native Authority Ordinance, of Chiefs alone as Native Authorities without reference to their Councils.

In more recent years the desire of the Chiefs for the advice and support of their Councils in the growing burden and complexity of administration has been recognised in the greater formality attaching to membership of these Councils which found particular expression in their use as electoral colleges for the House of Assembly in the 1946 Constitution.

The Committee noted that the appointment of Chiefs-in-Councils as Native Authorities, under the Native Authority Ordinance, would in no way affect the traditional status of an Emir as the religious head of his Emirate, but agreed that, in all purely administrative matters, such as the making of Rules and Orders and the appointment and dismissal of Native Authority Councillors, officials and employees, a Chief was accustomed to seek the advice of his Council. Both by tradition and by current practice, therefore, the relationship between Chiefs and their Councils would be more accurately described by the phrase 'Chiefs-in-Council', than by the existing appointment of Chiefs as Sole Native Authorities.

It was suggested that, in view of the fact that the term 'Chief-in-Council', which in English has a very definite and precise legal significance, is foreign to the Hausa language, it would be desirable to provide, perhaps by an amendment to the Native Authority Ordinance, a statutory definition of the phrase in order to overcome this difficulty: such a definition would specifically establish the right of a Chief, similar to that of a Governor-in-Council, for reasons stated to the Resident of the Province concerned, to diverge from the advice of his Council. If the Resident considered that the Chief was wrong in diverging from the advice of his Council he would advise the Chief accordingly. If the Chief disregarded this advice the Resident would report the matter to the Lieutenant-Governor-in-Council for decision.

If the Resident considered that a decision of the Chief-in-Council was likely to prejudice the peace, order or good government of the area, he could order that the decision be suspended pending his immediate report thereon to the Lieutenant-Governor-in-Council for his decision.

For these reasons, and on these conditions, the Committee agreed that there would be no objection to the employment of the term 'Chief-in-Council' instead of 'Chief', in the appointment of Native Authorities under the Native Authorities Ordinance. It was recommended that, where a Native Authority has heretofore been defined as a Chief, such Native Authorities should be invited to consent to the necessary amendment of the Public Notices concerned.

The other point covered the relationship of Administrative Officers to Native Authorities, and ran as follows:

It was noted that it was the first duty of the Administrative Service to act as the mouthpiece of government policy, but that they had, as representatives of the Governor, an overriding duty to ensure the maintenance of peace, law and order, and good government in all spheres. Administrative Officers had certain limited statutory powers and duties conferred by the Native Authority, Native Courts and similar Ordinances; besides this they had only advisory functions in respect of the Native Authorities of the Province to which they were attached, except in those Native Authority areas not sufficiently advanced to function unaided.

A number of the members of the Committee expressed the view that of recent years some Administrative Officers appeared to have exceeded their proper function as advisers to Native Authorities and to have taken upon themselves executive powers which belonged to the Native Authorities themselves. It was appreciated that inefficiency, negligence or misconduct of subordinate Native Authority officials or employees might sometimes justify direct intervention by Administrative Officers which would be reported to the proper quarter; it was, however, felt preferable that, normally, such action should continue, as in the past, to be taken by the Native Authority or his representative.

The Report was agreed unanimously.

78

The first delay in setting up the Select Committees had been due to the need for general consideration of the Potts-Maddocks Report and to various administrative difficulties and to constitutional changes and discussions.

The second delay followed the time taken in printing and circulating the Report of the Committee for discussion. But it was also held back by the first General Election and the meeting of the new House early in 1952, followed by its first Budget session and the creation of Ministries in their first and rather primitive form, all of which took place at that time.

It was therefore not until July 1952 that I was able to rise in my place and move the acceptance of the Select Committee's Report. Two years had rolled on their way and much had happened. We learned that the mills of Government grind slowly but sometimes surely. I said in the course of my speech:

We have of recent years witnessed the sweeping changes in the local administration in the Eastern Provinces and proposals for almost as drastic changes in the West. The North has nothing to match against these spectacular moves and it is perhaps because of this that it has become the fashion in other Regions to regard the North as backward and hidebound by tradition. Indeed, there are some people in the North who hold this view and who think that we should follow the example set by other Regions. Fifty years ago in the East the unit of local administration rarely extended beyond the village, whereas in the North our units covered much the same large areas as they do today. The East inherited from the past no such strong foundations upon which to build; hence the need to complete new structures. The daily growth of a tree passes unnoticed by those that see it every day and it is only by casting their minds back along the years that they can realise the extent of its gradual development. It is even so with our system of local administration. The traditional form has over the years undergone a series of gradual changes designed to adapt it to more modern conditions and conceptions of government. The old form is still there, though much changed, and still commands the old loyalties and respect upon which stable government so much depends. . . .

Conditions in the world today change much more rapidly than they used to do and this country has progressed more in the last ten years than it did in many years preceding. It follows from this that the rate at which the institutions which guide and mould our lives

79

adapt themselves to new conditions must be increased. Ten years ago there were not many who were adequately equipped to play a useful part in public life and to contribute their share to the solution of the problems which confronted the administration of the country at every level. Thanks to the schools and training centres there are many more today who are not only able but eager to assist our traditional leaders in the discharge of their duty of government; a duty which becomes more onerous as modern conditions render life more complicated.

Before the war the voice of this new class with its Western education began to be heard in public affairs and shortly the traditional Native Authority Councils were enlarged and enriched by the inclusion of some of its members. This was the beginning. . . .

Local administration is a dull and lifeless business, unless the people take an interest and an active part in it, and the task before the Committee was to find the best method of enabling the people to do this. The Committee came to the conclusion that this end would best be achieved by retaining and building upon the existing and largely traditional framework of village, district and Native Authorities. The Committee did not attempt to make recommendations which would be applicable to all Native Authorities, with their varying administrative structures; this was manifestly impossible. Instead, it set out statements of principles which it was thought would be of assistance in determining the broad lines on which development should be pursued.

These statements of principle include provision for elected village and district councils, for considerable delegation of responsibility to both, and for delegation of financial responsibility to district councils, which are, of course, already responsible for the management of district council funds. At the Native Authority level the principles to be followed in the creation of Outer Councils are set out, and it was recommended that Sole Native Authorities should become Chiefs-in-Council. This last measure would not be an innovation; it would give legal recognition to the current practice of Sole Native Authorities in seeking the advice of their councils in all administrative matters, which itself was in accord with tradition. This recommendation has recently been put into effect. . . .

The object to be achieved by a reform of local administration at this time is to enable the people to take a much fuller part in their own administration and thereby to bring home to them a realisation of their civic rights and of their duty to the State which is inseparable from the full enjoyment of those rights.

We can set about attaining this object in one of two ways. Firstly, we can copy the example of the East, wipe the slate clean, overthrow the present structure, forged as it was in the furnace of experience, and start afresh. Secondly, we can retain the present time-tested structure to which we are all accustomed and modify it to suit our new requirements. . . . Above all, the present structure is known to the common man, who is to be called upon at all levels to help make it work. From experience we know that it does work; it is something we have inherited from the past and to which we have added from time to time. It is our own. Would we be wise to do away with what we have ourselves built up in favour of a system of administration designed by people with different customs to suit different circumstances, or in favour of some other system not yet designed and quite untried? I do not think so, Sir, oh no, I do not. . . .

This motion was passed unanimously and with acclamation. A new Native Authority Law was enacted in the summer of 1954, just four years after the matter was first raised. This new Law brought into force the principles specified in the Select Committee's Report with some further improvements.

New mosque at Kaduna

CHAPTER 8

THE FIRST MINISTRIES

THE Constitutional decisions were taken at Ibadan in January 1950. They were debated in the three old Houses of Assembly and in our House of Chiefs and agreed without alteration. They were then brought up to the Legislative Council which voted its own abolition. After that they were sent to London where, after further discussion by letter, they were finally approved by the Secretary of State for the Colonies. There were no meetings between him and ourselves on this occasion. His lawyers then set it all out in an Order in Council; all this took much time and it was signed by the King and published in July 1951. During the drafting, verbal misunderstandings seemed to have crept in which meant departure in detail from the points agreed. It was unfortunate but it did not matter very much as changes were bound to come, but next time we scrutinised the drafts rather more carefully.

The Elections were held as soon as possible after publication, but it was not till January 1952 that the New House was sworn by Captain (now Sir Bryan) Sharwood-Smith, who, as Resident, Kano, and the Senior Resident in the North, was automatically President of the House. God willed that I should be elected a Member of this House along with the other fourteen Members from Sokoto; and I am glad to say I made my way of my own impetus all the way from the first 'village' level to the top of the Provincial College. There were then no 'constituencies' and we were all elected by the Final College for the Sokoto Province. I was at the head of the list by numbers of votes cast. The four Sokoto Chiefs were all Members of the House of Chiefs, so the Province did pretty well in the new set-up.

I had now determined to make politics a career for the next few years and was delighted when Sir Eric Thompstone included me among his proposals for Central Ministers. On the list with me were Abubakar Tafawa Balewa and Shettima Kashim. Sir John Macpherson was anxious to have me in Lagos, but my people would not agree to my going there and Mohammadu Ribadu went instead, so I was offered the post of Minister of Works in the Regional Government.

I had known Sir Eric well many years ago in Sokoto. Under the old Constitution he was the Chief Commissioner of the North and now became the Lieutenant-Governor; thus we went back to the time when I was at school, when we had had Lieutenant-Governors; in a few years we were to go back even farther, to a Governor in Kaduna and a Governor-General in Lagos as we had had in the early years of my life. It was Sir Eric's duty to form an Executive Council for the Region for the first time, but he left before the first meeting and so never presided over it.

We should think well of him, for his tact and scrupulous fairness took us through the period of the discussions over the new Constitution without friction and with satisfactory results. He was always calm and reasonable, and made an excellent chairman of the House of Chiefs which was ex-officio his post.

Executive Council, in this its first shape, was made up of not more than six from the House of Assembly, not more than three from the Chiefs, and not more than five officials. Those from the Assembly were:

The Wali of Bornu, my old college friend,
M. Bello Kano (now Makama of Kano),
The Makama of Bida (now Minister of Finance),
and myself;

and those from the Chiefs:

The Sultan of Sokoto,
The Emir of Zaria,
The late Aku Uka of Wukari.

83

The three Secretaries (Civil, Legal, and Financial) were Members, with two Residents—one because he would probably act as President when the Lieutenant-Governor was away, and the other for no particular reason that I can recall at the moment; maybe he was there as a learner. There was thus an unofficial majority of three.

We met in the dining-room of Government House in Kaduna, which was not by any means an ideal place for the secret meetings of the highest body in the Region. House-boys were constantly passing its doors and there was a hatch into the pantry.

The first meeting was held on the 6th February, 1952, just after Sir Eric had gone, and was presided over by Captain (now Sir Bryan) Sharwood-Smith, the new Lieutenant-Governor. We had just been sworn for the first time as Executive Councillors when the Private Secretary came in with a note. Sir Bryan glanced at the paper, lost his colour, and looked upset. Then in a strange voice he said, 'Gentlemen, I am sorry I have very bad news. The King is dead.' His voice broke and he could say no more, and we adjourned in some confusion. It seemed a most unfortunate omen to start our new Government on this tragic note, but, as someone said, we started with the new reign, a young Queen, and a new age.

You may ask how the Chiefs could come in to meetings when they had their Emirates to control and administer some hundreds of miles away. The answer is that they did not come in to all meetings; they only came to full meetings, as they do to this day. Ordinary meetings dealt with the more trivial subjects, and important matters were held over for the full meetings. A technical difficulty was that all Council papers were in English and were sent out to the Chiefs, who had to employ trusted scribes to translate their contents to them whenever they were received.

At their first meetings the House chose the Members they wished to send to Lagos to the House of Representatives. Sixty-eight were chosen and they came from both Houses, so

84

that the Chiefs found themselves sitting with the representatives of their own people and with the Yoruba Chiefs. Though there were technical arguments against it, it worked all right in practice.

I was among those chosen, and led the Northern Representatives. You will understand that we still had only a rudimentary form of party organisation; the East had their strong NCNC and the West were coming along with the Action Group. The Northerners, being people of the same outlook for the most part, clung together, and virtually formed a party, usually called 'Northern Bloc'. We all found it very strange and did not care for our stays in Lagos. The whole place was alien to our ideas of life and we found that the Members for the other Regions might well belong to another world so far as we were concerned. I was very glad not to be a Member of the Council of Ministers: as you have seen, I might have been one.

The Northern Peoples Congress grew out of a purely cultural society of that name. This had been started in Zaria by Dr Dikko, who is now an important figure in the Ministry of Health. After the 1951 elections—the electoral college ones—Abubakar Tafawa Balewa, who had been a Member of the original House of Assembly from the start and who always had a keen political sense, asked me to join this cultural party, later to become our own political party with the same name. Curiously enough, this is how the Action Group also started, for it is in origin the 'Action Group' of the Egbe Omo Oduduwa, a Yoruba cultural society. And they started at much the same time.

I agreed to do this and so later became President of the political Northern Peoples Congress, with Abubakar as Vice-President, and Ibrahim Imam, who since then has had a number of different political allegiances, as Secretary-General. We called it Northern because we wanted to unite the Northern people and at that time we were not looking much beyond our own borders. It had an immediate success and most of the Members of the Northern House joined it. Since then it has

85

remained unshaken, though other parties have blossomed and faded.

Our aims were very simple. To develop the country to the fullest extent in the shortest time; to preserve the peace, good order, and friendly relations between all our different peoples; to conduct an efficient and impartial administration; to ensure for all, freedom of thought and religion, to do good to all men. You will see that we were never militant 'nationalists' as some were. We were sure that in God's good time we would get the power. The British had promised this frequently and we were content to rest on these promises; there was plenty of work ready at our hands for us to do.

The Central Government had made a supreme effort and had completed in almost record time a fine and expensive building for our meetings. They persisted in calling it 'temporary accommodation', though I could find nothing temporary about it. The Governor presided over the first meetings, but we were fortunate enough to have a Mr (now Sir Edward) Fellowes, a Clerk of the House of Commons, to come to our assistance. From him we learned a great deal about decorum and procedure, and so did the man who was to be our Speaker in the North for so many years. We found that attending meetings in Lagos and in Kaduna and working through two budget sessions was rather too much and our work suffered in consequence.

Fortunately, Lugard Hall in Kaduna was by now complete and ready to receive the new House of Assembly. This was just as well, as otherwise we should have been homeless. We had in fact had a meeting or two of the old Assembly in it. There was then no floor and no panelling and, I think, no ceiling; we sat, rather lost in its size, in the lowest level of its amphitheatre on coarse, unfinished concrete. The acoustics were at that stage very poor, and it was all rather depressing and we wondered whether it would ever be finished. But it was finished in time for the new House and the result has always surprised us ourselves and has astonished visitors from overseas.

86

As a matter of interest, the present Chamber was designed to accommodate 80 Members, then nearly twice the requirement, and thus it was thought that a handsome margin had been assured. Before it was finished the number had gone up to 105, and in the end nearly 150 were crammed into it. When the new Chamber is finished for the Assembly the present one will comfortably seat the Chiefs.

Well, here we were, Ministers and Members of Executive Council, but we had no Ministries. We then found that, owing to a peculiarity in drafting, the Constitution did not say in so many words that we were completely responsible for the departments assigned to us (which is what we believed to be the case): we were only responsible for the 'subjects'. So the department (or departments) concerned went gaily on as though they had not heard of our existence. I am quite sure that so far as some individuals were concerned they were quite indifferent to our existence; even if they had heard of us they did not think we were worth consideration and, indeed, it may well be that there are still some of these. Some thought that the whole thing would 'blow over' if ignored; some thought, and some perhaps still do, that in some mysterious ways the Ministers are in the hands of their permanent staff and that British Administration would continue, though in a slightly revised shape.

The departments were very suspicious of the ministerial set-up, for they saw in it, and very rightly too, the end of the empires they were running. The Works were particularly obstructive and the Medical were not much better. The 'writing on the wall' meant nothing to them, and they thought that things would never change and that they would have direct control for ever. Technically, of course, they were very competent and we were lucky to have them. I have found that so many technical officers think that they can draw rings round anyone who is not technical, and by surrounding the subject in a fog of technicalities can stifle any suggestion by a layman or at least obscure it out of recognition. But they are not always right.

I have said that we were Ministers without any Ministries, and at first we scarcely had even an office. We were rather grudgingly given space in the buildings housing the department assigned to us. We had a Secretary each—an Administrative Officer—posted to us. Hardly anyone knew how a Ministry should work, but we soon found out. Some time after this it was decided by Sir Bryan that our status should be increased and that there should be a public appearance of such a change. We were then given more senior officers as Permanent Secretaries and we were also given European Private Secretaries from the Administration. But it was not until 1955 that the position was really cleared up.

At first we had very little to do and our Administrative staff, who were used to working hard, complained bitterly and intrigued to get away back to the Provinces. They were told that before long they would have more than enough to do; they did not believe it but it was true enough. I know some often used to read books in the office to pass the time. I did not blame them for this, for time must have hung heavily. I got hold of as many files as I could and read up all that I could lay my hands on.

The Wali of Bornu, Mallam Mohammadu, who had been Chief Scribe to the Bornu Native Administration, was Minister of Natural Resources—that is for agriculture, forestry, and veterinary. The other important natural resource was minerals including oil, but this was a Central subject and one we could not touch. The revenue from it was divided on a percentage basis. Actually the search for oil, though it had started in the East near Port Harcourt, had not then yielded any interesting results.

Social Services (an all-embracing title) came under the Makama of Bida. He had been a Native Administration schoolmaster in that town for many years with considerable success: he was headmaster of the Middle School for some years and later became Chief Scribe of the NA: after that he turned to politics. This Ministry included education and health and other subjects of that nature.

He had no say in higher education; there was only the new University College at Ibadan and that was Central. Since then there has been a sensational change and, as there is nothing to prevent the Regions having their own universities, they are all planning to do so at the time of writing. But at the time to which I am referring, the remark that before long each Region would have its own and that the one at Ibadan would not suffice was considered very laughable.

Bello Kano was given Community Development. This was an even more amorphous phrase and covered practically everything which affected the life and comfort and welfare of the individual in both urban and rural surroundings.

My Ministry of Works and Communications dealt with all buildings—their design, construction, and maintenance—required for or used by Regional departments. We were still, at that time, concerned with buildings for what are now Central departments, such as Post Offices or Police Stations: these came under the Federation later on, together with Trunk Roads 'A'—that is, the main routes of the country. In the first meeting of the new House the matter of poor roads was brought up and I replied to it thus in the very first speech I delivered as Minister:

> . . . there is a very large programme of road construction and improvement due to be carried out in the future. From 1946 to 1951 in this Region under the Development Plan, £727,151 were spent on the construction of new Trunk and Feeder roads and the improvement of existing roads. Under the revised Development Plan for the Northern Region during 1951 to 1956 it is estimated that a further £1,656,000 will be expended on improving the road system of the North. As these actual and estimated expenditure figures show, every effort is being made to obtain a satisfactory network of roads in the Northern Region. . . .

But I was sorely tried by lack of staff and supplies, as the following extract from the same speech shows:

> . . . several Members complained that shortage of materials and staff was always the excuse given for the delay in carrying out major constructional projects.

89

I know that many people both inside and outside this House are tired of hearing this phrase. But, Mr President, Sir, I will risk arousing the anger of the House by saying that this is not an excuse but a valid reason. Many types of materials essential for buildings, bridges and roads were in short supply during the years after the war and now, through the priority demands of the rearmament programme, they will again be difficult to obtain. Also, qualified technical staff are in great demand, not only in Nigeria but throughout the world. In many cases the salaries offered here by Government are not so high as those offered in other countries and as a result the technical departments, especially the Public Works Department, cannot recruit the staff that is required to carry out their programme of work. . . .

I did a comprehensive tour of the country and saw much that surprised me, especially in local development work. This came out in a meeting of the Assembly in January 1953, when I said:

I was one of those old critics who fought hard in their Emirates with the Administrative Officers. I did not fight because they were trying to take powers from my NA, but I fought because I thought that they were not doing much towards the development of my area. On the other hand I had congratulated some Administrative Officers who served in my Province before I became Minister of Works, but when I took the chance of touring the Plateau Province I said I did not thank them. I saw what an Administrative Officer had been doing there and everybody—any Member of this House—who goes there and is shown what Administrative Officers have done, would retain their services for years.

An Administrative Officer built a bridge with the aid of one artisan near a big town, and yet an Honourable Member from that area was complaining that Administrative Officers were useless. It would not have been built in Sokoto Province during the last five years. I assure the House that more roads and buildings have been constructed in Plateau Province by Administrative Officers than anywhere in the Northern Region. That was mainly because there were not sufficient technical advisers in the Province to tour all the Divisions. However, Sir, the Administrative Officers have contributed greatly to the development of this country, and I am sure most of the people have that contention at hand. If you have a lazy Administrative Officer and you see him idle in your own Province, I would not blame him. I have always brought it to the notice of my Resident and action has been taken. . . .

And later on:

During the course of my tour I found that those responsible for the maintenance of these roads did not realise their responsibilities. I came to a certain Native Authority and somebody remarked: 'Hello, this is the man we want to attack.' I said, 'Yes, and quite frankly I am going to retaliate on my contractors. Who is my contractor in the Provinces? The Native Authorities.' What he answered was: 'Let sleeping dogs lie.' Well, Sir, it is not just that I should tour the Provinces in order to see whether the roads are good or bad; if they are bad, I must try to make some sort of plan to improve them. One of my first recommendations to the Native Authorities was that their Councillors must realise that the sole responsibility of the maintenance of roads is on their shoulders: it is up to the Native Authorities to make the people in authority pay more attention to road maintenance. . . .

It was at that time that we introduced teams of mechanical equipment for rapid road maintenance and construction. On contracts I said :

Members often say, why not give out contracts instead of direct labour. Well contracts are being let. People think that there is very little difficulty with regard to contract work. I would like to oppose that. My reason is that I shall be without a house for the next three months. It is much dearer to build by contract too. I remember that the Public Works Department estimated that 4 houses were to be built for £30,000. Tenders were invited. One man submitted a tender for £32,000, another £56,000 and another £59,000. What a difference. . . .

And on staff:

I went on tour to a Provincial Headquarters and asked how many engineering and technical assistants they had. I was told that they had never had a volunteer from their Middle School. I went next morning to the school and gave a lecture. I was then in the company of a certain Minister in that town. He was surprised to see, later on, boys coming to say that they wanted to join the NA or the Public Works Department. If I can do so, so can you in your Provinces. . . .

Then there was the matter of housing—staff quarters, with a clear eye on the future:

In view of the outcry for Northernisation of the service I have decided, with the Executive Council, that all quarters for both senior and junior service officers will have 50% of them built in the Northern type, so that in future we may not have to convert all the houses into houses that would suit Northerners. . . .

During the time that I was Minister of Works, the department undertook and completed a number of major projects. Of these, the mass of buildings for the school, and college, and hospital at Keffi, the Institute of Administration at Zaria, and the Adult Education buildings at the same place were very important and extensive; on roads, work was undertaken on the new road from Kaduna to Keffi, in the Zamfara Valley, which came under me years ago when I was at Gusau, and on the short-cut west of Kaduna to Mando; and the large bridges at Mayo Belwa in Adamawa and at Foggo (910 feet in length) were completed, among a number of others. A great many other buildings—houses, offices, hospitals, and schools—were completed.

All water supplies for the Region were my responsibility and this was a serious matter. The British Administration had paid a great deal of attention to this vital service and had spent a lot of money on it, but the need was still most severe both in the large towns and the villages.

It was nothing for women to have to go four or five miles each way in the dry season to draw a pot of water; fortunately they actually thought it was nothing and took the position for granted. This was just as well but did nothing to absolve us from the responsibility for alleviating this distressing situation. This could happen just as easily in the comparatively well-watered country by the great rivers as in the arid North. I said in the House of Assembly:

It is difficult to make a programme for well-sinking. I cannot honestly say how many wells are going to be dug for such and such a number of towns. You can dig a well to a depth of thirty feet and get water and, in some cases, you have to dig for about 100 feet or more, and a further difficulty is that peasants are scattered about, one at a distance of a mile, and another at a distance of a quarter of a mile from his neighbour.

92

Again the sinking of wells was by no means the answer always. For some wells produced chemically tainted water and others were so deep that hauling a gallon was a matter requiring strong men and several minutes for each pull.

There is another difficulty about water supply. This is an entirely natural one and quite inevitable, but none the less difficult to deal with. However little water a village or town will use when it is difficult to get, the demand will rise steeply as soon as it is easily available. That would present no problem if it stayed at that, but in practice the demand increases very steeply and for some years it will rise in a geometric progression. Eventually it will slow down but we have not yet reached that point in this country. It is absolutely reasonable that this demand should rise like this; there is little question of waste, but from the Government point of view it is very difficult to meet it in one place without depriving another place which may be even worse off.

All the other activities of Government, and they are very numerous, came directly under the Civil Secretary or the Financial Secretary: they were, of course, British officers and held the highest positions in the service. The Legal Secretary was at that period only concerned with giving legal advice and drafting the few Bills we considered and other official documents. There was little legal work and I think he had only one assistant.

Fortunately these men were very competent, and energetic and sincere in their work. They were at that time easy to get on with and as co-operative as anyone could wish.

They counted as Ministers and stood up in the Houses of Assembly and Chiefs to defend the actions of the units answerable to them and to handle their business. The Regions were still answerable to Lagos for a good many things and could not deal with the Colonial Office direct nor with any other external body. All correspondence of this kind had to go through the Civil Secretary.

We were never quite clear about this title 'Civil Secretary' which was brought in at this time. For thirty years and more the man holding this appointment had been called the 'Secretary, Northern Provinces' and 'SNP' was a very well-known abbreviation all over the North—the other Regions had an exactly similar post. The Financial Secretary was new too, for he had been in the old days merely an Assistant Secretary, a subordinate of the Secretary in the Secretariat, but this change was sensible. The title Legal Secretary, who till then had been called Senior Crown Counsel, was more intelligible though peculiar.

But why 'Civil'? Perhaps it was an echo of the old days—but then Lugard had had a Military Secretary as well—or perhaps of Khartoum, but there too Kitchener had had a Military Secretary and the later Civil Secretary in the Sudan was a survival with a reason. As it was we sat with these three officials and the two Residents in Executive Council and very helpful we found them.

In a year's time we added two new Ministries—Health under Yahaya Ilorin and Local Industries under Peter Achimugu, both good men from south of the rivers. I dropped the word 'Communications' from the title of my Ministry (making no difference in practice to its responsibilities) and Makaman Bida's was renamed 'Education and Social Welfare'. Over this he continued to preside until the next Constitutional upheaval. In fact, he retained the Education side of it with great success until September 1957.

In April 1953 the Wali went back to Bornu as Waziri and Peter Achimugu took over Natural Resources as well as his Industries, but the latter went to a new Minister, Abba Habib from Dikwa, at the end of that year. At the same time—in April, that is—Bello Kano took over Works from me (but only for seven months) and I took his Community Development until I became Premier, when it was split up among other Ministries.

After many searchings of hearts and with much doubt a Ministry of Local Government was created in that same April. The other Regions had had such Ministries for some time, but

Sir Bryan was uncertain of the effect such a Ministry would have on the great Emirs. In the end, however, they took it in their stride as a necessary co-ordinating body. I was given this office, which I retained until 1957.

I will conclude this rather detailed list by saying that I went back to Works in November 1953, when Bello Kano, who had been a Councillor in Kano, became a District Head there as Dan Amar. I was Minister of Works for nearly a year after this (in addition to the two other Ministries), and then Isa Kaita from Katsina took it over as his first Ministerial appointment. In spite of fears to the contrary in some circles, we had no difficulty in finding people to fill these posts and, what is perhaps more surprising, there were no misfits.

CHAPTER 9

MINISTRY OF LOCAL GOVERNMENT

MY first Ministry was called Works and Communications and I formed it in 1952. The next year the title lost the latter word and became just 'Works': in April that year—that is, 1953—I took on in addition the new Ministries of Community Development and of Local Government. I don't really know how I managed all that, but I certainly could not have done it had things been as extensive as they are now.

The supervision and co-ordination of local government had been one of the most important of the functions of the Civil Secretary; and his colleague in Finance controlled the finances of the Native Authorities, as we call our local government bodies in the North. As I have said, the functions were handed over to me with some reluctance and considerable doubt.

You have seen that we had just had an enquiry into the Native Authority systems, and that improvements had been suggested, which were being carried out. This did not affect the fact that we were, and are, very proud of our Native Authorities and the Native Administrations they control. They have worked well, and we are sure that if it had not been for them we should not have progressed as far as we have.

It was notorious that between the wars many a government institution would languish for want of funds: if it was in the 'bush' far away, little interest was taken in it by headquarters, though there were plenty of 'explosions' if anything went seriously wrong as the result of the general lack of guidance and control. The best examples of these truths are the deplorable state of the general hospital in Kaduna in those days compared with the excellent ones in Kano and Sokoto, or the very

96

poor government school in our capital compared with a similar NA school.

The Provinces depended on what money they could get from Lagos, and there was not very much even there. For example, the total vote for the *whole of Nigeria* in 1938/39 for Education was £282,820, and for Health £446,632, and the cream naturally went to Lagos—what is the good of being a capital if you don't have first go at the money? And yet when we spend something extra on Kaduna the Provincial Members are on us like a swarm of bees. You will see how pathetic these sums are when you realise that the totals spent on these two subjects by the four Governments are about £19,000,000 and £8,000,000 respectively.

Fortunately, we had the NAs behind us to counteract the poverty of the Government. They were run very cheaply in comparison with Government and usually enjoyed the close personal attention of the Ruler and of the Resident, and so were more efficient and better looked after.

Most of the original roads were built by the Native Authorities also all the elementary schools (now called, quite incomprehensibly, junior primary schools) and dispensaries and markets, and indeed, most of the things that affect closely the life of the individual. The Native Authorities were, and still are, responsible for the peace in their area, as you have seen in my account of my duties as District Head. They are, in their functions, not unlike an English County Council, with some additional duties: for example, they appoint their own judges, for courts of all grades and powers, and supervise the work of the courts.

They are all of them based on historic grounds and their areas have historic boundaries. That is why they vary so much in size and population—from Kano with over three million people to Bedde with about forty thousand—and also why they have such awkward shapes. From the point of view of the Regional Government, it would be very much better to cut off some of the odd protrusions and incorporate them with more convenient neighbouring units—for example, there is one Dis-

97

trict of Bornu Emirate which is 260 miles away by road from the Shehu's headquarters. Any such interference with these boundaries would be quite impossible and intolerable, and would cause trouble out of proportion to the gain.

Lugard, as has been said so often, saw the administrative genius of the Fulani Rulers and their staffs: he utilised it as the mainspring of the Native Administration system, that he called 'Indirect Rule', and it has worked well since then. The only difficulty from his point of view was that the Fulani system did not cover the whole country. An attempt was made by the British to produce an imitation of Fulani Rule in what were then known as the 'pagan areas' and this failed completely.

There was a period of close enquiry and investigation in the late 'twenties and as a result Councils were set up to rule these areas, based as much as possible on an historic framework: these Councils have worked on the whole quite well to the present day, though there are obvious weaknesses. Perhaps the most curious development has been the demand from some of the Councils that their chairman should be made a Chief and should have a staff of office, which is more or less what the British had actually done and which they had had to abolish. On the other hand, this demand springs from the people, while the British arrangement was imposed from above.

I suppose that one of the most valuable features of the Native Administration from a wide point of view is one which no one would have thought of twenty years ago. That is the way in which the servants of the Authorities have come forward into the public life of the Region. Though we now have new blood coming direct into the system, until recently practically all the Ministerial (and many official) posts in the Region were manned by ex-Native Administration employees—and some are still so employed. After all, I am one myself and continue to appear in the Sokoto Estimates, though there is no financial provision against my name.

This was made possible by the very wise ruling that, though Government servants cannot stand for election to any legislature here, there is no obstacle to Native Administration staff doing so. Without that I don't know what we should have done. To say that we should have been 'in a hole' is an understatement.

There has been a good deal of criticism of the Native Administration system but there are no really cogent grounds for it. It is, I think, partially due to the quite disastrous attempt by the British Administration to force it on to the Eastern Region, where it was completely inappropriate in the form they employed, and on to the Western Region, where it is more appropriate but, owing to local peculiarities, never sat really happily.

The criticism is also partially due to those people who are never really satisfied unless power is concentrated at a centre. They speak of the 'inefficiency of small units', the waste of money and man-power and the 'inevitable' reduplication of jobs and equipment. This is, I feel, rather special pleading and possibly it is also fallacious. Anyhow, it ignores human nature and the inherent desire of people to run their own show in their own way. I have already given examples of what the Native Authorities could do better than the Regional Government, and this is equally true of other spheres.

It is only since we set up a Regional Government and got away from the shadow of the Lagos Government, call it what you like, that we have made real and substantial progress in this country. In the same way, though here the parallel is not exact, so long as Nigeria formed part of the British Empire, it could not get the chance it should have had to develop on its own lines. Again, for this same reason we have as part of our policy given District Councils money to spend on local matters.

Big units may be successful in commerce and they are naturally inevitable if you want to own, say, an air force—what Borough Council could do that?—but for the basis of ordinary day-to-day government they are, I feel, out of the question.

Our serious difficulty over our Native Authorities was twofold. Firstly there were such important differences in population and size and the state of development between them that sauce for the goose could not be sauce for the gander. The big ones had a huge pool of suitable men on which they could draw, and had enough revenue to enable them to pay large salaries to the right people. The others had neither the men available nor could they possibly find the money for really good men from elsewhere.

The other facet was the sharp and fundamental difference between the historic chieftaincies, especially those set up by the Shehu Usuman dan Fodio, and the tribal councils of the people we used to call 'pagans' for convenience. The Chief's position was clear and definite, and the only uncertainty was the man's own personality. He knew quite well what he was supposed to do, but whether he did it or not depended on himself. In some extreme cases it proved necessary to remove the man—and this has proved to be just as true under self-government as it was under the British Administration—but they were comparatively easy to deal with.

Serious difficulty often arises where the Chief, though inefficient or ineffective, has many good points and is personally very popular with his people. It is obviously much more difficult to remove such a man than the type I have just mentioned. In any case it is a confession of failure to remove a Chief. It can be said that a bad one should not be appointed, and an indifferent one can be improved by the actual weight of the office in which he finds himself and of its tradition, together with gentle guidance.

But what are you going to do to a bad Council? We have had several of them. When they are directly elected by the people the position is even more embarrassing. Obviously in the end they must be suspended; but at what stage should this be done?

There was one Council, of quite a large and flourishing place, who would never discuss anything of importance and, what was even more surprising, seemed unable to come to any decision on what they did discuss. This would not have mattered very much in some places, but in this town, for which they were theoretically responsible, there were large numbers of strangers and travellers and some kind of definite rule was very necessary.

It took quite a long time to make sure that they were not merely suffering from 'growing pains'. We hoped for a while that they would settle down and begin to do some good work. But they never did. At the end of six months we came to the conclusion that they were unlikely to improve, and they had to be suspended. It was very awkward and tiresome, as they were one of the earlier elected Councils.

Here another evil had raised its head. At the time of the elections for this Council a general inertia had settled over the place. One party was completely fogged by it, while the other woke up to the extent of voting in small numbers. Naturally, the latter got all their members in and there was no opposition to galvanise the Council. Anyhow, the standard of people elected was so low that even opposition would have made little difference. This does not often happen but it is typical of some kinds of Councils.

Another difficulty arises in quite a different way. An elected Council goes out at the end of its three years of life. Elections are held and not one single member of the old Council is returned. You then have a completely new council. They not only have no knowledge of, or interest in, procedure, but they know nothing of the past actions of the former Council. They then proceed to resurrect all the ideas and objections that had been raised three years before and which had been laboriously put aside after endless argument. What a waste of time!

We must have a look at what kind of Local Government I had to deal with; you must not think that the Native Administrations were always as they are now. They have developed, like everything else, from humble and quite simple beginnings to their present state, and they have not stopped yet. There are still further developments before them. But let us see what there was to build on.

Lugard's earliest form of administration was the Emir and his Council, hereditary members some of them, favourites others, and the scribes to take records. The Councillors owed no responsibility to anyone except to the Emir, whose hand appointed them and whose hand maintained them in their positions. They lived in the Emir's headquarters and hardly ever went out of it. The Emir consulted them on most things before taking action and usually took their advice. Most places had District Heads, some of them had what we should now call Districts, but some had only farms in the bush, though they were pretty extensive farms. They tended to live in headquarters: if they went to their Districts they might be forgotten. There was obviously a great deal of jealousy and intrigue—and I don't say that there isn't any now.

Then there were Village Heads; they were responsible for the peace in general, the apprehension of offenders, and the good order of their areas. For this they had no help from outside and very much the same thing obtains now. They collected the complicated system of taxes, which was replaced by the single general tax and the cattle tax. I don't know how they managed the quite difficult arithmetical side of the collection, but there is no doubt that they never erred in favour of the peasant, for they had to hand the tax on to their superiors and take something out of it for themselves.

What we call Native Courts existed then. As they now hear over twenty times as many cases as do the British type of Courts, you can see that they play an important role. The most sensible thing that Lugard did at the very start of the occupation was to prohibit the appearance of lawyers in these Courts: had they been allowed, the situation would have been administratively intolerable and the state of the litigant or criminal would not have been improved and would probably have been worsened.

The British Administration were very reluctant to take the risk of making changes in the Native Courts, since the system and the law they administer are so inextricably mixed up with the Muhammadan religion. But they managed to introduce a principle of appeals and laid down channels for appeal, which were of considerable service to the people, though not as much as they might have been had they been fully understood by the peasant.

In fact, they faced a great deal of active opposition in making this change and, besides that, there was a far greater volume of concealed opposition than they realised; though hidden, it was very strong. In Muslim Law there is no provision for an appeal and the Alkali's decision is final, except that he could send the case along for the Ruler to award the penalty, if he thought that the Ruler would be interested. In any case, death sentences could only be given by the Ruler, whose staff carried them out. Thus a man on a comparatively modest charge could do nothing once judgement had been given.

The British system of appeals worked all right in theory, but in practice it was not as smooth as it might have been; the delays were very serious and gave a pernicious example to the lower Courts, whose ideas of slow working would, anyhow, be hard to excel. There were occasions when the allowing of an appeal in, say, a murder case by the British Judges of the High Court (or Supreme Court as it was sometimes called) might cause real confusion.

It is easy enough to understand, and often quite inevitable, that a judge called upon to review a case taken under one law will find that steps prescribed by his own law may not have been carried out, or that the kind of evidence required in the lower court is not the same as would be required in the higher and so on. Thus a case might very easily get thrown out and the startled public in some bush village would see to their astonishment that young Audu, who had been taken away for execution for a crime well known to them and perhaps one which they had seen him commit, was walking about as large as life and as free as air. This would create difficulties which could hardly be explained away: the curious unpredictability of the white man in some directions was often all that could be claimed.

The Judges (or Alkalai) were appointed by the Native Authority and received their pay from the Native Treasury, like other officials, and still do so. No one outside the Emirate could say anything or interfere with them, and this is still the practice. In recent times, however, the appointments have to be confirmed by Kaduna.

In those early and uncomfortable days, there must have been a very great deal of work for someone in each Province, in sorting out all these posts and drawing up the first Native Treasury Estimates (about 1910, it was) and then someone else had to check them all through and co-ordinate them at head-quarters. We are lucky that the form of the Estimates was drawn up by amateurs and not by professional accountants: they are very simple and easy to understand as they are, and they have scarcely deviated from their original arrangement in the fifty years since they were first brought to the attention of a rather dismayed Ma'aji (or Native Treasurer).

He was an official of the old Fulani Courts and his title means the 'storer' or, literally, the 'putter away'. All the money was, in fact, in the hands of the Ruler, but the Ma'aji was the man who accepted receipts and made payments in the name of the Ruler. And that is just what he still does to this day. Until quite recently they were responsible for quantities of actual cash; sometimes, when the tax had just come in, very large sums indeed in shillings and pennies were locked away in their dingy mud 'strong rooms'. But now there are more banks and much is done by cheque.

There was a form of police known as Dogarai, who were at once executioners, escorts, watchmen, and personal guards of the Ruler. They all wore scarlet rigas (sometimes with another colour inserted) with great scarlet turbans, ill-balanced on their heads, and a huge sword. In some cases they had guns as well. Until the end of the 'twenties they were, for practical purposes, the only police in the North, for there were very few Government police and they were mostly on escort duty with Administrative Officers and as guards for Government cash.

At that time the best ones were taken out of the Dogarai to make a new force called the 'Yan Gadi' or 'Yan Doka', who were properly disciplined and gradually trained in ordinary modern police methods. They still belong to the Native Authority in exactly the same way as does a County Constabulary in England. There must be about 6,000 of them in 56 different forces.

The Chiefs always had their prisons, and pretty poor things some of them must have been. These have been expanded and modernised, and the warders are now centrally trained. In many ways prisoners are better off than people outside, they certainly get better food and housing than many of their non-criminal or undetected friends outside. And that was about all there was in the old Fulani Administration, plus one or two specialised people, such as heads of markets, court poets, and people who kept the trade routes cleared, more or less.

You will, of course, understand that in the areas outside the Fulani and Kanuri influence there was very little organisation of this kind, if any at all. The tribes were mostly small: if they were large, then there was some kind of clan system as a group. The tribe or the clan ran things their own way: they collected any money necessary, but we do not know on what basis this was done and whether or not there was any regular scheme; they dispensed justice according to the rules and customs of the tribe; they were very self-contained and most of them had little to do with strangers. There was thus no incentive to improve on their tribal methods.

But the coming of the British changed all this. Unfortunately they did not realise all these differences and sought to impose the Fulani ideas. These were resented at the time, as I have said, but now they are fully accepted and people, even primitive communities, are quite put out if they don't have the whole organisation. Whether or not they can pay for it, or staff it, seems of little consequence.

To this original framework have been added modern departments. I might perhaps say that the Native Authorities employed in 1962 about 37,000 people: I find this a surprisingly large figure. The informal gathering of children under the tree round the venerable Mallam, chanting the Holy Koran, has now expanded into formal junior and senior primary schools, where they get a good modern education.

There are now six hundred village dispensaries, which are much patronised by the local people: there were, in most headquarters, NA hospitals which were far better equipped than anything the Government could produce at that time. Most of them have been, unfortunately, taken over by Government recently. The Kano City Hospital, which grew up under the Emir's watchful eye, was bigger and better equipped than any other hospital in West Africa: the flexibility of the Native Treasury financial system made it possible to get supplies quickly and without reference to any carping superior, and so helped quick development and specialised equipment.

The Forestry, Agricultural, and Veterinary departments of the Native Authorities, have grown steadily and have done a great deal of useful work locally. This has been specially so in the planting of amenity trees in towns and avenues, the issue of 'budded' fruit-trees, and the battle against cattle diseases which plague the millions of head of cattle in this region.

A new line is a small survey unit for town planning and market lay-outs and the like. Kano has had, for forty years or so, an elaborate Survey Department, printing their own maps, and also an excellent printing press.

The Native Authorities for a long time have had their Works organisations, which have been responsible for maintenance and construction of buildings and roads and which have contributed greatly to the development of the areas. They also maintain and run the motor transport of the Native Administrations, which has now become a substantial fleet.

Kano put about £300,000 from their reserves in 1929 into water and electricity for the city and were wise to do so. Had they left it to the Government, goodness knows when they would have got the installation: they even employed European technical staff to look after this plant.

Most of the Native Authorities have realised that if they want to impress the public they must have good offices for their staff to work in. The days of the crumbling mud building, with its dark corners and uneven floors, has gone. They were useful in their time and served their purpose, but their passing is not mourned by anyone. Some of the NA offices are very impressive: they have not been extravagant, but have got good value for their money. In the same way, office accommodation in districts has been vastly improved. The Alkali can now see who is in front of him: he no longer has to peer through the gloom; gone are the vaguely menacing figures in the shadows; glass windows open and shut; the days of the ant-eaten shutter, hanging lopsided from a single rusty hinge, have gone for ever.

All these departments work in harmony with the equivalent Regional Ministries: they do not form part of the Ministry, but take advice and guidance from it and are also liable to inspection by the Minister's staff. They spend their own money in the direction the Native Authority wishes, with the agreement of the Regional Government. The Native Authorities must balance their accounts each year on the right side, but they say what they want to develop. In practice they all follow much the same line as each other.

All this makes a great deal of work in the Ministry of Local Government, and there are naturally constant queries from the Native Authorities, as well as to them, and every now and then a crisis which needs swift action.

At one time it was thought that when we became Independent, the post of Administrative Officer would become redundant and would gradually fade away. These posts include the Resident of each Province and the District Officer in charge of each of the forty-odd Divisions into which Provinces are divided. We have found with experience, however, that we cannot do without these officers. The East and West have made several experiments in this direction but they have not succeeded in doing without some form of Administrative Officer. A link of this kind between the Government and the local administration has proved to be essential.

We are doing all we can to replace the former British Officers by Northerners, and by the end of 1961 over half had been successfully replaced. While they represent the Ministry for Local Government in the field, as well as some other Ministries, they come under the Premier's Office direct for discipline and major policy and so keep the Regional Government in touch with local affairs.

It may be of interest to show the development of the Native Administration system from the time I went to Katsina College to the present day: the simplest way of doing this is to look at some typical figures.

		1926/27 £	1960/61 £
Kano Emirate	total revenue	119,630	1,777,135
	reserves	300,000	635,600
Sokoto	total revenue	79,187	1,041,910
	reserves	100,000	514,000
Bornu	total revenue	50,000	901,030
	reserves	75,000	950,000
Jemaari*	total revenue	1,274	14,557
	reserves	1,000	15,500
All NTs	total revenue	706,353	10,911,712
	reserves	1,200,000	7,000,000

* The smallest of the NAs.

As I have said, the Native Authorities run their own show as far as possible in their own way. The Regional Government avoids unnecessary interference into their conduct, but expects them to maintain their staffs and organisation at a satisfactory standard—that is, a standard satisfactory to the Ministry responsible for the Regional aspect of the same subject.

This is in itself rendered very difficult because of the variety of the Native Administration themselves. Obviously it is almost impossible to expect the same standard from a small Native Administration far away in the bush as one could from Sokoto or Katsina: they probably have not got the equipment and certainly have not got the right kind of staff or the money. But we do our best.

There is, too, another problem which is growing on us now.

That is, the more we encourage the democratisation of the Native Authorities, the harder it is for us to impose the Regional will on them. For they will quite naturally turn round and say, 'We have discussed this project thoroughly: we have the money and we have the staff, and yet you say we must not do it. What were we elected for, anyway?' Or conversely, 'We have considered your proposals about X and we are entirely opposed to them because of . . .' I know that in Europe the central governments are taking more and more interest in and control over local government activities, and 'advice' is becoming farther from its proper meaning. But people there are in a position to understand the subtleties of the matter, in a manner which I don't think you can expect here yet.

We give large sums to the Native Administrations in grants, especially for Education, Health, and police, and naturally expect that there will be reasonable maintenance of standards. There is in most cases, but inevitably some lag behind.

The Kano Mosque

CHAPTER 10

CRISIS IN LAGOS

THE new Constitution had been running for just over a year, but though things were smooth in the Regions, the same could not be said of the Centre. There were four reasons for this:

Firstly, the curious set-up in the Council of Ministers; secondly, the strong feelings running in Lagos and the big towns of the South; thirdly, the impact of the new political parties; fourthly, the different stages of development in which the Regions found themselves.

To take these in their reverse order, we were very conscious indeed that the Northern Region was far behind the others educationally. We knew that individually the educated Northerners could hold their own against the educated Southerners, but we simply had not got the numbers they had, nor had we people with the university degrees necessary as a qualification, at that time, for some of the higher posts.

For example, for years the British Administration had clung to the principle that no one could enter the Administrative Service, the rulers of the world—our world, of course—without a degree. The fact that at one time none of the three Lieutenant-Governors had acquired degrees seemed to be of little consequence in practice, and did not appear to vitiate the argument. The British allowed only a very, very few Africans into this sacred flock. No one remembered that, thirty years before this, an African had been Resident of the Colony—that is, in charge of Lagos and its surroundings—and others had been high in the Secretariat.

As things were at that time, if the gates to the departments were to be opened, the southern Regions had a huge pool from which they could find suitable people, while we had hardly anyone. In the resulting scramble it would, we were convinced, be inevitable that the Southern applicants would get almost all the posts available. Once you get a Government post you are hard indeed to shift and, providing there is no misconduct, the line of promotion to higher posts must, so far as possible, follow seniority. The answer was clearly that in these circumstances the Northerner's chance of getting anywhere in the Government service would be exactly nil.

Such a situation might, taken from a broad angle and in other conditions, have appeared to be quibbling and possibly rather childish. As things were here, it was a matter of life and death to us. For we were not only educationally backward but we stood at that time far behind the others in material development. This was due largely to our great size and rather scattered population, but also to the simple fact that we were a long way from Lagos. If the British Administration had failed to give us the even development that we deserved and for which we craved so much—and they were on the whole a very fair administration—what had we to hope from an African Administration, probably in the hands of a hostile party. The answer to our minds was, quite simply, just nothing, beyond a little window dressing.

The political parties in the South were more highly developed than were ours; further, they were more 'party minded'. The advantage to the party was their first consideration, and the advantage to the country a second, and quite a long way back too; we were still working as a whole and looking at problems as a whole. The Southern parties were, in fact, though they would not admit it, the followers of prominent individuals. Their business was to 'boost' that individual and do all they could to put him into national leadership and power. Our people had no thought of pushing the interests of the Sardauna, of Abubakar or of Ribadu, and so, there was no danger of a split, as there was in other parties. This, of course, could not fail to advance the interest and status of the more prominent party members.

This was made all the more striking because the parties had in truth little divergence in policy: they were all working for self-government and the exit of the British Administration. There were no clefts based on matters of principle, as there are between the British Conservative and Labour parties. Even NEPU, which was just starting in the North and which had different views from ours on the future of the Native Authorities —largely due to faulty understanding and personal experiences —was not widely different.

The cry of 'Self-government NOW' would always raise a mob in the Coast towns and the large centres of the Yorubas and Ibos. This was used by the leaders as a means of bringing pressure to bear on the Government and to create a feeling of a 'national' demand. No one knew better than the leaders that such a demand was not only inept but also quite impossible of fulfilment, since there was no organisation ready to take over. But, as you will see in a few moments, when it came to the crucial motion there was no talk of 'self-government now' and a date in three years' time was the best they could think of.

All this did not, however, stop them egging the people on to believe that they actually would receive self-government now, if they made enough noise, and that a new Jerusalem would be ushered in, in which all would be milk and honey, well below cost price. Fortunately, the people so deluded only formed a tiny fraction of the total population and in the end no serious harm was done.

The final point was quite different. In the newly created Council of Ministers, which met in a new building forming part of the Governor's office in Lagos, there were four Ministers from each Region's representatives in the House. The Southern Cameroons was at that time theoretically part of the Eastern Region and so one of their seats on the Council went to Dr Endeley from that territory, but without Portfolio.

This was obviously a stopgap measure to tide over the time until it was possible to have a majority party in the House, from which a full Government could be drawn in the best Westminster model. It recognised that in this newly introduced version of Parliamentary democracy there might not be any clear majority party and further that the parties might not be willing to join together to form a coalition to support a workable Government. I will come back to this matter later on as it still has an importance, though the Constitution has been changed.

In addition to these twelve Africans there were seven British officials. The Governor presided: with him were the three Lieutenant-Governors, the Chief Secretary to the Government, the Financial Secretary, and the Attorney-General. Normally, the three Lieutenant-Governors did not attend and the row of white faces was rather less impressive. They came in for special meetings, and were always present when the House of Representatives was sitting. All the six Europeans were members *ex-officio* of that body, and the Governor presided though he could delegate to others.

If everyone had been sensible this Council would have worked quite reasonably until the next step in self-government was decided. But it had no chance to do so. The Ministers from the West and the East were professional politicians: everything that was put before them they considered from a political angle. There was great suspicion, sometimes not even veiled, about the motives of the Europeans. For the most part this was quite unfounded and unjustified, for, though they could see the writing on the wall as well as anyone else, they were busily engaged in doing all they could to further the development of the country, both politically and materially.

With them were the four Northern Ministers. They were not politicians and wanted to get on with the jobs that had been given to them. Further, they warmly disliked the atmosphere in Lagos and the habits of the Lagos crowd. They thought things out for themselves and stuck to their conclusions. It was, of course, inevitable that quite frequently their opinions would coincide with those of the British officers, since both groups had the same objects in view. When this happened the other two Regions at once came to the conclusion that the simple-minded

Northerner had been got at and bulldozed by the unscrupulous Europeans to 'gang up' against the others. Nothing could have been farther from the truth. And besides that, the British officials did not by any means agree among themselves on some matters.

There was yet a further complication. Only one of the party leaders was in the Council of Ministers. Dr Endeley represented the Southern Cameroons as a Minister without Portfolio and was the sole leader of a party. The West were headed by S. L. Akintola (now Premier of that region), while his party leader, Chief Awolowo, Western Premier, was a floor member of the House of Representatives. The leader of the Eastern party, the NCNC, Dr Azikiwe, was not a member of the Lagos House at all and was the Premier of the East. When the Representatives were sitting he would, however, take his place in the public gallery and thence direct the operations of his party taking place on the floor of the House, and for this I must say he had a remarkable talent. Finally, the Northern Ministers were led in Council by Abubakar Tafawa Balewa: I was a floor member in the Representatives and left the affairs of the Council of Ministers severely alone.

I must explain that though for convenience I refer here to 'Western' or 'Eastern' Ministers, their functions were not Regional; it was their origin that was Regional. The departments that they controlled were of course Central and housed in Lagos. Their portfolios covered Labour, Fuel and Power, Transport, Commerce and Industries, Posts and Telegraphs; four had concern with Regional subjects such as Agriculture and Social Services, though they did not control them; and there were two Chiefs, the Oni of Ife and the Emir of Katsina.

There was the setting, and now let us have a look at what happened during the Budget session of 1953, on the 31st March and the 1st April. This proved to be the most serious crisis that we have so far been called upon to weather, and disaster hung over the scene in grim threat. God was pleased to turn it away from our unprotected heads.

During the meeting we were startled to find a private member's motion put down which read 'that this House accepts as a primary political objective the attainment of self-government for Nigeria in 1956'.

It was in the name of Chief Enahoro, a back-bencher from the Action Group, a very talkative man. By the way, I must make it clear that the use of the word 'Chief' in the Eastern and Western Regions is quite different from that in the North, where the holder of the title of Chief or Emir has very definite territorial authority and extensive legal rights. In its Southern form, the word, as I understand it, is an honour only, on the same lines as a British title: no authority is conveyed with it.

When I saw Enahoro's notice of motion about self-government, I saw him and asked him to withdraw it, as it would be very embarrassing to us if it were to be debated. He replied that, though it was in his name, it was in fact a Party motion and that it would be better if I would discuss it with his leader, Awolowo. Makaman Bida and I asked the latter to see us and he came alone. I said that on a matter of this importance it was essential that I should consult my people in the North before making any public statement, and that, if it were to be moved at this meeting, such consultation would, of course, be quite impossible. He said that he would have to consult his Party as they attached much store by it.

The next day Awolowo came again with a curious proposition. He said that his Party had agreed to put it off until the next meeting—the one likely to be held in August—*provided* that I would guarantee that at that meeting we, the NPC, would not oppose it. This was, of course, entirely ridiculous and we could not entertain it. Battle was therefore joined. Awolowo went off to make a plan with Azikiwe, but our simple little device fortunately defeated the whole project as you will see.

Tuesdays are normally Private Members' day in all the Nigerian legislatures, and the House of Representatives was no exception. This motion was set down for Tuesday the 31st

March. There were six other private motions on the Order Paper and this was the last of them.

It was stated later on that this position had been given to it by the Council of Ministers, to ensure that it would never be reached and would in consequence fall to the ground—in these circumstances it could not be moved again during the same meeting. In the Northern House such motions were taken strictly in the order of their presentation and only when there were a good number of them, and it was necessary to ballot, did the Northern Speaker permit any alteration in their order, however inconvenient it might be, and it sometimes was, to the Government. However, it seems that the custom in Lagos was different.

The first thing to strike the intelligent reader will probably be the mover. Surely such an important matter should have been moved by at least the leader of a party, if not by a Minister. And surely it should not have been moved at all unless there had been general discussion and agreement between all the parties. For it to be a matter of argument and controversy would not look at all good to the world at large. But none of these considerations appear to have arisen in the mind of the Action Group. It is quite clear that had it been discussed, as it should have been, before being presented to the public eye, it would never have reached the Table at all. I do not think that agreement would ever have been achieved.

The alleged 'unscrupulous attempt' by the Government to put the motion out of reach was defeated by the refusal of the movers of the six previous motions to move when they were called. Thus the field lay open for Enahoro (who had failed to move two earlier motions in his name) to introduce this political resolution.

When one thinks what a good speaker he is, this speech, on such an important matter too, was strangely uninspiring. It was long; it enlarged upon the obvious; it magnified the conspicuous; it slipped conveniently over the dangers that lay ahead; it took support for granted. The date 1956 was chosen because it was at the end of the life of the House and a point when a new Constitution could be conveniently introduced.

To bring it earlier would be to put a premature end to the life of this Constitution. Why he did not want to do that, though he yearned for self-government, was not clear to me; little did he think that the result of his introducing this motion would effect just that and little more in the direction he wanted. The date could not be later than 1956, for that would mean 'a further period of national slavery'—a remarkable description for a country whose inhabitants had complete and unfettered majorities in every council and legislature, a country in which no outside authority had the slightest say, unless an undreamed-of situation arose which demanded intervention.

He said some other remarkable things: here is one of them.

There may be some doubt as to whether any political party is fully representative of the people, but there can be no doubt whatsoever that any unanimous view approved by the majority of political parties must represent the true feelings of the politically conscious citizens of any country, and 1956 from this point of view enjoys the advantage of unanimity.

Did it, indeed?

He admitted that there might be 'one or two minor points to answer,' such as 'Shall we have enough knowledgeable men and women (by 1956)?' 'Are there any grounds for the fear on the part of some members of the North that they will be dominated by the South?' He did not answer these vital questions but left them to those who spoke after him. They were not mentioned again.

He then made two unfortunate and lengthy exhortations to official and special members to refrain from speaking or voting on this intimate subject—surely the last thing they would have thought of doing, as he might well have guessed.

His final paragraph started, 'The whole country—I even say the whole world—is awaiting the verdict of this House on this motion. News of what we say here today will travel far and wide.' It certainly did, though not quite as he had hoped.

117

His seconder, Awosika, contributed nothing at all to the question. He seemed obsessed by the 'slavery angle' and addressed us on the desirability of self-government in general, a matter on which we were all at least in warm agreement and on which we required no exhortation.

The question was proposed by the President, and at that point, I am afraid, I rather put the cat among the pigeons by moving an amendment to substitute 'as soon as practicable' for the date '1956'. This is what I said:

. . . We from the Northern Region never intended, nor do we intend, to retard the progress of any Region. Nor do we say that those who demand self-government, if it is for their own Region alone, are wrong. Far from it. For, after all, every community is the best judge of its own situation. In this regard, Mr President, the people of the North are the best judges of their own situation and we feel that in our present situation we cannot commit ourselves to fixing a date for the attainment of self-government. We are fully aware of all the implications involved and we want to make it abundantly clear that the destiny of the North is in the hands of the people of the North.

We of the North wish our form of self-government, once granted, to be such that its attainment should give us no cause for eventual regret. It would be very unwise, Sir, if, before we fix a date for attainment of self-government for Nigeria, we do not stop to think of the condition of things obtaining in this country today. It is true that we politicians always delight in talking loosely about the unity of Nigeria. Sixty years ago, there was no country called Nigeria. What is now Nigeria consisted of a number of large and small communities all of which were different in their outlooks and beliefs. The advent of the British and of the Western education has not materially altered the situation and these many and varied communities have not knit themselves into a composite unit. Sir, whatever Nigerians may say, the British people have done them a great service by bringing all the different communities of Nigeria together. . . .

The great day came with the introduction of the Richard's Constitution in 1947 when, for the first time in our history, indigenous citizens of the North sat side by side with the South to legislate for one Nigeria and share in the discussion of Nigerian affairs. That was in 1947. Meanwhile, Sir, our comrades in the South had been taking part in the discussion of their own affairs in the Legislature as far back as 1922.

Sir, the 1947 Constitution was to last nine years, very probably in order to give the North sufficient time to learn. That Constitution, Sir, was revised after the North had gained only two years' experience and now we have a new Constitution which has been barely a year in existence. I must say here, Mr President, motions like the one which I am now trying to amend, are deliberately designed to destroy the happy inter-Regional relationship which the present Constitution is rapidly building up. Though I realise that motions of this nature are merely an expression of opinion, yet I feel that they can serve no purpose other than doing harm and causing ill-feeling. I have my reasons for so saying. For many years the outside world has been led to regard Northern Nigeria as a backward country, where all the people are conservative to the extreme and unreceptive of modern ideas. One has only to read the local papers and to remember utterances made by some Southern Nigerians in the past for a confirmation of my statement. . . .

Before we commit ourselves and the people we represent in such matters, we must, I repeat, we must seek the mandate of the country. As representatives of the people, we from the North feel that in all major issues such as this one, we are in duty bound to consult those we represent, so that when we speak we know we are voicing the views of the nation. If the Honourable Members from the West and East speak to this motion unamended, for their people, I must say here and now, Sir, that we from the North have been given no such mandate by our people. No Honourable Member can therefore criticise the Northern Legislators for refusing to associate themselves with such an arbitrary motion fixing, as it does, a definite date for the attainment of national self-government. We in the North are working very hard towards self-government although we were late in assimilating Western education. . . .

It is our resolute intention to build our development on sound and lasting foundations so that they will be lasting. . . .

With things in their present state in Nigeria, the Northern Region does not intend to accept the invitation to commit suicide. Unless we Nigerians can prove to ourselves and to the world outside what we want, I cannot see how people can be expected to regard our demand seriously. It is not uncommon for people in this country, for a group of people to sit together and demand self-government. Some are even demanding it now, immediately. . . .

Any country which accepts self-government must do so with its eyes wide open and the problem, therefore, of one section of the country imposing its will on the others does not arise. I move this amendment, which, in my humble opinion, is much more appropriate if the question of self-government for Nigeria is at all to be discussed at this stage. I do so, Sir, without any fear or misgiving that if the original motion were to be carried, it would automatically be binding on all Regions. Far from it! As I said earlier in my remarks, a private member's motion is intended primarily to give that member and others an opportunity of expressing their views on a given subject. . . .

Numberless motions of this nature will not achieve self-government for the un-unified Nigeria. Self-government for Nigeria can be demanded and obtained only when its meaning is fully understood by all the mass of this country. Let all the implications be thrashed out and agreement reached by the leading citizens of all three Regions. This is the primary objective to which we have addressed ourselves and, in doing so, to show to the country our fitness to discharge the heavy responsibility we have begun to assume. Then, once this objective has been attained, we will be on the safe side in demanding self-government.

CHAPTER 11

MORE CRISIS IN LAGOS

M y old friend the ex-Waziri (formerly Wali) of Bornu supported me in quite a brief but powerful speech. His theme was that self-government must mean Government of the people, by the people, for the people, and, if this was so, the people themselves must have a great say in deciding when and how it was to be introduced. We in the North were trying to educate the public. By education we did not mean that we were going to make all the members of the public literate, but we were trying to give them enlightenment—cultured minds. We wanted the public to be able to sit and discuss among themselves what kind of government they wished. But on the present motion we appeared to be endeavouring to impose a certain kind of government, which they had not discussed.

Our amendment would give a flexibility and the date might conceivably be before 1956, it might just as well be after it. He said that we did not want any Region to wait for us and thus originated an idea which eventually blossomed out when each Region was granted self-government individually before the Federation received theirs.

He finished thus:

We in the North are men of practical experience and we wish to work on a sound foundation. We never believe in false propaganda and the mass of people will not accept any false propaganda. My Honourable friend, the mover of the motion, has said, if I followed him correctly, that the people of this country have been asked to discuss whether the people wish to accept self-government in Nigeria or not. I do not know whether he or the other Honourable Members in the West have discussed with the members of the public whether they are asking for self-government or not: as far as the North is concerned, as I have already explained, we are working for it, educating them, but at no time did we discuss with them whether they wish to have it in 1956 or any other date. Mr President, Sir, if we members from the North accept self-government in 1956 we are doing a very serious disservice to our Region. This is because I know there are very few educated elements in the country, who know the meaning of self-government, and this number is very, very small. . . .

We had arranged a further surprise for that morning and the motion that will now be mentioned was known only to myself and one or two others until this instant.

Up popped the massive figure of Ibrahim Imam—at this particular time he was on our side of the fence as Secretary-General of the NPC. He begged 'leave to move that the debate be now adjourned'. The President said quite gently that he couldn't do so until the question had been 'proposed' and then went on to propose the question. He suspended the sitting so that everyone could get their breath back.

These tea intervals, though not included in the Westminster pattern, often proved invaluable in crises, as I will tell you later. The House trickled back after a while, the President took his seat once more and the debate proceeded.

Before Ibrahim Imam could lever himself out of his seat, the Oni of Ife was on his feet. He said, 'I have been very worried for the past few days over the motion now being debated and in the circumstances in which I find myself I trust that the right course for me was to resign from the Council of Ministers.' And resign he had that very morning. That caused a real sensation in the House.

Ibrahim Imam now had his chance and moved again that the debate be adjourned.

To me [he said] a motion of such political significance and importance ought to have been discussed by all the Regions of Nigeria. Self-government for a population of over thirty million people is not a matter of little importance that can be taken up independently by one party, forming only a section of the community, because of political expediency, perhaps. . . . Speaking of independence in this way is a decision which can be regarded as an act of rugged individualism. . . . We should only approach the motion through brotherly affection and mutual understanding. But we have not been consulted or asked for our views and opinions before this motion was tabled. . . .

When some parts of the Northern Region have not got the word 'self-government' in their political vocabulary, we may well need time and opportunity to educate the members of the public in their civic and political responsibility. It is only after such preliminary spade work that we shall come forward with any audacity or confidence to ask for a time-table setting out the main stages towards self-government.

The motion should be now adjourned until the three Regions can form a national front with a view to agreeing among themselves, sinking their differences, grievances, prejudices, both tribal and political, suspicions and fears and agree on the fundamental principles of self-government.

His speech was punctured by disturbances, but he was used to that, and he sat down in uproar. His supporter was Sani Dangyadi from Sokoto. You will remember that he was the Headmaster of the Sokoto school when I was a teacher there, fresh from Katsina. Now he was a Sokoto Councillor. He looks like an old man and very frail and speaks with a very quiet voice in slow gentle English. At this particular moment he was still a little ruffled over a small scene which had occurred round him earlier in the morning.

It would be a gross mistake [he said] if we were to commit ourselves as requested by the original motion. In this world of uncertainty, who will venture to take such unplanned responsibility? In the face of all these glaring prospects that may tend to deceive the minds of some Honourable Members, anything may happen.

Without giving time for the President to propose the question, Chief Awolowo rushed in with a long and indignant speech. He said that it was unprepared and he was obviously thrown off balance by the swift turn of events in the House. It seems almost inconceivable to me that his party should have come to the House in the expectation that there would be no opposition to the motion, and that he should have had no speech up his sleeve. But that seems to have been the case.

We were taken back to the slave-trade and after some eloquence it was suggested that the value of the slaves taken out by the British was far higher than any contribution she had made since the occupation. Any development work which had been done was because the officials were paid salaries to do it. He maintained that Britain was in illegal occupation of the country and should go; on the other hand he liked business men, traders, and missionaries, and had no quarrel with British officials, who come here to earn their money. His quarrel was with the British Sovereignty and his real demand that the country should be able to vote for its own Governors and Governor-General. 'For,' he said once more, 'power corrupts and absolute power corrupts absolutely. However, he did not indicate who it was that had absolute power at that time: I could think of no one. Then he made an observation about the bones of the revered Shehu Usuman dan Fodio which brought me to my feet in anger: the President made no ruling and he continued his remarks.

Two things he said deserve to be remembered. Firstly:

Our Northern brothers should not bother themselves about the conference of the whole country, the conference of the masses and so on and so forth. Who are these masses? The generality of the people are *not interested in self-government or in government generally.* What they are interested in is their food, shelter, clothing, to get married, bear children, and drink plenty of palm wine, and, if they have the money, to drink some gin as well. It is the Walin Bornu, Sardaunan Sokoto, Awolowo, it is Mbadiwe—these are the people who are interested in self-government.

A little astonishing from a man who prided himself on his democracy, I thought.

The other one was:

We should be free to say our mind on this issue without being fettered, and the North should be free to say its mind without being fettered. At division time we know by the look of things that we will be beaten but we are not afraid. It will go on record that A, B, C, and D voted for freedom for their country and that E, F, G, and H voted against. We find that the Northern majority is not only being used in having their way, but is also being used in preventing the majority from having their say.

I found it rather difficult to follow all this as I was pretty sure that they would not vote: I also could not see that they were 'fettered'; our motions did not prevent a good deal being said by skilful debaters and there was no doubt that they were that all right. And who was 'using' us? I suppose they meant that the British officials were doing so. How they got the idea I do not know. The British were, of course, more friendly to us because, as they said, 'we talked the same language', but so could the Southern parties if they had wanted to. And in some ways it would have been better if they had.

I must here make it quite clear that there was never any occasion at all in which we, or any one of us, were persuaded by British officials to vote or act in a manner contrary to our own feelings. We were, quite naturally, always prepared to listen to what anyone had to say, but after we had considered their opinions we came to our own conclusions and stuck to them. As I have said before, the fact that our conclusions more often coincided with the British views than did those of the other parties was because we tended to think along the same lines in our own minds. It had nothing whatever to do with any mental compulsion or servility.

It is a mistake often made to think that our natural courtesy implies that we feel ourselves to be in any inferior position to those to whom we are being polite: the fact that we are polite does not mean that we are necessarily in agreement. Our courtesy is, I think, not unlike that of the British people, though of course it is by no means the same thing. But, however it may be, the fact remains that our being polite does not mean that we have no minds of our own. Strangers often make that mistake, to their own cost.

Anyhow, Awolowo had already made up his mind to walk out, but when he discovered from signals that the NCNC still wanted a say, he refrained and listened to K. O. Mbadiwe the next speaker, a member of that party.

He took a different line and did his best to flatter the North, but it was shallow stuff and, as he knew well enough, it could make no difference to the outcome. Most of his speech was, in fact, quotations about the beginning of the United States of America which, though a parallel situation to ours, did not really advance the debate very far. Sandwiched into this was a denunciation of our educational system.

We are suffering [he said] from this woeful education, that has made us to have such little minds, such little vision; your brother is suspicious of you, your countryman is fearful of you, the North is suspicious of the East, and the East of the West, the West of the others. Why? Is it because we cannot meet? No. It is because of the type of puny unimaginative education that has been dosed on this generation, and we want to eradicate that type of education so that the light may be seen, and men may be set free.

There was quite a lot in this, but then he went off on another quotation about the USA. I have wondered why some Southern members are so fond of quotations: surely if a thing is worth saying it is better put in one's own words?

His concluding remarks were difficult to hear owing to the noise, and they did not take us any farther. He then left the Chamber at the head of the NCNC, with Awolowo and the Action Group, and left us to it. I can never understand the mentality of those bodies who 'walk out' from conferences and the like. Nothing whatever is gained by this manœuvre. It is quite impossible to run anything if parties walk out at the crucial moment. It merely means that they are not prepared to face criticism, opposition, or even defeat like men and, what is perhaps more important, it lays them open to the charge of failing to be present to intervene at the next stage in the proceedings, which may well be important. Anyhow, they walked out, but there was still a residue of Southerners, besides the solid mass of the North.

It was striking to me that no one had produced any reasoned argument against the adjournment and no one had suggested any date for its resumption. But, of course, there is no doubt that everyone had been caught on the wrong foot.

At that time the NCNC had split, not an unusual situation, and the smaller group opposed to Dr Azikiwe's larger one called itself the National Independence Party. As the main party had walked out, they of course had to sit with us and make the best of it. Jaja Wachuku was the spokesman for this group, an ingenious man, quick to take advantage of any situation that might arise to further the ends he was interested in at the moment.

He thought that the important thing was to get the Ministries working properly. We had only the previous day passed unanimously a motion calling on the Government to amend the Constitution to give authority to the Ministers, who had at that time (owing to the peculiarities of legal draftsmanship) only casual authority over their Departments. (Little did anyone then realise that it would take the best part of six years to get the Ministries fully integrated.) He felt, and very rightly, that we should first concentrate on getting this done before we demanded full self-government. And, when it came, it should come for everyone and not only for individual Regions. (Again it was odd that no one thought that the inevitable line would be for Regional self-government as a first preliminary to that of Nigeria as a whole.)

He thought that the motion was a matter for consultation between the parties and not a line to be imposed by one group: he thought too that self-government was a thing to be worked for and not be merely voted on for publicity's sake. I agreed warmly with one point: 'Mr Enahoro said one of the objects of this motion is to assess the honest feelings of all sides of this House. Why should he make that statement and then not be prepared to sit down to hear these honest feelings?'

He finished up with some resounding remarks about the future of Nigeria and the United States of Africa which seemed to me to be a little premature at that particular moment in our history.

Isa Kaita wound up for us in a short and simple speech.

No one person or party has all the answers [he said]. Among the essentials of a successful democratic government are tolerance, respect for other people's ideas, and ability and willingness to make compromises. Unfortunately, some of us, like the people who have walked out from this Honourable House, are inclined to be very intolerant of views different from our own. There must be a realistic approach to the problems of development and finance and there must be genuine unity at all levels behind the demand for self-government. We are not in opposite camps with any party on the question of self-government, for we do not differ in our desire to attain it, we only differ as to the time factor and methods of approach.

And so the adjournment of the debate was put and passed unanimously, for there was no one to vote against it.

That afternoon we went into the financing of the College of Arts, Science, and Technology, and passed two small Bills.

In the evening some of our members were abused by people in Lagos and in some cases there was quite a demonstration against us. The next morning when we came to the House there was more trouble. The Northerners were distinctive in their *rigas*; the others for the most part wore European clothes and we were conspicuous. The crowd outside the building on the Racecourse cheered the Southern leaders but gave us a rough time.

After prayers Edward Fellowes, the President, read a letter from the Governor saying that on the previous morning he had received, and accepted, the resignation of the Oni of Ife—a Minister without Portfolio from the West—that Bode Thomas, Akintola, and Arthur Prest had written to him in the afternoon resigning their offices as Ministers of Transport, Labour, and Communications respectively, because they felt themselves unable to abide by a decision of the Council, and that he had accepted their resignations. You will see what the decision was in a moment.

Six Southern members refused to ask the questions down in their names, still sulking from the previous day, but Michael Audu Buba, quite unabashed, charged in with what, at that stage, seemed a hopelessly irrelevant question, about postal facilities in Pankshin and Shendam, his own rather remote constituency. That is typical of Parliamentary procedure. The sublime and the ridiculous, the tragic and the comic, hustle their way shoulder to shoulder through the columns of Hansard.

Then Bode Thomas rose to make an explanation on his own behalf and on that of Arthur Prest, who was ill. Bode Thomas was not a likeable man. He was a clever lawyer but was ungracious and arrogant and never went out of his way to help: it is not surprising that the Action Group thought a lot of him, for he was the kind of political bulldozer they admired and wanted. They have named a dredger after him in Lagos harbour —it is not inappropriate when you think of its functions. He thought that we were a lot of uneducated savages and never attempted to conceal this opinion. He is dead now, but no one was really surprised that a veil of mystery and suspicion cloaked the circumstances of his death.

Akintola was a very different kind of man; he was very quick, and could be friendly and interested in all around him.

Bode Thomas did an extraordinary thing. He told the House what had happened in the Council of Ministers about the Enahoro motion and even alleged that the Governor, as President of that Council, had endeavoured to persuade the Council that they should not take part in the debate on this motion.

The usual practice is for the Council of Ministers (and Executive Council) in considering private members' motions to decide whether an answer is required and, if so, who should give it and in what form; whether it can be accepted or whether it should be rejected. In this case His Excellency obviously felt that this matter should be left to floor members and that Ministers should not intervene: revision of the Constitution was not a Ministerial subject, but it is noteworthy that the motion did not 'pray the Government to take steps to'. It set down a bald fact.

After much argument it seems that His Excellency said he would put it to the vote. The Western Ministers said that the officials should abstain. Bode Thomas exclaimed, 'They who would not have the courage to come here and speak their minds should not sit behind closed doors to use their six votes to try and tie down people from speaking their minds.' He was getting very hot and excited and at times it was difficult to follow what he was saying.

The Governor took no notice, he said, and the six officials voted for abstention with the four Northern Ministers; the West voted against, plus Dr Endeley; and the East abstained. The furious Ministers told the Governor that nothing would stop them coming to the House to speak on the motion. Pressure was applied to them, but they resisted it.

We do not think [said Bode Thomas] it is necessary for us any longer to stay and work with people whose intentions are to be guided by those who have vested interests in the prolongation of British rule in the country. We refuse to associate ourselves any further, Sir, with Africans who have not got the guts to speak their minds about the time when their country should have self-government.

By that he meant, of course, the Northern Ministers. Little did he appreciate what way the Northern 'guts' would take the debate and that there would be no opportunity for the Western Ministers to speak on it.

He then went on for some time on what had been happening in the Council of Ministers: how the Northerners had always voted with the officials; and how the Ministers had no real responsibility, a matter which had already been debated. He was called to order by the President but went on remorselessly and with great heat.

We did not mind what he said about us—that was, of course, part of the game—but we, who were ourselves Ministers in our own Regions, were aghast at the shameless way in which he had broken his sacred oath. The proceedings of Councils of this kind must be utterly secret: it is impossible to carry on a Government successfully if the discussions taking place under the solemn oath of secrecy, which each Member takes freely on assuming office regarding all that happens within the walls of the Council Chamber, are made public. It is only by the unanimous decision of the Council itself that such can be disclosed and there would have to be some astonishingly good reasons for such a course. Bode Thomas had obviously forgotten his oath and so had Akintola who spoke after him.

He spoke with just as much heat and followed the same lines as Bode Thomas, complaining that he would not be 'muzzled'.

I cannot [he said] sacrifice the freedom of Nigeria for the mere pleasure of preserving my office as a Minister. I am not appointed an Imperialist Minister to do the will of the Imperialist agents in Nigeria. I represent the people of Nigeria. To me the will of the people of Nigeria is the supreme law. I have no part with anyone who would prevent me from doing the will of my people and that is the reason why I have considered it honourable to take my exit from the Ministry of Labour.

He said it was a Government by blackmail by the skilful Imperialist Government. He saw vested interests and clever machinations at work everywhere, plotting and undermining and setting one against another.

If I had felt as he did I should never have had a wink of sleep. It was good oratory and he never missed a point, but did he really gain anything? I wonder. The hand of God was moving as always, using us men as its pieces on the wide field of the world events. Nothing which we could have said or done would have moved the date of Independence forward, or put it back a single hour from the moment in which it was ordained from the dawn of time itself. Bode Thomas and Akintola were, like all of us, in the inscrutable field of God's will. So we must not blame them or think harshly of what they said on this momentous day.

Njoku, NCNC Minister of Mines and Power, rose to explain the part that his fellow Ministers from the East had taken (or failed to take, according to how you look at it).

We felt [he said] that any attempt to remedy the situation must be made outside the Chamber of this House. We, like the [Western] Minister, reflected on the events that have taken place in the past fourteen months, i.e. since this Constitution came into effect. We knew to what extent all of us had aimed to co-operate in serving this country. We knew that the North had come with us on a number of issues.

Only last Monday I moved a motion which had the full support of all the Ministers, including the Ministers from the North, and we felt, Sir, that that was ample evidence that it was possible for the country to achieve all its wishes in the time that it thinks necessary to achieve it. We feel that because a man has been asked today what he will do tomorrow and he gives the answer 'no', that does not mean that he cannot reconsider the matter. There is plenty of time between now and 1956. . . . It has been possible by persuasion and talks round the table to get agreement on a number of issues.

Very sensible and level-headed it was to listen to, and quite short.

Since these were Ministerial statements it was, of course, not possible, under Standing Orders, to hold a debate on them, though obviously many were itching to have their say. It was probably a very good thing that at that stage this rule was sharply applied by the President, otherwise the position might have grown much worse, for all were labouring under the heat of the moment.

Arikpo, an Easterner, who was Minister of Lands, Survey, and Local Development, managed to get a few words in sideways as it were. He rose to move the adjournment *sine die* on that day. But before he did so, he regretted the impossibility of a debate. 'I would have been very glad,' he said, 'of the opportunity not only to reinforce the statements made by my colleague the Minister of Mines and Power, but to give the lie to some of these statements.'

When the question was proposed, Wachuku was on his feet like a flash. He wanted an opportunity for debate; the unity of the country hung in the balance unless the statements were contradicted—but it might have been even more in the balance if they had been argued perhaps—he did not want such statements, some of which were true and some not true, to go on the record: then he managed to get in a little about his own party and got called to order.

Isa Kaita in his calm, cold way settled it all:

132

I rise to support the motion. It is not because I want to go back to my home, but because the motion is reasonable and should be adopted. It is said that you can take a horse to water but you cannot make it drink it. If the West and a section of the East feel that only their case should be heard and that they are not prepared to hear the other side, well, why delay the House?

I then made the shortest speech that I have ever made and possibly one of the most important: 'I rise to associate myself with the last speaker. The mistake of 1914 has come to light and I should like to go no further.' I was referring to the Amalgamation that took place in that year between the old independent governments of Northern and Southern Nigeria. I was very angry and so were all of us. The air-conditioning in the great blue and white Chamber seemed to be turned off: the violence of feelings had stirred up much heat.

No one else spoke and the motion was passed without division or adverse vote. And then in the usual inconsequence of Parliamentary procedure that I have already mentioned we went on to round off the Committee of Supply. Four heads of Estimates were proposed and passed without any comment at all.

Four indignant (or sullen) members failed to rise to move their motions and we went on to a ridiculous motion about nudity, which had bedevilled us during the last part of the meeting. The Southern members were very hot under the collar about this and wanted laws to be passed thrusting hundreds of thousands of our fellow-subjects into unaccustomed clothing, which they did not want at that time and which, in any case, they could not afford. A great deal of nonsense was talked and Arthur Benson, the Chief Secretary, made a most absurd speech which failed in its aim. The Southern people seemed to object more to the taking of photos by white people than the absence of clothing.

We in the North were against this motion. Though we did not care for the habit, we have always disliked bringing in legislation which cannot be enforced, and which is obviously against the popular feelings of the people to whom it would apply; anyhow, we thought that the matter was covered by existing laws, which had been allowed, for many years, to lie dormant; we were sure too that with economic development the whole situation would gradually change itself—it has done and is still doing.

Jaja Wachuka was once more on his feet and moved an amendment which toned down the original motion but improved things as far as we were concerned. It was carried without argument, and a good thing too, for we had wasted a lot of time on it a few days earlier. And, as I thought, nothing ever came of it.

The House adjourned at 11.05 a.m. and we went out into the screams and insults of the large crowd of Lagos thugs waiting for us in the courtyard. I can tell you we were all very glad to get into our special train that evening and head for the high hills and plains of the North.

We never liked our sojourns in Lagos and this had been worse than usual. The Lagos politicians had certainly gone out of their way to stir up trouble for us. We found that it was by no means over when we pulled out of Iddo station. Whenever the train stopped we were surrounded by angry crowds of demonstrators. Even when we slowed down by village crossings we were assailed by boos. I was warned before I left Lagos that it would be unwise for me to leave the train, but I was not going to be cooped up for fear of a lot of scallywags of railway employees. I got out at each stopping-place to stretch my legs.

We hoped that when we crossed the border that we should be all right, but all the way up the line, even to the last station before Kaduna, the railway people and Southern elements gave us no peace.

CHAPTER 12

CRISIS IN KADUNA

THIS journey just about finished it for us. We were all not only angry at our treatment, but indignant that people who were so full of fine phrases about the unity of Nigeria should have set their people against the chosen representatives of another Region while passing through their territory and even in our own. What kind of trouble had we let ourselves in for by associating with such people?

Lord Lugard and his Amalgamation were far from popular amongst us at that time. There were agitations in favour of secession; we should set up on our own; we should cease to have anything more to do with the Southern people; we should take our own way.

I must say it looked very tempting. We were certainly 'viable', to use the current phrase; we could run our own show; the Centre would have to hand over to us our share of Nigeria's accumulated sterling assets. We had the men and production and minerals and the will to act.

There were, however, two things of the most vital importance in our way. The first was that the greater part of the revenue of Nigeria comes from customs duties collected on the coast on all goods brought over the wharves. Obviously we would have to collect our own duty at our own borders. This would be more difficult than collecting at the waterside, but it was not impossible. But would an unfriendly South permit the free passage of our goods across their lands and the transit of our vehicles to carry those that were not moved by train?

The second difficulty was similar to it. Would it be possible to send our goods down to the coast for shipment by rail or road, and what guarantee would there be that they would get there at all? We depend on the railway for the greater part of our transport and that is Federally owned and operated; we would have to use the Southern roads and they are built and maintained from Southern funds. On the other hand, we could use the River Niger and there we would be liable to no one, but there was no really good port at its mouth and it might even be necessary, at times, to force a passage of the narrower sections.

There was, indeed, the rub. We had no sentimental illusions about leaving the others: they had acted in such a way that it was abundantly clear to us that they would sooner see the back of us; but what about this transport difficulty?

We therefore had to take a modified line. We must aim at a looser structure for Nigeria while preserving its general pattern— a structure which would give the Regions the greatest possible freedom of movement and action; a structure which would reduce the powers of the Centre to the absolute minimum and yet retain sufficient national unity for practical and international purposes. This policy was gradually developed among us and we went over the Region canvassing our constituencies and influential opinion on its merits. We received a great deal of substantial support and reached a point at which we felt it desirable to put the matter to a vote after wide and public debate. Accordingly both Houses were summoned to meet on the 18th May; this was just over six weeks since we left Lagos. In that time we had done a good deal.

Two days before this meeting—that is, the Saturday—trouble broke out between Kano City and Sabon Gari, the area outside the walls occupied by 'native foreigners' (mostly Southerners). This was the culmination of a series of incidents in the past few weeks which had had their origin in the troubles in Lagos. While the Action Group in Lagos had been the prime mover, they had been supported by the NCNC. Here in Kano, as things fell out, the fighting took place between the Hausas (specially from the 'tough' suburb of Fagge) and the Ibos; the Yorubas (of the Action Group persuasion) were, oddly enough, out of it. Very large numbers were involved on both sides and the casualties were severe in numbers, though not in proportion to the crowds involved. The rioting went on all through Sunday and into Monday morning: peace was reluctantly accepted by the combatants, though they were in fact very tired by then. In the end there were 31 deaths and 241 wounded. The number of police injured was very small and no troops were employed, though we had them standing by.

This was the first time that anything of this sort—that is, real intertribal fighting—had taken place since the British occupation. And it was most disquieting. We were very nervous for the Plateau Province where there were some 40,000 Yorubas and Ibos and large numbers of Hausas. But firm handling of the situation nipped it in the bud.

When the House of Assembly opened, the Civil Secretary made a statement on the riots up to that actual hour, for there had been more fighting that very morning. The Civil Secretary was responsible at that time for law and order and so it was of no concern to any Minister, though that did not mean that we were not very worried about it. The statement was received in silence and no questions were asked.

I moved a formal resolution thanking the British Government for a fine copy of *Erskin May* they had presented to the Legislature and then the House adjourned, without a date fixed.

An hour later the House of Chiefs took over the Chamber: all they did was to listen to the same statement by the Civil Secretary that we had heard before they too adjourned.

Thus we had all Members of both Houses in Kaduna, and the next three days were spent in anxious consultation and discussion in a series of private meetings of all Members. By the end of this time we had come to almost unanimous agreement on the course of action to be taken and were able to ask for both Houses to be reassembled, the Assembly on the 22nd and the Chiefs on the following morning.

There were two motions in which we had formulated our general wishes. But before the first one was moved, the Financial

Secretary managed to get a Report of the Joint Standing Committee on Finance passed without argument—an unusual occurrence with us.

Yahaya Gusau introduced the first motion. He was then a floor member but is now a Permanent Secretary and an O.B.E. He was also a Member of the House of Representatives and was in the House at the time of Enahoro's motion. His motion was just the reverse of the latter and said that the Northern Region is not ready to commit itself to a fixed date for self-government in 1956. We felt that we had to get this absolutely clear before we went on to the next one, which was about the future form that Government would take.

Yahaya explained that the whole matter had been discussed everywhere by all classes of people, and that there was general agreement that we should not be tied down to a fixed date. He laid down four points:

First, that I am a firm believer that freedom is the heritage of all men of all races, and that, although my motion does not demand self-government in 1956, it does not mean that the North will never demand self-government, nor does it mean that the North will never be ready for self-government.

Secondly, I am a firm believer that the three Regions of Nigeria will for ever remain inter-dependent for various and obvious reasons.

Thirdly, I am a firm believer that the whole tribes and the whole nations of the whole world aim generally towards a common organisation for a much better and speedier way of solving common human problems in furtherance of the progress and the advancement of mankind.

Fourthly, I believe that any tribe or race can govern itself in a certain way. At the same time I believe that certain criterions are necessary for establishing sound modern democratic government. Although I believe in all the four things I mentioned, yet I am also aware of certain fundamental facts. I am aware, Sir, that this complex world requires complex administrative machinery which among other things requires certain qualifications and long established experience.

He went on to say:

I am aware, Sir, that it will be abnormal to try to force three brothers, especially in an African society, to have their first wedding

138

the same day, for certainly they come of age at different and long intervals. [Hear, Hear.] It is equally unfair to expect the three brothers to start and finish a hundred yards race at the same time for the fact that they attain different physical development. I am also aware, Sir, that in forming a nation, one should not solely aim at improving the intellectual and artistic attainments, the more visible ones, but one should also remember the traditions and the customs and moral training, which are undoubtedly the most important but which are usually trodden upon in haste.

In 1948, Sir, we, the Northern Leaders, started the first widespread and respected organisation in the country, the Jam'iyyar Mutanen Arewa, or the Northern Peoples Congress; we realised then that it was sheer madness to talk of politics. We realised that there were things more fundamental to concentrate upon, namely the fight against the three evils—corruption, laziness and ignorance. We believed that healthy politics would not develop in a country where the three evils were rampant. Though much has been achieved since then, yet the three evils still remain unconquered. Unfortunately the Jam'iyyar Mutanen Arewa has not been able to continue solely on its first party policy but, due to unforeseen circumstances, has to engage itself in politics.

Is it wise to ask for big things when you are not in complete control of the little things? When we were talking about rough roads and broken bridges last time a Member said, 'You have rough roads and broken bridges and you now demand better ones. In my area we have not even got bad ones. Will you please give me your bad ones?' Is it not madness for the North to ask for self-government at a time when the majority of the Junior Service in the North are filled entirely by non-Northerners? The British Government will fail in its duty if it gives self-government to Nigeria as an integral part at a time when the North is still incapable of taking its full share in the educational, economical, political and administrative activities of the country and at a time when the common man in the North does not know his rights, much less how to ask for them.

We do not, however, like to hurry unduly, nor do we like to force anybody behind to move necessarily at our own pace.

I then intervened in the debate as there were special aspects of the problems that I wanted to underline.

Mr President, Sir, I rise to speak on this historic motion which has roused a lot of bitterness and hatred in all sections and tribes throughout the three Regions. May I say that there is no great difference between us and the other Regions, each one of us wants self-government. The argument among us arises as to the time. In my view there are two points we have got to tackle rigidly and as soon as we have a firm grip on them, then self-government is at hand. With your permission, Sir, I would like to talk to you about them in detail although they have already been touched on by the mover of the motion.

They are the Northernisation of the Civil Service and of Local Government Services. The Regional Government is fully aware of the need for the Northernisation of all grades of the Civil Service of the Region. As far as the Senior Service is concerned it is the policy of the Regional Government to appoint a Northerner wherever he can be found. As proof of this I am pleased to be able to tell the House that within the last two months we have had fifteen Northerners appointed to the Senior Service compared with twenty-nine over the past five years. How are we to carry out this policy of Northernisation in the future?

There are two sources from which we may recruit for the Senior Service—from the experienced Native Administration officials and from scholars who have completed their University studies. We hope that Native Administrations will help by making available some of their experienced staff. There is, however, a grave danger that the efficiency of the Local Government system will be lowered if too many of its best employees are absorbed into Government service. It must be remembered that an efficient Local Government is required for self-government.

Members should not make the mistake, or let others make the mistake, of thinking that our policy of Northernisation with a view to self-government means that any Northerner can be promoted to the Senior Service without any qualifications. To lower the standards of entry would be fatal; self-government is not possible without a Civil Service which keeps to the highest standard of efficiency and incorruptibility. Let us not think the road to Northernisation is easy; it is not. It means hard work by everyone concerned.

Then I turned to Local Government and said that we would have a new Native Authority Bill before long (as I have already mentioned)—and that Chiefs were converting themselves of their own will from sole Native Authorities to Chiefs-in-Council; thus a decision would be that of the Native Authority Council, as a whole, and no longer of the individual Chief. We were aiming at strengthening councils at lower levels and better training for NA staff. As we would inevitably be forced to take away many of their best men for the Government service, it was vital to ensure that the remainder should be properly conversant with their duties.

To this end [I went on] the Clerical Training College at Zaria is being greatly extended and will be known in future as the Institute of Administration. Apart from the present clerical and training courses there will be a Native Treasury Diploma Course in Accounting which will be gradually raised in standard to something approaching the Institute of Municipal Treasurers and Accountants in the United Kingdom, and there will also be courses for Local Government staff. These courses will be of a practical nature for district heads, district scribes and other Native Authority officials. Summer schools will also be held at the Institute for Chiefs and Native Authority Councillors in order to keep them informed of developments in Local Government reform. Courses will be held for all types of Local Government administration, and special attention will be paid to the needs of the more backward areas.

Another factor, Sir, which is most important is the interest that the public takes in their own Local Government affairs. To encourage the public to take this enlightened interest, the Regional Government has given the highest priority to the Mass Literacy Campaign. It is also hoped that the campaign will assist in producing an enlightened public opinion, which will help to expose the evils of bribery and corruption. The Regional Government, Sir, is well aware of these evils and intends to make every effort to stamp them out. Bribery and corruption are by no means confined to the Local Government bodies, but whenever anyone is found guilty of these offences he must be adequately punished.

And finally I gave a much needed assurance.

In connection with our policy of Northernisation, I would like to assure the expatriates working in the Civil Service of this Region that their interests will be safeguarded. The Region needs their services, and they can be assured that in the future they can make a career in this country and confidently expect to be well treated when we attain self-government. But I would like to make it clear that we only want those who are efficient and hard-working, have the interests of the North at heart, and are willing to be sympathetic towards our ideas and customs. The same applies to the Africans of the other Regions who are now working in any capacity in the North, or whom we may recruit in the future.

Three members who automatically opposed the Government—we had no formal opposition in those days—spoke unconvincingly; they added nothing new and merely said that many people really did want self-government, a matter which we have never denied. They drew on themselves the rather obvious retorts that they had not consulted their constituencies or they would not speak as they had, or alternatively that they were talking at the dictation of another party, not an unusual occurrence for these people. There were some cases in which complete speeches had been sent to them. This was made quite obvious since, when they read them, they did not trouble to make the minor adjustments needed to make them fit with the subject under debate.

Six members spoke in favour of the motion; they had consulted their people and were convinced that it was the right course. They all came from different Provinces and spoke for different kinds of people and were surprisingly representative of vast areas. While one of them was speaking a great gale blew up, windows and doors slammed and crashed, papers were swept off the members' desks; messengers rushed hither and thither to make doors secure; for a time it was difficult to hear what was being said.

Abba Habib from Bornu hit the nail very squarely when he said:

This motion before the House has given me the fullest chance to state why we do not want self-government in 1956. Because our Southern brothers seem to have underrated our intelligence, they have ridiculed us in the eyes of the public and in their newspapers. We have been accused of being 'stooges' of the Imperialists while they have not shown the slighest desire to co-operate with us and work with us for the mutual progress of the country as a whole. . . .

They think because they have a fair number of trained staff to man their services, knowing very well that the North is appallingly short of such staff, they are trying to seize this opportunity to dictate to us their will, which we are quite prepared to reject. If our Southern brothers are sincere, and have the sympathy of the North in their hearts and of Nigeria as a whole, they should have properly consulted us and had our difficulties thrashed out before fixing the very date—1956—and stating the motion as irrevocable.

Michael Audu Buba referred to the debate in Lagos (where he had spoken):

We did our utmost to get them to give us time to consult the people, but nevertheless, those members did not agree. They seemed to have in their minds the idea of hurrying this motion—this made us suspicious that something must have been at the back of their minds. That is what prompted a member from the North to move that the motion be adjourned until the next meeting. When we returned to our Region, I for one toured the whole of my area in my province and there I consulted many people. Their desires were for us to develop the North and give them things that would promote progress in the country, and that is a vital point upon which we are concerned and upon which we should concentrate our efforts.

The motion was carried without a dissentient vote.

The next day being a Saturday, we met early and proceeded straight to the second motion. This was rather long and involved but, as it is very important, I have no hesitation in quoting it in full:

WHEREAS the constitution established for Nigeria in 1951 provided for the establishment of a central legislature and executive with full legislative and executive powers over all matters throughout Nigeria and also for the establishment of a legislature and executive in each Region with limited executive and legislative powers subject to the control of the central legislature and executive;

AND WHEREAS the representatives of the Eastern and Western Regions in the said legislatures desire to progress towards self-government in Nigeria at a pace which is not in accordance with the wishes of the people of the Northern Region;

AND WHEREAS the composition of the central legislature and executive and their powers over the affairs of the Regions are such that the wishes of the people of the Northern Region in relation to their own affairs and to the future of Nigeria are not capable of being satisfactorily realised;

AND WHEREAS the wishes of the people of the Northern Region with regard to the staffing of the public service in the Region are being prejudiced by the attitude of the representatives of the Eastern and Western Regions;

AND WHEREAS for the reasons before mentioned the existing constitutional arrangements have become unworkable and it is in the interests of the good relations of the peoples of the three Regions that new arrangements should be made;

BE IT RESOLVED that this House prays His Honour the Lieutenant-Governor to set up machinery for the consideration of popular opinion upon measures to amend the constitutional arrangement for Nigeria on the following principles:

(1) Each Region shall have complete legislative and executive autonomy with respect to all matters except the following:
(a) Defence;
(b) External Affairs;
(c) Customs;
(d) West African research institutions.
(2) There shall be no central legislative body and no central executive or policy-making body for the whole of Nigeria.
(3) There shall be a central agency for all Regions, which will be responsible for the matters mentioned in paragraph (1) (a) to (d) and any other matters delegated to it by a Region.
(4) The central agency shall be at a neutral place, preferably Lagos.
(5) The composition, powers and responsibility of the central agency shall be defined by the Order-in-Council establishing the new constitutional arrangements. The agency shall be a non-political body.
(6) The services of the railway, air services, ports, electricity and coal mining shall be organised on an inter-Regional basis and shall be administered by public corporations. Such public corporations shall be independent bodies governed solely by the statutes under which they are created. The Boards of such corporations shall be composed of experts with a minority representation of the Regional Governments.
(7) All revenues shall be levied and collected by the Regional Governments except customs revenue. Custom duties shall be collected at the port of discharge by the central agency and paid to each Region. The administration of the customs shall be so organised as to ensure that goods consigned to each Region are separately cleared and charged to duty.
(8) Each Region shall have a separate public service.

BE IT FURTHER RESOLVED that should general support be accorded to these proposals they be forthwith communicated to the Government of the United Kingdom requesting that Her Majesty be advised to amend the constitutional instruments accordingly.

This, as you will see, was our compromise on the suggestion of secession from Nigeria, as it was then. The Central Agency was to be an executive committee, appointed by the Governments of the Regions and would be non-party. These Governments would be quite independent of each other and would have no common services beyond those in (1). It was a novel idea developed in general party discussions, and it might have worked. Obviously there were not lacking difficulties, but they could have been cleared up, and naturally there was more to examine than appears in the text.

This was moved by Ibrahim Imam in a brief speech. It was for the most part devoted to expanding the words of the motion and the intentions behind it, but it included these two paragraphs which gave the reasons for our taking the action that we then thought necessary:

The first is the unworkability of the Constitution by the intervention of the party policy of the Action Group on the system of the central legislature in the Constitution. No party is in power in the Centre and so any party insisting on putting across its party policy in either the Council of Ministers or the Central Legislature will definitely result in a possible crisis, as during the last session of the House of Representatives. The motion, brought before the House of Representatives recently by a member of the Action Group, was a result of action taken by the Action Group during their party meeting at Benin. The members of the Action Group insisted that they had already made up their minds and that their decision was irrevocable. This clearly shows that the party was insisting on putting across its views whether the House liked it or not. . . .

The second reason, Sir, is the underrating of the Northerners' intelligence by the Southern legislators. The contemptuous attitude of the Southern legislators to the North in the House of Representatives was such that anything said in the House was regarded as having been put into our mouths by the 'Imperialists'. We were, as such, regarded as undesirable partners. In this aspect it was difficult on our part to come to a compromise with our Southern brothers with a view to working the Constitution successfully.

Mohammadu Lapai, who is now Emir of Lapai in Niger Province, put it like this:

Firstly, the present Constitution gives more power to the Centre and this fact gives rise to the possibility of attaining a united government for Nigeria. In a self-governing Nigeria the North would certainly not fare well for it might not be possible for it to go along with the other Regions. Hence our wishes would be that full autonomy be given to each Region so as to make the Centre weak or loose.

Secondly, it is proper and constitutional that each Region should progress at its own pace so that no one territory will be a drag on the other.

Thirdly, the attitude of the Members in the House of Representatives, from the West and the East, is so hostile to expatriate officials that the latter are being discouraged from coming over here to join the Nigerian service. . . .

The speeches in the House of Representatives are usually poignant and will not induce foreigners to come into Nigeria at all. Psychologically speaking the more Southerners are employed the less will Europeans want to serve the Nigerian Government, and the more opportunity would the Southerners have of becoming the overlords of the country. The North has the greatest need for expatriate staff now and is bound to suffer without them and would be forced perhaps to take local people in place of them.

Fourthly, the Nigerian Legislative Council was first set up in 1922 and since that time the South has been gaining the art of democratic government. It was only in 1947 when the Constitution came into being that the North first participated in the Legislative Council Meetings, thus you will be able to see that the South had twenty-five years start over the North in application of parliamentary procedure.

Fifthly, as far as the history of Western education is concerned, the first Mission School was started in the Southern Provinces in 1842 and the first government school was started in the North at Kano in 1909. Thus the South has had about seventy years educational advancement on the North.

The Central organ would have somebody at its head with Nigerian representatives as assistants only: the representatives would be Regional. In this respect the Central organ would have to receive its powers from the Regions and must also be subordinate to the Regional Government. On the other hand if Macpherson's Constitution were to work, live and grow, Nigeria could look forward to nationhood, whereby we could have Regional and Central Legislatures with their executives, and a possible Governor-General, as in Canada or Australia, but unfortunately the relationship between the Regions has been so much poisoned and the Constitution itself has been so much scotched that the possibility of a united Nigeria has been doomed.

Abubakar Imam, who had been Editor of *Gaskiya*, our Northern newspaper, described the position very picturesquely as follows:

146

We thought we were travelling with friends, though the other friends had been travelling for about seventy miles before we had started. Now these friends looked around and said to us, 'Friends, come on!' We answered them, 'We are coming.' The North was walking before, but it started to run. The other partners said again, 'Come on!' We replied, 'We are coming! we are coming!' They said again, 'Come on! come on! We are going to the garden of self-government.' The more they called, the more we ran. At last they looked round and said to us, 'We are going on without you.' So you see, it is they who broke the Constitution and not we the Northerners.

Quite a number of Members spoke in support and only the two Plateau Members, who had spoken against the previous motion, were opposed to it. They did not add very much, beyond pressing for a united Nigeria and a reconciliation between the parties. Two other members from the Plateau spoke in the other sense.

The motion was carried unanimously, so far as the voices went. Then, in the same inconsequential way that we have seen before, Makaman Bida, the Minister of Education and Social Welfare, rose and moved good wishes to the Queen on her Coronation, so soon to take place.

We adjourned at 11.40 and the House of Chiefs, who had been waiting in the lobbies, moved in. The Emir of Gwandu (that is, the late Emir Yahaya) moved the 'no self-government in 1956' motion straight off after prayers.

In the House of Chiefs it has become the custom to speak briefly, since the matters have almost always been thoroughly argued in the House of Assembly before they are put to the Chiefs. It is sometimes thought that the fact that few of them speak, and none of them speak for long, means that they are taking no interest. This is far from being the case. They take an interest, but they do not waste time. Quite a number of them were members of the House of Assembly before they succeeded to Emirates and Chieftaincies, and they are fully conversant with procedure and the finer points of Parliamentary life.

The second motion, that on the Central Agency which has passed into our history as the 'Eight Points Motion', was pro-

147

posed by the Emir of Katsina, who was present at the debate in Lagos. Quite a number of Chiefs spoke on the matter and there was general agreement, though there was among a few a little doubt over the meaning of some of the details. However, it passed without a word of opposition.

In those days we, the Ministers, were not automatically members of the House of Chiefs as we are now and only the three Europeans were present with, of course, the three Chiefs who were Ministers without Portfolio: they conducted the proceedings.

The next step came surprisingly quickly and we found ourselves invited to London to take part in a Conference on the Revision of the Constitution.

Lugard Hall

CHAPTER 13

THE FIRST LONDON CONFERENCE

THE debate in the House of Representatives had its reper-
cussions elsewhere too. The British Government in Nigeria were
very worried and Sir John Macpherson took prompt action to
stir up the Colonial Office to do something about it. And they
must have worked unusually fast, for on the 21st May, just after
we had passed the first motion, and just before we had reached
the Eight Points, the Secretary of State for the Colonies announced in the House of Commons that the British Government
'had regretfully decided that the Nigerian constitution would
have to be redrawn to provide for greater Regional autonomy
and the removal of power of intervention by the Centre in
matters which could, without detriment to the other Regions,
be placed entirely within the Regional competence'. This was
a complicated and pompous way of saying that we might get
something of what we were asking for.

We did not know of this statement at the time of the Eight
Points debate, but I am certain that it would not have made any
difference to us if it had been known. It would still have been
necessary for us to have made our points very clearly.

Immediately after this we received invitations to go to
London for discussions. There was a good deal of argument
about the numbers of people who should go, but we reached
agreement in the end, and, indeed, it did not take as long as it
might have done. There were five delegates each from the
major parties, two from the National Independence Party
(Nwapa's), and one each from the Cameroons and the NEPU.
The Secretary of State (Mr Oliver Lyttelton) had four officials
from the Colonial Office, and the Governor of Nigeria attended

in person. And there was a cloud of people called 'advisers'. There were forty-six of these and I cannot help having a feeling that some at least of them went because they wanted a free trip to London. Quite a number of the party had never been to Europe at all and it was a great experience for them. The weather was good: in fact, it was the right time to go to England.

We travelled by chartered planes and this too was a new experience for some. The whole of the NPC delegation and party was accommodated at Jermyn Street, where we were very comfortable and well looked after. We met at No. 10 Carlton House Terrace, a government building overlooking St James's Park. There we held twenty full sessions, as well as many committee meetings.

The proceedings were far from smooth. The Action Group was still smarting very severely from its injuries in the Lagos debate. They seemed to have little sporting spirit and approached every problem in an attitude of bitter wariness. The National Independence Party was not much better. Both these expected to get their way all the time and if they failed to do so they became 'upset' and both parties 'walked out' from several meetings. What they did not appear to appreciate was that we, the NPC, had the most to lose if things went wrong, and that we would then be, as they say, 'out on a limb'; and yet we never made a scene or even an excitable speech.

I did not open my mouth during the first five or six days of the Conference. This gradually alarmed the other delegations and the Colonial Office people. They feared that the Conference might break down and come to no conclusion. It was only when I finally agreed to the Federal principle that confidence returned to the meeting. I was very disappointed that we had to modify our Eight Points programme.

In the end we got quite a lot of what we wanted, but nothing like the Eight Points with which we had set out from Kaduna. However, as you will see, we did not do too badly. We got more than any other party achieved.

The first and most important point was to clear up the relations between the Central Government and the Regions. The British Government had already said that they would agree to changes, and so it was up to the Conference to decide the extent.

It was agreed that the Regions should be as independent as possible, and there was a long argument as to whether specific functions should be allotted to the Centre or the Regions. As things were we had at that time a list of 'subjects' which were considered Regional. This obvious method had failed and so the alternative should be tried. This meant that a list had to be drawn up for the Centre and that everything else should be Regional—this was called technically the allocation of the 'residual functions'.

In some ways it was easier to draw up this list than the other had been. Naturally the Centre must be responsible for the matters which affected the whole of Nigeria—that is, defence, external affairs and trade, civil aviation, banking and currency, tele-communications, railways and harbours, and the corporations (electricity and broadcasting), and some other minor matters. This is more or less the position to this day, with a few amendments in detail. The only one which we regret was the allocation of Trunk Roads 'A' to the Centre; this has been a constant cause of irritation and worry ever since.

In addition to this list of functions the Conference came to the conclusion that there should also be a 'concurrent list' of functions which could be discharged by either the Centre or the Regions. The most important of these were higher education and industrial development: in case of conflict in these matters, the Centre would prevail.

You can imagine what a lot of talk there was over these details before the lists were finally agreed. At times I thought that we should never finish, but Mr Lyttelton (now Lord Chandos) was a fine chairman and commanded the greatest respect from all of us; the successful conclusion of business was largely due to his personality and quickness of mind.

It was agreed that the Central Government should become the Government of the Federation. Let me say that was no mere empty form of words. What it meant was that the Federation would get on with its own share of work and responsibility, and would leave the Regions strictly alone to deal with theirs. The Central Government at that time could, and did, run things in the Regions; the Governor of Nigeria was supreme and had the right to throw out Regional laws if he wished to do so. So far as we were concerned only one of ours was rejected: it was not an important measure and, anyhow, it came just at the change of the Constitution, so it didn't matter very much. The Regional Lieutenant-Governors were subordinate in every way to the Governor at Lagos.

To make things quite clear the Conference recommended that the Lieutenant-Governors should become Governors, with full and independent authority, and that the Governor should become a Governor-General as the head of the Federation. The Regional legislatures should become sovereign, and no power in Nigeria should be empowered to alter their decisions on their own subjects. As we were not yet independent, we had to agree that the 'reserved powers' should still rest in the Governors, the Governor-General, and Her Majesty, and the Queen's right to 'disallow' legislation still remained.

Another consequence of this change was that the staffs—that is, the Public Services—of the Regions and of the Federation were made entirely independent of each other: they were to be separately recruited and transfers could not take place without agreement, both of the employing Government and of the officer concerned. Each Service would come under an independent Public Service Commission, which would be divorced from politics and political control. At that time, however, the Governor could still use his discretion in staff matters—he cannot do so now. Before this was decided there was one Public Service for Nigeria and any public official could find himself in three or four different Provinces, some in different Regions, in a single tour; now they are confined to their own Region.

Federal Officers are, of course, still liable to transfer anywhere in Nigeria.

This matter of a separate Public Service was important for us. As you see, it made it possible for us to select whom we wished for our jobs here, and made it impossible for the Federal Government to flood us with Southern staff to the exclusion of our own people. That was one of our greatest fears and one which was entirely justified. Each Region and the Federation would have its own Public Service Commission.

It was agreed that the seats in the Federal House of Representatives should be based on one member for each 170,000 inhabitants, and that their elections should be separate from those to the Assemblies: in future, no one should be a Member of both Houses. The first suggestion was that we should keep to the old form of selection and that the same method of choosing members should continue, with the addition of some form of Upper House with delaying powers. This produced an explosion from the Action Group, who left the Conference in a body. The scheme mentioned above was a compromise brought in to get the Conference together again.

It did not matter very much to us which way it was, and we saw that it was not really satisfactory to have the same people in both Houses, as I have already said earlier on. We were, however, a little worried at the prospect of having to find twice as many suitable men, as candidates, as we had done before. We were to supply 92 members in this new House (the others being 42 for each Region, plus 6 for the Southern Cameroons and 2 for Lagos), as well as the 131 for the House of Assembly. The idea was that we should use the same electoral college system for the House of Representatives as we had for the Assemblies, but with different membership.

The Governors would no longer be members of the Council of Ministers nor of the Representatives: that reduced the European members to the three officials (and the Governor-General, who would preside in the former). The counterparts of these were retained in the Northern Executive Council and Assembly, but not in the other two Regions.

The number of Ministers in the North was increased to thirteen, of whom not less than eight had to be active: the others were Chiefs, without Portfolio. The heads of Regional Governments became Premiers, but there was still no Prime Minister in Lagos; that development came later, as did the name Parliament for the Lagos Houses (while 'Legislature' was retained for the Regional Houses).

An important matter on which there was general agreement was that the Ministers should be given the full responsibilities of their posts and should not continue with the truncated powers that had somehow or other got into the previous Constitution. They should not only be responsible for their subjects but also for their departments. In practice it took some years and a good deal of effort to secure this, simple as it may seem to be.

There were a number of quite serious matters as well as these. For example, there was the perennial matter of money. It was decided to set up a Fiscal Commission to enquire and recommend as to how the Regions should be financed and what proportion of the general revenue they might reasonably claim.

The question of the control of the Nigeria Police provoked a lot of discussion, and it has continued since then. In the end it was decided to have one Force, but the Regional Commissioners would answer to the Governor and he to the Governor-General (in this respect only). The administration of justice was not cleared up entirely, though the greater part of a good report by a sub-committee was accepted.

The biggest uproar took place over the future of Lagos. At that particular time it formed part of the Western Region. The Action Group naturally clung to this position with all their strength of hand and voice, especially voice. The others (including ourselves) just as strongly, though for quite different motives, wanted it to be a separate territory. Finally, and quite unexpectedly, everyone agreed that they would hand the problem to Mr Lyttelton and that they would abide by the decision of Her Majesty's Government. At the end of the meeting the Secretary of State announced the decision in an able memorandum. This was that the Municipality of Lagos should be Federal Territory and should cease to belong to the Western Region.

An historical remark here may make the position clearer. The Island of Lagos was annexed in 1861 to the Crown of England in order to deal with the slave trade, of which it was at that time a centre. In subsequent years a long strip of land, 150 miles long and about twelve miles wide, running along the coast from the present Dahomey border to the east was also annexed. I suppose that the real reason for this was to secure Lagos from attack from the mainland—the strip was a little thicker north of Lagos—and also to control the long thin 'lagoon' which runs from Porto Novo to the Niger Delta three hundred miles away, and which carried then, and still carries, a considerable 'coastal trade'.

For ninety years, therefore, this had been a British possession and used to be quite independent of the interior governments. It was called the 'Colony of Lagos' and its inhabitants felt themselves superior, as British subjects, to the 'natives' of the interior. It seems odd to think of this in these days, doesn't it? In 1914 the title was changed to the 'Colony of Nigeria'—the rest of the country was the 'Protectorate of Nigeria', after the amalgamation of the Northern and Southern Nigerian Protectorates. It was run during this present century by, first of all, an Administrator and later a Commissioner, who came directly under the Governor of Nigeria. It never formed part of the Yoruba country to its north until the formation of the Regions, when the mistake was made of incorporating Lagos in the West.

Since that time its retention has been obstinately fought for by the West. They even went to the length of offering land and money to help in building a new Federal Capital elsewhere (but naturally it would have to be somewhere in the Western Region). This idea had often been considered. For example, when Lord Lugard amalgamated the North and the South, he actually planned the new town of Kaduna as capital of the whole of Nigeria. It was, I understand, turned down by the Colonial Office as it was a two-day journey from the coast and their precious despatches would take that much longer to reach the Governor and replies would be delayed as they would not catch the same boat—though, in fact, as it was, they seldom managed to do so.

It was a great pity that this ruling was given by the Colonial Office; much future trouble would have been avoided. Kaduna, being in the middle of almost uninhabited bush, would have been ideal for this purpose: there is a fine water supply and vast areas for expansion, with ample room for as big an airfield as anyone would want; 2,000 feet above the sea and a fine climate. In fact, it had all the things that Lagos has conspicuously lacked, and it would have lacked the biggest menace in Lagos, the city riffraff who have made life there unbearable for respectable people.

It was reconsidered again, I believe, by Lord Milverton. It was found that to move the headquarters of the essential departments of government would cost a million pounds, and this was apparently beyond the country's purse. No one had thought of the huge sterling balances that were piling up. Our new general hospital in Kaduna will cost over £2m. before it is finished: a capital city costing less than that would have been cheap. Incidentally Mr Lyttelton said at this London Conference, 'my own view is that the argument which cites cost as militating against moving a capital is frequently over-stressed'.

The matter was of great importance to us, because included in the Municipality of Lagos are the wharves at Apapa, on the other side of the harbour, and it is across those wharves that a large part of our Regional imports and exports must pass. It is true that quite a percentage is moved at Port Harcourt, but the bulk comes through Apapa. Who, therefore, holds Lagos also holds Apapa and could withhold our trade. With our relations at that time with the Action Group as they were (and have been since then), we felt that we should be in a better position if this vital area were to be under the Federal Government, in which we would have some say, even if we were not in power, than that it should be under other control.

We were therefore much relieved at the Secretary of State's decision, but the Action Group, who with all of us had agreed to abide by it, behaved in a way which can only, and with charity, be described as childish: they suddenly, and with little apparent justification, bearing other things in mind, announced that they could do nothing about accepting the decision without referring it back to the Region—and to whom would they 'refer' it? After all, the bulk of their party leaders, and of the Western Government itself, were present in London at that time.

I have taken rather a lot of space over what may seem to be a comparatively small matter, but it is one which we felt to be important. I must add that, even as it is, the position is not satisfactory. Lagos has grown considerably to the north, outside the municipal boundary, and these suburbs are in the Western Region—this must be embarrassing in many ways to many people; further, the essential Lagos airport at Ikeja (14 miles out) is not in Federal Territory as it should be.

We realised that it was inevitable that some delay would ensue before the new Constitution could be brought into force, and, until that happened, things would have to go on as they were. This meant that the Council of Ministers would be short by the number of Western Ministers who had resigned, unless new ones were to be appointed. We were greatly surprised when we found that the four Ministers—who had resigned amid such excitable and emotional scenes only four months ago, who had protested with such vehemence at the treatment they had had from the 'Imperialist Officials', who had made public the inmost secrets of the Council, and who had imputed the basest motives to our Northern Ministers on that Council—now, without any apology or public statement, wanted to be reinstated.

At first we felt that we should not condone such conduct and, when we said so, the Action Group 'walked out'. But on consideration we saw that it would only be a matter of months before

157

the new Constitution would require a complete reappraisal of the situation and that, for that period, it might be as well to let the Government carry on in the simplest way possible, which was to restore the *status quo*. Restoring the *status quo*, however, would in no way serve to obliterate from our minds what had happened: it only served to make up our minds that it would not be permitted to happen again. There was much relief in the Conference when we announced that we withdrew our objection, and the Action Group reappeared at the table.

The two Southern parties had managed to get 'self-government in 1956' on to the agenda as a formal item: the British Government were obviously not enthusiastic about this. They did not want to part with Nigeria until the necessary preliminary steps had been taken to ensure a successful administration after Independence. Nigeria is too big and too important, and too many people are involved, to use it as a stage for amateur administrators. Since we were not ready at that time to contemplate a fixed date in 1956 and since we were the largest section of the country, the British Government naturally tended to hang back on this issue.

There are those who say that the British 'always want to hang on to Colonies'. While there is, of course, a section of the British people who understandably feel this way, and some of them feel it very strongly, I am satisfied that the vast majority of those who think about it at all are more concerned with the effects of independence on the people so freed than on themselves and on their own interests. With the vivid picture of the Congo disaster before our eyes, we should be able to understand that the Administering Power cannot be too careful in making this grave and far-reaching decision. Once the decision to grant independence has been made, it is quite impossible to put back the hands of the clock. What is written must indeed be done.

The final solution was actually what we had suggested at one point and which had been derided as impracticable. That was that each Region should be given self-government when it felt ready to take it on its shoulders; this self-government would cover all the activities that fell legally into the Region's range: in this it would be supreme and free from any outside interference—save only that it could do nothing to prejudice the Federal Government in carrying out its own lawful functions.

In fact, as everyone knows, even the other Regions did not get this self-government for another five years, and we were a year later. No one can honestly say that the public was, by any measurement, the worse off for this delay, though it is true that the process of 'Nigerianisation' might well have been faster than it was in practice, and that some deserving people had to wait for the appointments they now enjoy.

To round off this matter I should add that in March 1957 Chief Akintola moved in the House of Representatives, to secure Independence in 1957. Jaja Wachuku then moved to amend this to a demand for Independence within the Commonwealth in 1959. This was accepted by the mover. Abubakar Tafawa Balewa, then Minister of Transport, said that the NPC agreed to 1959, and so the matter was in the end amicably concluded, except that we did not actually get it till October 1960.

We decided to have another meeting for further review of the Constitution before the end of August 1956—that was, in three years' time. But before that it would be necessary to meet again to finish off the financial arrangements and also to go through the final draft of the Constitutional Instrument. It was agreed to do this in January 1954 and Mr Lyttelton kindly said that he would come out and preside over it. We were glad to hear this as we admired him very much. He is a big man physically, with a comprehensive intelligence. Being a big man myself, I find that I can get on with big men better than I can with small ones—but I must draw a certain line, for the big men must have big minds. I have no use for men who are merely big and I have no use at all for people who are stupid and I seem to be forced to come up against numbers of them. Nor can I tolerate lazy people, who have the brains but won't use them, or won't take responsibility where it is handed to them.

At this conference we came across the menace of British hospitality in full swing on a large scale for the first time. Much as I like the hospitality of the *kind individual*—and this goes for all of us Northerners—we cannot appreciate the hospitality that is handed out on these occasions. The official parties are too lavish and too big, and one can never make really successful contacts beyond passing remarks. In the end we used to arrange turns amongst ourselves so that some would make an appearance at those parties which were inevitable.

Further, none of us Muslims are permitted to drink stimulants at these parties, or anywhere else, and though we cannot object to others doing so, we can never really approve of it or enjoy it even by proxy. Again, by nature we go to bed early and do not care at all for 'late nights'. Here we part company with our Southern colleagues, many of whom never seem to go to bed until the early hours of the morning and who like what is oddly called 'gaiety', which is, in fact, only an expensive way of wasting time. All my life I have worked whenever I could do so, and that has meant keeping regular hours and not wasting time. I agree that 'in Rome' one must, to some extent, 'do as the Romans do', but the better 'Romans' will obviously not press you to do what you do not want to do.

There is one kind of 'London party' that none of us can tolerate, and that is the party given by a business firm or organisation. This is not 'hospitality' at all, since it is entirely paid for by the firm or body and therefore its expenditure is only incurred in the hopes of an ultimate profit. They do not call in the blind and the maimed to these parties—if they did so they would be fulfilling the commands of God—but they call in others who, like themselves, are surfeited with such parties, and then, in the noise and confusion, they try to 'interest us', as they say, in certain enterprises and projects which would, if they came off, bring much profit to themselves.

They do not realise that we are not traders or merchants and have no desire to be such, and, indeed, if we were, would we choose such peculiar conditions in which to do business, business which might involve vast sums of money, and other people's money at that? This picture is not at all exaggerated: I myself have been 'approached' at such parties with the most startling, and, of course, most expensive, schemes, and so too have my colleagues in the Ministries. We have plenty of skilled people who understand these things and who should be 'approached' in the first place and on whose recommendations we will make our decisions in the peace and quiet of our offices.

Then, too, unless we are very careful we become the target of fanatics of all sorts—those who are wildly on our side (to an extent that they themselves cannot possibly appreciate) and those who are just as vehemently against us. They come from every walk of life—there are plenty in the House of Commons and there are some too in the Lords—up and down from any level they try to reach us, to advise and exhort us and, quite often, to admonish us on some course we have never taken or some action we have no intention of pursuing. We receive letters, too, from all manner of people asking, in some cases demanding, all manner of impossible things.

But I must not paint too black a picture, for we do meet interesting and helpful people; we do think that some conversations are stimulating and worth while; we do like seeing certain kinds of things, though we tend in this to be more practical than artistic. Indeed, I fear that we are often a grave disappointment to many of our good friends, for Islam does not encourage appreciation of art, except in its own stylised forms; and though we are deeply interested in our own history, it does not go far enough back for us to be interested in those great antiquities that thrill European people so profoundly.

And that was the first of the London Conferences. There were four others before we came to our final goal, but I will not go into them in detail and will content myself with passing mentions. This was the decisive meeting, and the others in fact stemmed from it and their conclusions were logical developments: there were no structural changes, as it were.

The Lagos Conference was duly held and we had to accept

the financial scheme which was, as was quite inevitable, heavily weighted in favour of Lagos and the Federation. The East and the North did not do well out of it at all. We, and the other Regions, found ourselves paying for those things that the citizens of Lagos should have been paying for if the Municipality were to be financed as others are.

CHAPTER 14

START OF AN ERA

THE new Constitution arising from the crisis came into force at the end of 1954. It had not otherwise been a very eventful year, though we had had at its beginning two tragic losses. The Emirs of Kano and Gwandu both died. Referring to this tragedy I said in the House of Assembly, 'The late Emir of Kano, Bayaro, was one of those just and pious rulers whose integrity and impartiality are unquestionable ... people wonder whether such a ruler can ever be replaced': of my kinsman Gwandu, 'He died as he lived, in the course of serving his people.' They were both succeeded by members of the Assembly, men of much ability, but the late Emirs will ever be remembered amongst us as outstanding personalities.

At that Budget Meeting I was Minister of Local Government, Community Development and Works, which was quite enough for any man to have on his plate, but help was in sight, for shortly we would have two more Ministers.

We were going to get an independent Regional Public Service, and this caused a good deal of fluttering. I said in the House:

... That caused a lot of alarm amongst the Southern workers of the Region. They did not know what the future held for them, and, in view of that, I unofficially approached both the House of Assembly and the House of Chiefs, sitting here in private, to ask for a mandate to give assurance that their services are required in the Region and their lives are secure. I came to this House and made a public announcement which was printed in the papers and also printed by the Government, and circulated to all the Government employees of the Region. . . .

We cannot run the country without the requisite people to run all our services. This was not only the view of the North—it was the view shared by all the delegation who went to the Conference. . . .

We declare our intention to ensure that the interests of overseas officers, who continue in the future to serve in the public services of Nigeria, will be fully safeguarded. We hope that the conditional principle of promotion according to qualifications, experience and merit, without regard to race, be maintained. . . .

We came back to this matter six months later:

. . . Nearly every week I get over 100 applications from Northerners for employment but people think that being a Northerner is the only qualification required during this period. These letters mostly come from people with Elementary IV qualifications, asking either for Senior Service posts or Chief Clerks' jobs in the Administration! May I appeal then to the Schoolmasters to speed up production of Middle IV's and Middle VI's. I assure you that the North is for the North and we are trying to do all we can to speed up Northernisation as quickly as possible. . . .

I have already said that the new Native Authority Bill was brought in at this time and was passed after a good debate, and without serious opposition.

I had been questioned as to why we were building houses for police officers:

. . . We have got to do so, the maintenance of law and order is the first duty of every Government. Buba sleeps outside his hut with 5,000 head of cattle. He sleeps quite well without being afraid of being attacked. Buba has no defence for keeping his cattle. It is because the rogues are thinking of those in authority, such as Emirs, Council Members, police, judges and everybody who contributes to the maintenance of law and order, that he is not attacked and his cattle taken away by force. We are asked why these houses are being built. You cannot expect to call a man from thousands and thousands of miles to come and work for you and make him live under trees. . . .

Funds were provided for the extension of the former clerical training school at Zaria into an 'Institute of Administration', which is one of my own pet schemes and which I am glad to say has done so very well since then. I said:

. . . The buildings are ready and we hope to cater for 180 clerks as against the 120 that we have been taking in the past. Now, a Member has asked why we are going to bring in Administrative Officers as well as Native Authority Headquarters' staff in order to attend a course there. The Junior Administrative Officers, who will spend most of their time on tour, are only going to go to the Institution in order to have refresher courses on what is being taught to these Local Government officials. It is no good our trying to teach all the Native Authority officials, who would be going back into the Provinces, Emirates and Districts to spread what they have learned, if those who are going to supervise what they are going to do later are not kept in the picture as to what has happened. So that is why we want all the Junior Administrative Officers to go to this Institute and have a brief summary of what the Native Authority officials have been taught. Of course, it is our earnest desire to see that these Native Administration Headquarters officials take the duties that the Administrative Officers perform now off their shoulders.

During the course of my tour as Minister of Local Government I have often told Native Authority Council Members that the work at present being performed by Administrative Officers is the type of work that they are supposed to do themselves. I hope that the Council Members will bear this in mind, that when they go on tour they will ask what complaints there are, instead of the Administrative Officer doing so, and should enlighten the people as to what is happening in the world and do everything that they can to hasten the development of this country to the final goal, and that is self-government. . . .

The announcement of a new Public Service brought in sheaves of applications. I had again to take a firm line:

. . . May I warn Members that being a Northerner is not a qualification. Many people have taken it for granted that 'so long as I am a Northerner, I must be given the privilege of being a Northerner'. If he is a genuine Northerner let him prove that he is the type of person who has come forward to work for the people and not for himself. I should like to assure Members of this House that it is the intention of this Government to hasten as quickly as possible Northernisation and that is why we have been encouraging all the forthcoming scholars who wanted to go overseas for further training and that is why we pressed for a separate Civil Service Commission for the Region so that we can preserve the North to the Northerners. . . .

I went on a visit to London in July in order to have a change of scene and a rest from day-to-day problems that beset me in Nigeria, wherever I may be. A complete change like this seems to me to do noticeable good.

On my return I found that the question of daily paid labour was becoming once more important. I said at the September meeting:

My Government is not prepared to enter into any political auction sale at this stage. It has to prepare *before* it announces. . . . Since we came back from Lagos I have had many letters from Trade Unions and other leaders in both the South and the North. This is a letter I got from the Public Utility, Technical and General Workers Union. . . .

'There has been much talk and writing about the 5s. or 7s. 6d. minimum wage for daily paid workers in the country. We wish to declare the stand of the Union with regard to this issue which has gained much attention from the Public. This is because our Union controls a membership of over 16,000 daily paid and unestablished workers. The idea of an increase in the minimum wages is welcomed. As a matter of fact, the need for 6s. or 7s. 6d. relief to the suffering workers is long overdue. A worker on the daily labour grade is only entitled to an increment of a penny in four years. The introduction of a minimum wage is, therefore, not a scientific plan to relieve him of his economical strains. Another point that is of significance is the question of security. Our Union would like a guarantee from the Government that the minimum wages to be decided upon should be applicable to both Government and mercantile workers.'

Now this Government, Sir, thinks it ridiculous to just come here and move a motion, without first consulting the persons who would be responsible for the payment of the wages. If the Government adopts the motion and says they are willing to pay so much to the Government worker and will subsidise the NA's, who is going to subsidise the ordinary farmer? Have we consulted all the mercantile employers, have we consulted the miners and other people who employ labour in their areas? Sir, this motion, which was tabled in the House of Representatives, was similar to that of self-government, where people were being rushed like mad people into legislation without an adequate opportunity to consider matters carefully. I assure the Honourable Members that we have not overlooked this matter and it is receiving our early attention.

The new Constitution brought many changes and there was a good deal of really hard work to implement it correctly. The only real relief was that we were not due for a General Election until the following year, 1956; to have had that as well would have made things very hard for all of us.

ıx(a). With Sir Rex and Lady Niven. Checking watches at the laying of the foundation stone for the Blind Society at Kaduna

ıx(b). Addressing a political meeting

x(*a*). With my fellow pilgrims at Mecca

x(*b*). Girls' education is worth watching

xɪ(a). I go to the nets . . .

xɪ(b). . . . and play fives

xii(a). I open a village school . . .

THIS FOUNDATION STONE
OF
AHMADU BELLO COLLEGE
WAS LAID BY
THE HONOURABLE
ALHAJI SIR AHMADU BELLO K.B.E. M.H.A
SARDAUNA OF SOKOTO,
PREMIER OF THE NORTHERN REGION
17TH OCTOBER 1960

xii(b). . . . and start a University

XIII(*a*). I watch a potter at work . . .

XIII(*b*). . . . and look at the Government Press with Private Secretary Isa Dutse, so tragically killed in a motor accident in 1961

xiv(a). I look at a model of the new Kaduna Hotel

xiv(b). We are developing mechanised farming

xv(a). Aerial view of Kano and the mosque

xv(b). Aerial view of Lugard Hall, the legislative buildings in Kaduna

xvi(*a*). Salute of allegiance at a Salla Jahi

xvi(*b*). Fishing by moonlight on the Niger near Lokoja

On 1st October, 1954, I became the first Premier of the Region and two new Ministers were appointed. They were for North Cameroons Affairs and Social Development and Surveys.

The first was to try to give the Northern Cameroons, which was under Trust from the United Nations, through the United Kingdom, a more co-ordinated development plan in every possible sphere than had been possible with various activities scattered through other Ministries and offices, without any common denominator. It should have been done before, but it was better late than never. This came under Abba Habib, himself a man from Trust Territory.

The other was the old Community Development, combined with Social Welfare, and the addition of Surveys—now handed to us as a Regional subject—tacked on, because there was no other convenient Ministry to take it. Shettima Kashim, who had been a Lagos Minister until the end of 1954, took over this new office.

This is a list of the Ministers at that Budget Meeting in 1955:

Premier	Sardauna
Education	Makaman Bida
Natural Resources	P. S. Achimugu
Trade & Industry	A. Turakin Zaria
Works	Isa Kaita
Development & Survey	Shettima Kashim
Local Government	Sardauna
North Cameroons Affairs	Abba Habib
Health	Yahaya Ilorin

We appointed four Parliamentary Secretaries—such an innovation this was that it was a long time before they really understood what their functions were supposed to be—and seven Permanent Secretaries from the top rank of the Administrative Service, thus following on logically from our beginnings. My own Secretary was R. E. Greswell, an officer as tall and as big as I am myself, and one on whose ability and integrity I have always placed the greatest reliance. His imperturbability was a great asset in some of the crises that blew up so easily in those days.

We also set up a Privy Council to advise on the exercise of the prerogative of mercy, formerly in the Governor's discretion with the advice of Executive Council. It did not live very long and disappeared with our self-government: it is not a satisfactory scheme and other arrangements have now been made.

There had been, from time to time, a good many attacks in the press and in public speeches on what by then had come to be called 'expatriates'—that is, the Europeans working in this country. It was in itself not only an unhappy phrase but also an inaccurate one. The attacks had been sheer politics: in most cases they were completely unjustified and, of course, were bitterly resented by the very people we wanted to keep to help us through the difficult country that lay ahead of us on the way to self-government. I felt that some reassurances should be given publicly.

The release of numbers of officers from the Sudan Government service following its reception of Independence seemed to us to give an opportunity for getting not only more staff, but staff used to dealing with Muhammadans and fluent in Arabic. This also gave us an indirect chance of saying that we welcomed European assistance and that, provided it was suitable and followed our ways, there was no need for people to be apprehensive of the future. This was set out in a letter to the London *Times* early in February 1955, signed by my Ministerial colleagues and myself:

Sir, we, the Ministers of the Northern Region of Nigeria have read with great interest the letter in a recent number of *The Times* describing the formation of an Employment Bureau for officers who have lately left the service of the Sudan Government. The Bureau has already been informed that this Region has a very large number of vacancies in a wide variety of professional and technical posts and would welcome suitable British Officers of the Sudan Service who would like to resume out here the careers of their choice. We realise, however, that officers who have had the unhappy experience of finding that, as a result of rapid political developments, their services are no longer required in one part of Africa may well hesitate to expose themselves to the possibility of a similar misfortune on the other side of the Continent.

We therefore beg the hospitality of your columns to make public our solemn and sincere assurance that such officers need have no such fear in Northern Nigeria. We frankly admit our earnest hope that the Civil Service of this Region will contain an ever-increasing number of our own young men; but the number of Northerners who now hold University degrees, or similar high professional or technical qualifications, is few indeed and the numbers coming forward for some time are certain to be quite inadequate to meet the expanding needs of this Region with its population of 17,000,000. We are also firmly determined not to impede the progress of neighbouring territories by enticing away any of their own all too few indigenous senior staff.

We thus must look primarily to overseas for our professional and technical staff and we wish it to be widely known that a welcome, and a future, await all suitably qualified overseas officials who are sincerely prepared to serve the needs of our people. We should particularly like to have those with experience of the Sudan which, as several of us from personal experiences know, has so many features in common with our Northern Region.

To obviate any misunderstanding about this letter I thought I would mention it in the debate on the Speech from the Throne. After giving an explanation of its terms, for the benefit of those (a large number) who had not read it, I said:

Sir, many of those tested and experienced officers we are now looking forward to, to help us, are all coming out here mostly on contract, so that they could do the work and when the time comes for our people to return, they will replace them. I see no fear in inviting foreigners to come into this country. Who says that self-government means getting rid of foreigners? [Cry of 'Nobody'.] In that case nobody is to deny inviting those people to come and work for us. Shall we close all the hospitals when medical officers go on leave? What about the health centres that are being advocated? How can they be opened if there is no staff to man them? How many Northern doctors are returning this year? None. It is not the fault of the present-day government.

This meeting in 1955 was the first Budget Meeting of the House of Assembly under the new Constitution and my colleagues and I were now armed with full Ministerial powers. We had received a gracious message from the Queen and in proposing a loyal reply I said:

. . . 'Her Majesty's confidence in us faithfully to discharge wider powers and greater responsibilities under the revised Constitution will be our inspiration during the coming year. We have watched with keen interest Her Majesty's tours in countries in the Commonwealth of Nations. We have prayed for her safety through these long journeys which she has made. We pray, now, Sir, that in the near future Her Majesty may visit us in this Region so that as many of our 17,000,000 people as possible may see their Sovereign for the first time and declare their loyalty and devotion to her Crown. . . .

Towards the end of the year we were delighted to hear that our wishes were to be fulfilled and Her Majesty proposed to visit us in the following year. I will tell of this in the next chapter.

It was at this Budget Meeting that the President of the Assembly wore his new robes of green velvet and gold, for the first time. We had refused to follow the other Regions in this matter. Their Speakers then wore, as they still do, robes made in the pattern worn by Mr Speaker in Westminster. These robes, apart from being in an entirely alien tradition and style, involved the wearing of full court dress under them, if they were to be 'correct'. We felt that this would be quite out of place for us and that the robes by themselves over a Northern *riga* would be inappropriate and would look very awkward. We therefore produced an entirely new style, which could be worn with comfort and dignity equally by the British President of that period and his probable Northern successor. We were glad when Her Majesty was pleased to express her approval on her visit.

As a matter of interest I might say that the Expenditure Estimate presented at this meeting was for £12,377,019, very nearly twice the total pre-war figure for the whole of Nigeria.

An incident about this time, which gave me much personal satisfaction, was the decision, by its committee, to make the Northern Nigeria Society for the Blind independent of the British Empire Society, with which it had been associated for the two previous years. I have always been much concerned with the condition of the blind in this country—unfortunately we have rather large numbers of them, and nothing very much had been done for them in the past; such action as there was, had been local and haphazard. I felt that we should make a serious effort to help these people, and so founded this Society. At this particular time we opened a vocational training school in Kaduna which has done very well.

A Senior District Officer, Captain G. D. C. Money, was one of the few people who interested himself seriously in their welfare and that was because, I believe, he was afraid that he would go blind himself. I remember that on one of my visits there I was much impressed by a blind boy whom Money had trained in Maiduguri: I found him working, and very efficiently, as the NA telephone operator. Money's death in 1954 in Zaria, after he had retired, was a loss to the North. I think an attempt was made to teach the blind useful crafts in Kano about 1948, but it came to an untimely end as the two European experts were not altogether suitable.

We had two important losses in 1955. In April, Sir John Macpherson, the new Governor-General, who as Governor of Nigeria had helped us through our teething troubles and whose initiative had always led us surely through the mazes of political development and complexity, retired on pension. Fortunately, we were not to lose touch, for as Under-Secretary of State at the Colonial Office he continued to do his best for our advancement. Another loss was the retirement of H. R. E. Browne, who had been Civil Secretary for some years, and on whose courtesy and intelligence we relied, at times quite heavily, in these difficult years. We appointed a new Chief Justice—the North had not had one since 1914—and also a Northerner as our Commissioner in the United Kingdom.

Just after the Budget Meeting, with the Emir of Kano and M. Musa Gashash, a Member of the House of Assembly, I went on a visit to Tripoli, Cairo, and Saudi Arabia. I found this most interesting.

We were very well received in all the places we went to. It was in the latter part of April that we took off on this trip, of which the real object was to see for ourselves the conditions of the pilgrimage in Arabia.

Sir Eric Thompstone and C. R. Niven had severally already been on this errand some years before and had done a good deal to clear things up and make the journey easier—from the official point of view—for the pilgrims. But we felt that it was important for us, as Muslims, to investigate for ourselves, and, as it was six years since the last of these visits, it had become quite essential. About the same time we sent Letchworth, the Resident of Bornu, direct to make official contacts on the more formal side.

In Tripoli we saw a fine demonstration by their police; they had been commanded and trained by Alan Saunders, who had done so much for our own Police just before the war, and we went also to see a British cavalry regiment and their splendid horses. We were interested too in the ancient Roman city of Sabratha, forty miles away to the west of the town. It is so well-preserved that we were able to appreciate a great deal of what it must have looked like. I was not feeling very well when I started out from Kano and during the first period in Tripoli, but my health fortunately improved as the journey went on. We met and were entertained by many Tripolitanian notables, including the Prime Minister, the President of the House of Representatives, and the Governor of Tripoli, and were shown many interesting institutions.

We had a surprising reception in Cairo, surprising because we were strangers from a country remote from them, though of course we had a contact in the Nigerian students studying from time to time at the Al'azahar University. We only stayed the night there and went to Jeddah the next day. We were greatly interested by this strange town of lofty buildings, five and six floors high, standing on the seashore with the desert skirting closely round it.

As I have said, there were points we wanted to discuss. They were the need for proper arrangements for the reception and guiding of Pilgrims, for accommodation and for medical facilities. We felt that, if we could see officials and Ministers responsible for these subjects, the difficulties might be cleared up.

We were most kindly received and, almost from the start, we were assured that all we wanted would be put into effect, as soon as official communications were exchanged between us. All were careful to insist that everything in Jeddah and Mecca was tuned to the successful handling of the many thousands of Pilgrims who throng the place every year. We went to Riyadh and saw the King, who was most gracious to us, and then to Medina, where we spent the night in the open, in preparation for the Friday prayers.

In August we went for the first time on the Holy Pilgrimage— that is, the Emirs of Kano and Gwandu and myself with Isa Kaita and Sheik Ibrahim; Mohammadu Ribadu came from Lagos and the aged Shehu of Bornu and his Waziri joined us at Maiduguri.

We noted that improvements had already been put in hand in respect of pilgrims' accommodation. It was good to see that electricity and water supplies were installed in Jeddah and Mecca, and so the previous high cost of drinking water disappeared.

It was estimated that at that time there were 700,000 pilgrims in Mecca. The handling of these vast and devout crowds is, believe me, no mean feat, and we have the profoundest admiration for the way in which the Saudi Arabian Government tackled it. I would rather not have that task to face, and you must not forget that it only happens once a year and lasts for only three or four days. The rest of the time Mecca is a quiet oasis town in the desert. So the vast organisation is purely temporary and all the more difficult for being so.

This was a busy year for us and we seemed to be seldom at home. We had only been back from the Holy Pilgrimage for two weeks when the Emir of Gwandu and myself set out again. This time we went to Cambridge for a 'Summer School' on Local Administration. These were arranged from time to time by the Colonial Office and, quite apart from the discussions that went on for most of the day, we enjoyed meeting people from all over the 'Empire', as it still was called at that time. It did us much good to discuss our problems with these people and find that they themselves were perplexed by difficulties similar to our own, and that the answers they were arriving at were sometimes much the same as our own.

We were pleased, too, to find that they were quite visibly impressed by the progress we had made in our system of local government, when we explained it to them. They seemed to have had little idea of the state we had achieved, and the vast sums of money that were paid out by the Native Authorities on their own schemes and at their own initiative. We all came back greatly strengthened in the belief that we were approaching the development of local government practice in Northern Nigeria on sound lines and in a manner best suited to our traditions and to our country.

This trip was prolonged after the Conference into a tour of parts of Europe, in which we travelled over one thousand miles by car and traversed Holland, Western Germany, Italy, and Switzerland. We were very well received and well treated in all these countries, as of course we were in England, but the one which appealed to us the best was Switzerland for its cleanliness and fine air, for the beauty of the country, and for the industry and courage of so small and isolated a people. We have since then encouraged all kinds of our people to travel as far as they can through foreign countries.

During 1955 the new Governor-General, Sir James Robertson, arrived among us. From his first appearance he impressed us with his strength of character and common sense: we felt that he was very suitable for the post—not an easy one to fill.

CHAPTER 15

HAPPY AND GLORIOUS

In January 1956 the preparations for the Queen's visit had reached such a pitch that few people in Kaduna and the places she was to visit thought of much else. Activities of many departments became so much diverted to this end that they came almost to a standstill as far as other ordinary routine matters were concerned.

It was surprising what a variety of people were affected; for example, you would not think at first sight that veterinary officers would be particularly involved. And yet practically every one of them was working at high pressure. It was their task to ensure that the thousands of horses setting out to converge on Kaduna were in good condition and that they would reach their destination without trouble or sickness. Of these columns, a number had set out from their homes as early as December 1955, for the farthest had 600 miles to cover. Many of the marchers were elderly men and were a cause for anxiety, but they could not be dissuaded. Though they held important positions, they preferred to travel with their men. As it turned out, surprisingly few were the worse for their long journey. And don't forget that they had to trek back the same distance after the Durbar.

There was so much to do in Kaduna itself that many officers were brought in to help their colleagues. They were not reluctant to come in, for it guaranteed them a place and accommodation for the great event, which otherwise might have been very difficult. So difficult did it become that we had to 'ration' the numbers of people, and accommodation was so full that quite important people were content to sleep under trees in the open.

175

The last time any ceremonial of this kind had taken place in Nigeria was on the visit of Edward, Prince of Wales, and that was as far back as 1925. That time he only went to Kano and travelled there by train from Lagos. The great Chiefs were assembled to give him their homage, but in 1956 few people could remember in detail what had been done and so we had to start from scratch. I was in my last year at school at that time and well remember the stories we were told by those who had been present. My half-brother had, of course, gone to Kano with the Sultan and it had cost him a pretty penny. He said that he didn't want to get mixed up in that kind of thing again for some time. In fact, he never did. But whatever they said, it was a great adventure and experience for many people, indeed for most of them, for few people at that time in the upper classes moved far away from their homes. It was to be, comparatively, quite a long time before there developed that fluidity of movement and that ease of travel that has now become a commonplace here.

Anyhow, the position was now quite different and we were all of us determined that we would organise and stage the finest demonstration that it was possible for us to achieve. We wanted to put on a spectacle in the Queen's honour that would not only be entirely Nigerian, and of course Northern, but one which would be unique and unrepeatable elsewhere.

In my New Year Message I said of the Queen's visit:

Let us show them the loyalty and respect that we feel for them in a calm and peaceful atmosphere, undisturbed by political strife or domestic quarrels. Let them see us and remember us as being the happy inhabitants of a country united together as brothers and not as political enemies, nor backward and irresponsible citizens. Let us ensure that Her Majesty departs with a fine and lasting impression of the North.

We were not yet independent and, though we were given a free hand on most things, the Governor, Sir Bryan, was not keen to give us our head on this visit and he kept a tight hold on many details: his orders would make unexpected appearances, often adding to the general turmoil rather than reducing it. He was, of course, to be Her Majesty's actual host and he was her own representative, so there was really little that we could do about this attitude, and on the whole I must say things ran very well in the event. It was inevitable that he accompanied the Queen closely all the time, and did not give us Ministers, responsible though we were, much opportunity.

Bruce Greatbatch, then a Senior District Officer (now my Secretary), who had been with Sir Bryan in Sokoto, was put in general charge of these arrangements, assisted in Kaduna by numerous committees; these were in many cases duplicated by local committees in the Provinces. He had a number of officials specially seconded to him. The most important Northerners involved were the Ministers, who presided over the various committees, and I dealt with the general one. The complexity of the schemes and their details were astonishing. When it came to the visit itself, to the spectator there were no hitches and arrangements appeared perfect, but there were some anxious moments behind the scenes. There is nothing odd about this: all important functions have their anxious moments.

Extensive alterations were made in Government House, but this was Sir Bryan's own responsibility and I had nothing to do with it (except to provide the money). Naturally there have been many opinions about the final results. On the whole the feeling was that they were not very successful; but then the house is an awkward one and difficult to adapt without pulling a good deal of it down. The public rooms have always been wrong and the bedrooms out of proportion. One cannot say, however, that enough trouble was not taken in this respect.

When you think that the Queen's own party consisted of nearly thirty people—some of them very important ones too— and that there were over one hundred men and women from the world's Press and Broadcasting services and that we had only the old Catering Rest House to use as a hotel, you can understand some of the difficulties. In addition, several hundreds of people came on invitation, either officially or privately, such

as Members of the Assembly and of the House of Representatives, and Provincial Officials and Foreign representatives.

Thousands of schoolchildren, boys and girls, were brought in
by road and rail. We thought it right that they should have their
share in this great and unusual event. The problems and com-
plications involved in their movement to and from Kaduna
were immense, but were successfully overcome. The accommodation and feeding of all these children and six thousand men
and nearly three thousand horses of the Provincial Contingents
was comparatively easy: the children were accommodated in
schools and at the Trade Centre, while the men lived in a special
camp of grass mats down by the river; there was no serious risk
of rain at that time of year, though the danger of fire and epi-
demic was grave and gave us food for thought. So did water
supply: huge pipes had to be laid to new areas, and miles of
smaller pipe and hundreds of stand-pipes were needed.

However, God was very kind to us and there were no losses
through sickness or accident to man or beast. Incidentally, it is
interesting to note that during the whole period of the Queen's
visit in the North, no cases of crime were reported to the police
in the places she was visiting. This was also true of the subsequent Royal visits. When you think of the thousands of people
of all kinds who flocked into Kaduna, Jos, and Kano on that
occasion and the way in which most people left their houses to
attend the parades and so on, this remarkable absence of crime
is to be a matter of continuing astonishment and gratitude. It
seemed as though a kind of peace, not of this world, came over
the country—and it was just as well that it did. It did not
endure for long after the Queen's departure.

Other political leaders and myself had actually signed a
formal agreement that we would eschew politics during the
visit, and I must say this was faithfully respected by all throughout the country and was a wise move. The police were fully
extended on their unusual and exhausting duties, and I
doubt whether they could have dealt effectively with any
serious outbreak of crime. They were reinforced by Native

Authority Police, but even so there were not really enough to go round.

We took elaborate precautions against disease, and all in Kaduna were asked to report any illness at once to the health people: there were vaccination teams on every road into the capital, and every traveller arriving was checked for immunisation against smallpox, and was vaccinated on the spot when it was seen to be necessary. Rabies was another fear, and all stray dogs were destroyed and warnings were broadcast to dog owners. We had extra fire-fighting equipment and trained men brought in to reinforce the Kaduna unit, but God ruled that they were not needed.

The routes the Queen was to use were decked out with banners and tall standards, and gay arches crossed the streets. There was a splendid one on the crossroads near Government House made by the students of the Trade Centre. The huge jewelled crown rotated in the floodlights until some interfering European put it out of action.

As you will remember, the Queen's aircraft flew direct to Lagos, so that our first meeting with Her Majesty was on our own airfield outside Kaduna. As the Governor aptly said in a message to her, we 'awaited her coming with mounting joy and enthusiasm'.

This was no exaggeration. Some people, especially Europeans, will think that I have my 'tongue in my cheek' when I say this, but, believe me, we were deeply moved here in this country when we were awaiting her visit: even after the years that have passed since then, and all that has happened in them, we have exactly the same feelings about that visit, and would have them again should we be so fortunate as to repeat the privilege. We were proud and happy: and this applied not only to the few, such as myself and some of my colleagues, who had the honour of meeting the Queen in London, but also to many hundreds of thousands to whom she was a distant figure, but well-known through countless photographs and moving pictures. The thought that she was actually to come among us in her own person was bewildering and breathtaking in its gratification.

None of us realised that the charm and graciousness that was so evident and compulsive when we had met at close range would be equally effective over vast crowds of people, alien to her race, in thought and speech and background. And yet it was so. To me it is well-nigh inexplicable. It is easy enough to understand the effect the Queen would have, and does have, in a European capital, but to repeat and even surpass this effect in the capitals of Africa and Asia as she does is another matter. As you will remember, exactly the same effects were felt by the multitudes assembled to greet Her Majesty in India and Pakistan as were experienced by our people here.

Anyhow, she arrived safely and four days of excitement put our arrangements to the sharp test of public practice. I will not go through the brilliant ceremonies day by day, since they received such wide publicity at the time, but will mention one or two striking points.

Firstly, our arrangements worked very well, though I think that there was too much emphasis on security: many of the wire fences seemed unnecessary and in practice were so forbidding that the Royal car sometimes drove down avenues almost entirely empty of spectators.

Security was so thorough, even at the rehearsals, that I had difficulty in getting through myself. Some wit said, 'I hope the Queen has the right sort of label, or she will never get to her seat at the Durbar.' But it was a big responsibility for those concerned and, by and large, it was carried out effectively.

One of the most successful events was the miniature village prepared by the Education people as a background to school-children, boys and girls, demonstrating all the activities of village life. There had been some adverse comment that the programme did not allow of the Queen seeing a typical village (not so easy to find a village quite typical of all the varieties we have in this great country): this living model formed a convenient substitute for the real thing. The Queen was so interested in her tour round these groups of young people that, for the only time, the time-table ran a little late.

The most exciting incident was at the end of the Durbar when the old Mai Fika led a wave of galloping horsemen, who, in their enthusiasm ignoring white lines and stewards, swept in, a wildly cheering mass, waving swords and spears right up to the steps of the dais; they drove the Press to take refuge on the islands arranged for the photographers, and officials fell back against the stands. This was quite unrehearsed, but most effective. By this time the camera men were running out of film. The whole thing had been more spectacular than they had expected.

The most impressive ceremony was, by its nature, unseen by the public. This was the gracious visit to the combined House of Chiefs and Assembly, which had of necessity to take place inside Lugard Hall. There, after paying our due and heartfelt tributes of loyalty, I said in my Address:

> We are seeing the distinguished successor to a line of Kings and Queens who have contributed so much to the unity of the free world. . . . We recall, only too vividly, the recent years of peril, when only the fact that we were one of many links in the chain of the great alliance preserved us from catastrophe. It is important to remember that there would be little talk today of constitutional advance and economic progress, but for the unity we then displayed.
>
> Northern Nigeria came into being through the accident of history. the courage of our distinguished ancestors and the foresight of your public servants whom your forebears sent to this country. . . . We have yet to combine the various elements into a single whole. . . . We seek unity but not uniformity. . . .
>
> I and my colleagues have learnt that the art of modern government is a difficult one. We are a proud people and our Chiefs and their servants have long been experienced in local government. It is therefore natural that we should be determined to assume more and more responsibility for the conduct of our affairs.

The Queen said in the course of her reply:

> After a little over fifty years of British Administration, your country is now approaching self-government. . . . It is fitting that we should remember the public servants who in close association with the Chiefs have laid the foundations of good government, and the mis-

sionaries, teachers and technicians who have brought the benefits of education and commercial prosperity to the Region. . . .

The struggle against ignorance, disease and poverty will require, for years, your industry and application. I am struck by the evident determination of the people to educate their children. Without this, economic development cannot be achieved. The education of women is very important. I am pleased to hear of the steps you have already taken and the future plans you have made for this. . . .

I am sure that the Government of the Region will always allow men freedom to worship God in the way the conscience of each dictates. Tolerance is necessary, not only in religious matters, but also towards those whose views and traditions differ. It is by this spirit of understanding that the people of varied races will be brought together.

She read this in the crowded Chamber, under the sweltering heat of the great lamps in the gallery. Accustomed as I am to heat, I must admit I felt it keenly, but the Queen, as the phrase is, 'never turned a hair' and looked as cool and composed as though it had been a pleasant summer afternoon at Windsor. Her diamonds and jewels flashed in the glare of the lamps like lightning across a rippled lake: her beautiful dress spread about her like a brilliant waterfall. We had never seen anything like it and could have sat there till evening drinking it in. But of course she had to leave: the lights were dimmed, and it was over. When Her Majesty left Kaduna, people felt quite lonely without her, and yet she had been with us for only three days.

There was to be a quiet week-end at Jos and she stayed in the Governor's cottage under the great rocks of Tudun Wada. There were no incidents here except that a new electric cooker caught fire, fortunately without injury or awkward consequence. The Duke went off and looked at tin-workings, but the Queen had a complete rest in this secluded place.

On the Monday she flew down to Enugu and stopped at Makurdi for half an hour. This meant that the Governor had to fly ahead of her to receive the Royal party there and take leave of them as they left the Region. It was hot and sticky after Jos, but she drove round the airfield and greeted the local Chiefs and people: they had gathered in thousands for this great event.

I did not travel with the Royal Party on either of these visits, nor did any other Minister.

We didn't see her again until she stopped in Kano ten days later on her way home. It was very hot, but she drove round the city and visited the Emir, spending some time in his house. Here an adult education class was in action and interested her greatly. Tens of thousands thronged the streets and the Emir had brought in horsemen from all his districts. As a result there were more than twice as many horses lining the streets than we had gathered together at the Durbar. There was much less security and hundreds of thousands of excited Kano people saw the Sovereign at very close range: there were no incidents and away from the Royal route the city was calm.

The great aeroplane roared up into the black night and she was gone from us, but not from our memories and our hearts.

The visit had been a great success and all concerned deserved warm congratulations. It is noteworthy, however, that while a number of Europeans received medals and presents from Her Majesty, the Emir of Zaria was the only African to receive a medal in recognition of his services.

CHAPTER 16

A GENERAL ELECTION

THE remainder of 1956 seemed to be rather flat, though some important things happened in its course.

At the 1953 Conference it had been agreed that another should be called in not less than three years' time: here was 1956 and we were looking forward to a conference in mid-September. There were a number of points outstanding that demanded early attention. For example, the Federation had no Prime Minister, there were still British Officials in the Council of Ministers and our Executive Council; the future of the public services was not clear nor was that of the judiciary, and the control of the police was still a matter of keen controversy. We wanted to enlarge our House of Assembly, and the East, after years of hanging back, now wanted a House of Chiefs, though the status of their Chiefs was uncertain to say the least of it; there was talk of a Senate at the Centre; and, gravest of all, the fears of various minorities had grown steadily, though unreasonably, through the last five or six years and it was vital to alleviate them as soon as we could—though what we could actually do about them was hotly argued.

But there was a political crisis in the Eastern Region, one of those in which people 'walk out'—which had the unexpected, and indeed unprecedented, effect of leaving the Regional budget in the air unpassed and therefore unenforceable. The Governor was then compelled to use his reserve powers, an unheard-of event, to ensure that government staff would receive their salaries, and that the Ministers and the Parliamentary Secretaries would receive theirs; had he not done so they would have all gone without for the time being. The Appropriation Bill was therefore, by the special powers of the Constitution, pushed through a House which declined to meet. It would have been almost amusing, if it had not been so serious. What made it odd was that it was not the Governor's own budget—it had been prepared by the Ministers in the ordinary way. It is true that there were a few amendments that were unpopular and it is true that the Governor was not getting on very well with his Ministers, but these together did not amount to sufficient justification for this peculiar political conduct.

The West were dismayed by the NCNC victory in their own Region at the Federal Elections and rushed a Dissolution hoping to catch the NCNC on the wrong foot, engaged, as they thought they would be, in a General Election in the Eastern Region. This Election, in fact, did not take place at that time in the East. But a situation was already developing. Allegations had been made about Dr Azikiwe's actions in connection with the African Continental Bank: in June the Eastern Opposition put down a motion on this which was ruled out by the Speaker. This caused great political confusion and a sense of crisis continued for some time until it blew up later on into a General Election. This Election completely vindicated him and put his party back in power.

These events had the ultimate effect of postponing this London Conference. While it was a great pity, it did not in the end delay the grant of self-government to any appreciable extent and certainly had little practical effect in the North.

Anyhow, we had plenty to do; the Governor in the Speech from the Throne at the budget session laid stress on the need for 'a spirit of unity and common purpose'. I embroidered this in my speech on that occasion:

We are not facing an enemy. In fact we are surrounded by friends —people in other countries of the world, and in the United Kingdom in particular, who are anxious to assist us in any way they can. They want to help us to move forward, united and strong, so that we can take our place as an equal member of the Commonwealth of Nations.

No, Sir, we are not facing any living enemies, who wish to harm us or who wish to weaken us. The only possible enemies to the people

185

of the Northern Region are two: Ignorance and Fear. Ignorance produces Fear. Therefore if we kill Ignorance, we kill Fear.

Let us together then press forward with our *Yaki da Jahilci.* ... War against Ignorance. Let us, in a true spirit of unity and common purpose, each and every one of us, do all we can to explain to the people of the Region the TRUTH. ... I repeat, Sir, the TRUTH. The people themselves—if matters are properly and truthfully explained to them—will not hesitate to say what *they* want in the way of constitutional changes in 1956.

We in the Northern Peoples Congress will *not* make any important decisions with regard to our Constitutional future, unless we have first consulted the people. We are not just a Town Peoples Party; we are not just a Students Party; or a Party of men of learning. We are everything. We are the Northern Peoples Congress and Northern Peoples Party. We act on the wishes of the Northern people.

Very near to our hearts was then, as it is today, and indeed will be for many years until it is fully accomplished, the matter expressed by the cumbersome but inevitable word, 'Northernisation'—that is, the filling of posts in this our Regional Public Service by the sons and daughters of the North, duly qualified by education, training, experience, and intelligence. I summarised the position then reached:

Let me quote to the House some figures. When I and my colleagues in 1952 first assumed Ministerial responsibilities, there were 1,633 Northerners in the Junior Posts of the Public Service and 25 Northerners in the Senior Posts. What is the position today? 2,356 Northerners in the Junior Posts and 62 Northerners in the Senior Posts. This is an increase of 48 per cent Northerners in the Junior Posts; and 148 per cent Northerners in the Senior Posts. We have therefore, Sir, achieved something towards the Northernisation of our public service.

A few days later, regarding enterprises backed by the Regional Development Corporation, I said:

We realise that overseas personnel will be required to fill senior managerial, technical and professional posts in the first instance: but we would like to see as many suitable Northerners fill these posts, when they are adequately trained.

I went on:

Our public utilities are already largely reserved for operation by public bodies; but we have no plans for nationalising industry beyond this. Nor do we foresee any such proposal arising. Neverthe-less, so that there should be no doubt in the minds of overseas in-vestors that this region will provide safeguards for the interests of investors in the event of an industry being nationalised, we would like to make it clear that fair compensation, assessed by indepen-dent arbitrators, would be paid.

Overseas capital designed to expand trade facilities in the less developed parts of the Region which are at present not adequately served would also be welcome. There is good scope for commercial organisations dealing on a wholesale and distributive basis in tech-nical goods which call for highly skilled after-sale service.

For many years the problem of the administration of Kaduna had occupied the minds of the British Government of Nigeria. Kaduna is a purely artificial town. In 1913 the great plains which now embrace our capital were virtually empty. There were a few very scattered Gwari villages, but until the railway went through them on its way to Kano from the coast, there was no common link between them. They came into the area of the Zaria Emirate, which, one of the old original Hausa States, stretched a hundred miles away to the south, and east-wards to the escarpment of the higher Plateau. Here the Emirs of Zaria had raided for slaves in the old days: it still remained part of their fief.

The railway crossed the Kaduna River, quite a substantial obstacle, by a six-hundred-foot bridge. From some quite early date in its consideration some far-sighted official had proposed and other far-sighted officials had agreed and approved the theory that some day a railway would have to be built from the coast of what is now the Eastern Region, towards the North, as part of the essential railway framework for the whole country. It was decided that the junction should be just south of the Kaduna Bridge, for naturally no one advocated the building of a third expensive bridge over the same river. The other one at Zungeru became inevitable once it was decided to link up the Lagos Government Railway, as it was called, with the inde-pendent railway in Northern Nigeria, known then as the 'Baro-Kano Railway' on which the Kaduna Bridge was sited.

187

Soldiers of the Northern Nigeria Regiment were stationed at Kakuri (near the Junction) when the bridge was built, and before long this became the military headquarters, at first of the North and later of the whole of Nigeria. These dispositions give good evidence of the small extent to which the British relied on the soldiers for internal security. It was only during the last war that the officer commanding troops, then a Major-General, went to live at the Governor's capital and not here in Kaduna, where his predecessors, who were full Colonels, lived for so many years. This was the strategic centre of the country; and if troops were required they could be moved with greater facility along either of the three major arms of the railways from Kaduna than from any other point.

Lugard was, by training and experience, a soldier and considerations of this kind were always in his mind. But he was also a great administrator and he realised that the choice of a site for a capital was of importance politically. Though Zungeru was his early love, he soon found that it was unsuitable for its purpose. Zaria or Kano were the obvious places to be considered: both were reasonably central; both had good communications; both had good climates, Zaria being on the whole the better from a European point of view. But Lugard saw that it would be a mistake to put the headquarters of an administration in the same town as the residence of a Chief. However careful the administration might be to avoid such an effect, it would, he felt, be quite inevitable for the Chief at the capital to acquire an importance that would not be his by right of native precedence, but only by administrative chance and foreign convenience. Conversely, the presence of the Government Headquarters in the same town as the Emir's residence could not but become a source of embarrassment to the latter. Jos might have been considered, but the country was still unsettled and little thought seems to have been given to it.

In the House I said in this connection:

. . . For our part, my colleagues and I, in our short experience of Ministerial responsibility, are heartily grateful that we are able to work here in Kaduna without the close presence or influence of purely local interests; we have in fact been placed in a position where there is full opportunity to think and work in the best interests of the Region as a whole. . . .

Lugard therefore decided to build in the empty plains, and the obvious place was by the bridge over the Kaduna River, where the soldiers had already put their offices. There was a good deal of argument about which side should be used, but the northern bank was finally selected and that is where we are now.

Kaduna has grown from 4,336 people in 1939 to 73,346 in 1960. It covers eleven miles from north to south and five miles from east to west. The place is still growing and is likely to continue to do so. The industrial area to the south of the river is attracting factories. These, of course, attract labour and so do the new government activities, both Regional and Federal workers bring their families, and they too must be fed, and so the town grows almost daily.

Until 1956 the area covered by Kaduna was considered to be a part of Zaria Province. The Zaria Native Administration had a sub-office here and the Emir's staff ran the place under one of his senior officials: all this came under the Resident, Zaria, who used to come in on tour and stay here. On the other hand, the Lieutenant-Governor could scarcely help taking an interest in the town that lay at his very gates, especially as regards planning and buildings and, of course, keeping the peace, sometimes quite a tricky business, and that involved the Civil Secretary and his Office. The only people who had no say were the Ministers whose capital it was.

It was abundantly clear that the time had come to clear up this situation which in practice was even more confusing than I have sketched out above. We decided to set up a 'Capital Territory' which would include the whole of the built-up area and the vital airfield: this would be excised from Zaria Emirate and would come under the direct control of a designated Minister (in practice, myself). The Administrator of this Territory was to be a senior Government Officer, but his staff could be drawn either from the Government or the Native Administrations. The area had been policed by Nigeria Police so far as the 'Government Station' was concerned and by NA police in the remainder of the African town. Now his police were to be Nigeria Police and they, of course, are Federal; here lay hidden a source of future difficulty.

He was to have an advisory board—in fact, more than one—but these were to have no powers: here we followed precedents in Canberra and Washington, but did not go as far as they do, for there the citizen is deprived of his franchise.

The Bill setting up this Territory was passed in due course; there was a certain amount of argument, but the opposition centred on the composition and powers of the councils and they could be dealt with fairly simply. They did not attack on the more vulnerable points, such as law and order or finance. But that has always been their way here.

To anticipate a little, I must say that five years of practical working has shown us that a revision would be necessary and at the time of writing, new proposals are being drawn up which will put it on rather sounder lines for the future.

My colleagues and I attach the greatest importance to Kaduna. Not only is it our capital, containing our homes and our Ministries, but also it should be the commercial centre of the North. As I said when opening a commercial motor garage here:

I strongly believe that Kaduna is the 'showroom' for business in the whole of the Northern Region. It is here that the representatives of the people come from time to time to attend the Legislature. It is here that the Chiefs, who provide guidance in their Native Authority Councils, also come to attend the Legislature and to attend Conferences. It is here that the heads of Government Departments reside, and it is here that Government decides what type of equipment and material it will purchase for the development of the Region. . . .

We, the independent government, have adorned it with fine buildings and have more in mind and we expect commercial firms to do the same. But buildings are not sufficient; the capital must be efficiently conducted and its people must be happy and contented.

In May of that year there was a lot of trouble in Bornu and a number of important NA people were arrested on various charges, but most of them were connected with receiving money. My old friend, Alhaji Mohammed, was forced to resign from the post of Waziri, and it was lucky for him that he did so or things might have gone worse for him. He was endeavouring, in his honest way, to bring in reforms for which the country unfortunately was not ready. The Bornu people are the hardest in the country to administer, but we always find that if the Shehu is left to 'have his head' he will usually bring things through all right. Some British officers could not understand this, simple as it is, and, by interfering at the wrong time and in the wrong way, made things not only difficult for the Shehu and his people, but also for themselves, and, of course, for us here in Kaduna. I doubt whether Sir Bryan ever understood the Bornu mentality—he had never served there; sometimes we felt that he did not really appreciate their great qualities.

Fortunately, the incident was cleared up without any rioting or bloodshed (not like a later incident), and after a while we were able to find a very suitable post for the ex-Waziri as Pilgrims Officer in Khartoum. And, talking about the Pilgrimage, I was able to take part for the second time in this holy journey. Conditions had not improved very much and, indeed, they were more than primitive. However, we were able to take with us a Nigerian doctor in addition to the usual dresser.

Perhaps I should explain about the Pilgrimage for the benefit of non-Muslim readers. The Holy Koran enjoins upon all good Muslims the duty of undertaking the Holy Pilgrimage to the Holy Places in Saudi Arabia at least once in their lifetime. This applies not only to men but to women also, for they too can be Pilgrims. The Pilgrimage involves the journey to Mecca, usually through Jeddah, ritual observances round the Kaaba, the journey to Arafat, the holy mountain. After this, most people make a trip to Medina, where the Holy Prophet lies buried.

King and commoner, poor and rich, all are equal at the actual rites; no display is permitted; no special privilege is allowed; all must wear the pilgrim's simple white cotton cloth.

To go once is to achieve merit in the future life: to go more then once secures for the pilgrim still more merit. There is no limit to the number of times anyone can go and I hope to go whenever it is possible for me to do so—in fact, I have already performed this sacred duty seven times. There is, however, a very wise and stringently enforced rule laid down by the Holy Prophet: it is to avoid abuses and vexations. The intending pilgrim must save enough money to take him to Mecca and bring him back home again.

It is regrettable, but unfortunately true, that many unscrupulous people make illegal gains by 'fleecing the pilgrim' and taking from him on various pretexts as much of his savings as they can. I believe that much the same thing used to happen on pilgrimages to Christian shrines. While there is no doubt that such people will suffer severely hereafter, this thought does little to mitigate the anxieties and sufferings of the pilgrims at the moment.

The Governments concerned are doing all they can to stop this evil practice, but it must be admitted that many of the pilgrims are gullible and easily convinced by the smooth tongues of the swindlers. It therefore becomes necessary sometimes for pilgrims to work on their homeward journeys. This has, oddly enough, operated in favour of the Sudan. Thousands of ex-pilgrims have worked, and are still working, on the great Gezira cotton scheme—the Sudan Government's most successful project—indeed, it is at least questionable whether the scheme could have been developed as it has without Nigerian labour.

We went to Mecca via Cairo: we had only passed through there before and now we wished to see the historic places. Though we were travelling quite informally as simple pilgrims, Colonel Nasser very kindly received us, and entertained us hospitably. Little did we know that while we were away in Arabia, this visit was going to cause a blow-up. Cairo radio, reporting our interview with the President, made a solemn announcement that I had invited him to visit us in Nigeria. He had, of course, invited me to return officially. British relations with Egypt were at their worst at this particular moment. The Governor was not at all pleased, and poor Makaman Bida, who was holding the fort for me in my absence, caught the full fury and had to issue a Press release denying the allegation, without, however, having any real knowledge at all as to the facts of the case. We were startled to hear about all this when we got home, as we had had no idea of what had been going on.

In June we announced that an election would take place in the forthcoming dry season. It was the fifth year of the House and a General Election was legally inevitable, but there were not lacking those who thought that we would go on as we were until we achieved Regional self-government.

At that time we still thought that there would be a London Conference before the election, and at that Conference we hoped that we would be able to get more members approved for our House of Assembly. But shortly after our return the Secretary of State, in consequence of the difficulties in the other Regions, since the prolonged enquiry into the affairs of the African Continental Bank was still unpublished, decided that the Conference must be postponed. At first we thought that it might be held in January 1957, but the upshot was that it did not take place until the end of that May. The result of this postponement was that our General Election had to be carried out under the 1954 Constitution. That meant that we still had to use electoral colleges, with registration areas only in the more advanced centres. And it gave us a hitherto unused increase in elected members—from 90 to 131; this was a step in the right direction, but nothing like what we had in mind for the future. As things turned out we did not achieve the full result until 1961!

After a good deal of discussion we decided to limit the electoral colleges to two tiers, in place of the four we used last time. This was made possible by adopting single-member constituencies throughout the Region, instead of the group election of Provincial members as had obtained before. This arrangement was a definite improvement: it also made the operation of political parties fairly easy at all stages and introduced the right spirit of competition. The Registration System (i.e. with ballot boxes) was extended to eleven centres of trade and industry. On the whole the campaign was rather leisurely and I remember that the Press brought accusations of lethargy against the parties and their officials in the constituencies. The fact was that we had left rather too much time and some people either lost interest or were slow in acquiring it. However, things accelerated themselves by the time the elections themselves came on in November and there were little signs of apathy by then.

The parties were: my own Northern Peoples Congress; the Northern Elements Progressive Union (NEPU); the United Middle Belt Congress (UMBC), and a number of tribal parties on rather a small scale and with a sharply restricted area of appeal. NEPU have a gift for 'alliances' which never seem to do them any good and are so involved that nothing whatever is to be gained by bringing them back to memory at this stage. The UMBC was anything but 'united' and little splinters were constantly splitting off and getting in the way, not only in our way but also in that of the people supposed to be on their side.

NEPU talk a great deal, but I have never been seriously worried by them, nor have I been impressed by their powers of leadership. I sincerely wish, however, that they could avoid rudeness and provocation in their election speeches and indeed in all their political actions. There is no call for either. I can see little real virtue in insulting elderly Alkalai, who are only trying to do their duty conscientiously in difficult conditions. Why NEPU should strike surprised, and almost grotesque, attitudes of outraged modesty when these old gentlemen show their teeth from time to time is beyond me. Rudeness has never really gained anything worth while.

Our election manifesto relied on our achievements which, though they were not spectacular, were considerable: our plans for the future were far-reaching (and since then have been largely fulfilled).

Our main objective—as, of course, must be the object of every right-minded government—was, and still is, security, peace, happiness, and progress. To achieve this we stressed the extension of education, especially that of craft schools at comparatively low educational levels with the introduction of more and more industries—at that time the Textile Mills were still on the drawing board and sack, paper, salt, cement, and flour works were in contemplation and a steel plant was a large and shadowy dream. New roads and irrigation schemes were, we thought, important, and of course new hospitals and dispensaries, for without these no country can be thought to be truly developed, and the people must be kept healthy. Again, without a vast and vigorous attack on public ignorance we could not take the people with us on our rapid forward march, and this included action against corruption and improvement in Native Authority Councils.

The latter of these presents little difficulty. But corruption is a big matter and one which had given us a lot of anxious thought and I must, at this point, be permitted to digress for a moment. It is all very well to say 'abolish corruption' as though it was a thing that can be cut off by turning a tap or pressing a switch. No, it is a matter which springs from the very roots of human nature. Is there any country in the world which can honestly and convincingly claim to be absolutely free of corruption? I doubt it very much. Some are obviously better in this respect than others, but so long as men and women are what they are, there will always be those who will hold back some service for their own gain, who will eagerly press some service so that they can reap reward, who will from their wealth or position claim services or priorities to which they are not entitled. These rewards and gains need not be financial: they can be very subtle and inconspicuous, but they are there all the same.

In my opinion all that a Government can do is to frown on these practices and endeavour to keep them in bounds. We do, however, take the strongest exception to the way in which many Europeans regard all Africans and African Governments and Institutions as incurably and profoundly corrupt. Not only is this most unfair, and quite unfounded, but it shows again an automatic tendency to look down on Africans just because they are Africans. After all, what are Europeans? They have, so far as I know, no general standard of honesty or probity pattern: they vary greatly among themselves, not only class by class, nation by nation, but by individuals in the same class. All Europeans were not at Eton or Harrow or Winchester—and even their old boys have been known to fall from grace—and there are plenty of different standards in different grades of society and in different countries. An automatic judgement to the prejudice of Africans is no more justified than an automatic exaltation of 'Europeans', whatever they may be. Anyhow, we are determined that, so far as we are able, no one shall profit by corruption and that it shall not become a byword among men.

We concluded our manifesto by reiterating our determination—not an empty one by any means—to develop the principle of democracy and to overhaul the government machine so that it could in due course be accelerated to the pitch required for the self-government that we had promised ourselves in 1959.

We said: 'These promises are made with the full knowledge of what is within the financial resources of the Region and its executive capacity. They are not merely empty vote-catching dreams, such as are offered by our loud-mouthed and irresponsible opponents. Above all, they are not promises which, if carried out, would involve a heavy burden of taxation on the people, as appears likely in other parts of Nigeria.'

By the beginning of November the rural elections were practically complete and we knew that whatever happened to the remainder, and in the towns, our victory was assured. The towns voted on the 15th November. There was no trouble and for that we thanked God. We were successful in nine of the nineteen seats and these included, to our astonishment, the four Kano seats, which till then were thought to be the very citadel of NEPU: their leader, Aminu Kano, was among the defeated. It is odd to me that he has never been a member of the Northern Assembly: in some ways this is rather a pity, as he might have learnt what applied politics are and how different they are from the kind you shout about in the market places. He is at present a member of the Representatives, but is too far from home to have much effect.

The final state of the parties was NPC 100, plus 3 Independents who came over to us: NEPU/BYM had 8 members and the others 20. The two last groups made up an opposition (though not very united) and Ibrahim Imam's long and lonely vigil, as the *sole*, but by no means negligible, 'opposition' was over. Not that the change made things any better for him, for in fact he had still to carry the whole weight of opposition, while the others argued among themselves and made more futile and pointless speeches in the House than sensible ones.

Meanwhile, the tragedy of Egypt was going on. Fortunately, the elections took people's minds off the dreadful hash that Great Britain was making in the Middle East, ending in the deplorable and wholly unjustified attack on Egypt which did not even have the merit of efficient planning and determined execution. We were greatly relieved to learn that Sir Anthony Eden had had to retire from the control of this ridiculous and humiliating disaster—one which need never have happened if there had been a little less arrogance on *both* sides.

The new House was sworn in in mid-December 1957, and set off on its five-year journey in good heart. I said:

I have a special word of welcome to Members—I mean new Members, to whom I say, not only welcome, but also congratulations. I congratulate them on winning their election campaigns and also bringing to the Legislature of the Northern Region some measure of opposition to the established Government.

I and my colleagues here on the Government Bench do not fear the opposition—rather, we welcome it.

(Mallam Ibrahim Imam: Hear, hear.)

197

A young man who is allowed to have everything in his own way, and is never subjected to criticism, becomes spoilt and weak.

(Mallam Ibrahim Imam: Good talk!)

Similarly a young Government, if it is not faced with an intelligent and constructive opposition, soon lacks incentive and inspiration. All I pray, Sir, is that in the heat of future debates we shall, none of us, lose sight of the fact that we are all here, whatever may be our political party, with one common goal to which we strive— the maximum good for the maximum number of people in this Region. We have our political differences but I am confident that these will never stop us from getting together in order to make our country a really great one. I am confident, too, that as in the past we shall experience in this Chamber in the future a true sense of co-operation and good humour in all business which we undertake.

The Executive Council was then made up of the three British officers, and

Local Government & Works	Sardauna
Education and Trade & Industry	Makaman Bida
Land & Survey, Social Welfare & Co-operatives (a new Ministry) and North Cameroons Affairs	Abba Habib
Health	G. Ohikere

Further changes were, however, brought in at the next Budget Session.

Ministers without Portfolios:
  Sultan of Sokoto
  Emir of Kano
  Aku of Wukari
  M. Ibrahim Gashash

Aminu Kano, rather rashly, wrote to the papers that the urban results proved that, had the ballot box been in use throughout the Region, we should have suffered severely, even if we had not been defeated. Five years later he was to regret these words.

CHAPTER 17

THE SECOND LONDON CONFERENCE

By the time we came to the Budget Session of 1957 Ghana had gained her independence, the first of the African states south of the Sahara to achieve this prize. I moved to congratulate the people of Ghana on this great success and, in the course of my speech, I said:

... The dangers are indeed formidable, and Ghana will have many hard tests to face. Perhaps the sternest test which Ghana will have to face is the preservation of democracy. It is up to the Leader of Ghana to resist all anti-democratic influences; and to resist using undemocratic means to retain control over the country. Nigeria herself will have to face such a test, time and time again during this century.

The second test which confronts Ghana is the danger of internal strife. It will be many, many years before the peoples of Africa will respect political boundaries higher than tribal boundaries. For many years the Leaders of countries in Africa will have the difficult task of welding together the peoples of their countries within the political boundaries which have been artificially decided upon by the Colonial powers within the last hundred years. One must not forget that the only Commonwealth country in modern times where the transfer of power has not been followed by bloodshed is Ceylon. We shall therefore pray most earnestly during the months ahead that Ghana will take her place in the world without suffering communal strife or internal unrest.

The third test, Mr President, which the new state of Ghana will have to face is the test of external influence. There is no doubt that Ghana will be called upon to join some Pan-African or some Pan-West African Movement. There will, for example, be a strong inclination to join any movement that protests against the racial policies of the South African Government.

There is also ever present the external pressure and influence of the Communist world. Finally, there may be opposition to the present Leaders of Ghana from other African Leaders who have their own ambitions. . . .

Reading these words again now, I see that there is quite a prophetic strain in them.

Later on I had an interesting trip to Ghana. We were most kindly received and were shown everything and even travelled as far north as Tamale. We were impressed by the thoroughness of the organisation of the PCC, though, I must admit that we were not impressed by its desirability, and could understand how it was that Dr Nkrumah managed to get everything his own way. We were surprised at the large numbers of Hausas and other northerners living in Ghana, and I should think that most of them came to see us. We were quite overwhelmed by the presents they pressed upon us and, as we were travelling everywhere by air, we were sometimes quite embarrassed by them, especially by the kind people who gave us a large ox at the last moment.

Meanwhile, at the end of January, Mr Lennox-Boyd stopped in Kano for a day, in order to 'relax', we were told. His relaxation seems to be very like mine—just going from one thing to another. But we were glad to see him as he has a very heartening personality. We did not mention the forthcoming Conference, though no doubt the Governor and the Governor-General, who had come up specially, did not abstain from doing so—curious how the old habits remain. We seem to get on well with big Secretaries of State; Mr Lennox-Boyd, now Lord Boyd, is a big man like Lord Chandos, and they both seemed to have a broad point of view; for this we were very grateful. It was to be very helpful to us in the Conferences.

I handed over the Ministry of Works to Abba Habib, but kept Local Government until our return from London, and for a short time was in charge of Land and Survey. These double jobs were not only very hard on the Minister, but made the organisation difficult. However, it was not until the end of the year that we started to 'integrate' the Departments into their Ministries, so we did not have the full weight of responsibility that was to be ours from 1958.

Abba Habib continued at the same time with North Cameroons Affairs and Makaman Bida also had two (Education and Trade and Industry); Musa Gashash, an experienced Kano trader, came in as Social Welfare and Co-operatives. We were at that time limited by the Constitution to six Ministers from the House of Assembly. In September we were able to spread our wings to the full extent: like those of the butterfly, they took time to expand properly and stiffen enough to carry weight.

That year our Regional Budget stood at about £21m. £4½m. went on Social Services, £1¾m. on Natural Resources, £2m. on Works maintenance, and £3m. each on roads and new buildings. One of these latter, though it was not in the estimates at the time, was to be the new State House on the northern outskirts of Kaduna. This proposal raised a wild storm of vindictiveness from our political opponents who were pleased to think (and apparently believed) that this was to be a house for my own gratification. They would not accept the plain fact that there was simply nowhere in Kaduna large enough to accommodate 400 people at an entertainment, and during the rains they would have to be under cover; there was nowhere to put up distinguished guests whom we wished to honour— Government House was not big enough and the Catering Rest House, the other alternative, was substandard.

It is true that the State House was planned with rooms for myself and my family, but in fact since they have been completed I have never occupied them, preferring, as I do, my own former house. On the other hand, the public rooms have been used scores of times for large receptions and smaller dinner parties and have amply justified their cost. No one mentions it now and those who were foremost in attacking the idea are far from pleased if they are left out of an invitation list.

The whole scheme has now been completed by the transfer of the Executive Council chamber and offices to the new site from Government House. When the Governor ceased to preside over the Council, it became inappropriate for the meetings to continue to be held in the shadow of Government House.

This new mass of buildings now makes a distinguished group in the modern style, and when the new Legislature is complete the Northern Region can well be proud of its architectural setting. I am one of those who feel that, however efficient and intelligent an administration may be, it cannot fail to be enhanced, both in spirit and in the public mind, by housing it in fine buildings.

Shortly before the delegations went off to London for the Second Conference, we were present when the new airport at Kano was opened. This was, of course, a Federal matter but we must give credit where so much is due. It cost well over a million pounds and was worth every penny. It was no little matter to raise Kano from being rather a 'bush' airport to the real international status of one of the best in Africa. The traffic has always been quite heavy at Kano, but the buildings were far from satisfactory. That was four years ago. I find it interesting to hear now that the accommodation is already considered to be too small and the runways too short.

Soon after that we left for England by sea. We found the voyage very restful. It is good to be in a place where the number of those who can reach you are limited to those actually on the ship. I find the greatest inconvenience I have to suffer, as Premier, lies in the number of people who manage to get into my house during the course of a day. It is quite impossible for us to employ the British methods and refuse, however courteously, to see them; that would be most impolite and would be bitterly resented—running as it would do against all our customs and habits.

You would think that things would be better in London but, believe me, they are not; in fact, they are rather worse. There are hundreds of students who feel that they must come and greet me, and they do so at all hours of the day and night. And besides these callers, the telephone is constantly ringing—mostly strangers who wish to get in touch about something or other (usually of more importance to themselves than to me). It is difficult for my secretaries to identify people swiftly, and we would not like to turn away an old friend or someone who might be of real value to us.

This time we stayed at St James's Court, which was very comfortable and the staff were very helpful, as indeed they should be for the price we paid. The only drawback was that the reception people and those on the telephone exchange could seldom identify us by name or title; they got confused very easily, and I am afraid that many messages must have gone astray. One of my friends was rather startled to find that, instead of speaking to me, he was engaged in conversation with Chief Awolowo, Premier of the Western Region, a very different man. After all, what is the difference between a couple of Regions to a girl on a telephone switchboard in London?

The meetings were in the gold and scarlet of Lancaster House, which makes a convenient and splendid setting, and incidentally is one of the very few places of this nature where you can park a car. Her Majesty's Government gave us a party one night here and it was memorable for the entertainment provided. Someone of intelligence had persuaded the Scots Guards to send along their pipers to play for us in the garden. We really enjoyed this: they looked so magnificent, and their music is so similar to our own that we were grateful for this forethought.

The meetings covered the last week in May and most of June. There seemed to be a crowd of people at them—55 delegates and 44 advisers, plus numerous secretaries and assistants—and this naturally protracted the proceedings a good deal.

The Eastern and Western Regions were to receive their self-government at an early date, but we did not press for the same for us before 1959. We asked for, and received, special modifications in our own existing Constitution as an interim measure. The House of Chiefs was to be increased to include all the First Class Chiefs and 47 others, and the Assembly would be raised to 170 elected members, plus the Speaker, as he was to be called, the Attorney-General, and not more than five special members (to be appointed by the Governor) continued as before. We were not able, in the long run, to take advantage of this increase until nearly five years had passed, for, as you have seen, we had just had our general election.

Executive Council was also increased considerably: there were to be not less than twelve Ministers from the Assembly in addition to the Chiefs (not more than four) and the Attorney-General, who was perforce a British officer, since we had no legal men of our own sufficiently qualified. The Governor continued to preside, though in the other two Regions he was no longer present and the Premiers presided themselves.

The Civil Secretary and the Financial Secretary vanished from the scene and their functions were divided up among the Ministries. Makaman Bida became the first Minister of Finance and has filled that office ever since with great ability. At that time P. H. G. Scott left us, a man of great industry and cleverness, unfortunately accompanied by a sarcastic tongue and a love of intrigue: these two in the end spoilt him for us. This was in many ways a great pity.

The Civil Secretary became the Deputy Governor, with no work to speak of and only the right to act when the Governor was on leave. At first the appointment had its uses but, as things progressed, so its value declined and in the end it outstayed its welcome. Looking at it now one realises what a valuable post was that of the Civil Secretary, for he could co-ordinate all government activities and keep an eye on the departments, especially through his subordinate the Financial Secretary.

With the formation of Ministries, which are independent bodies, the co-ordination can only be undertaken by the Premier himself (not by his Office, which is in effect another Ministry), and that puts a further strain on the Premier and he has quite enough to do as it is. The Secretary to the Premier cannot, of course, interfere in any way in the other Ministries, for they are all (including their Permanent Secretaries) under their own Ministers and must look to their Ministers for guidance, instructions, and control.

At this time a most useful step was taken in the setting-up of a Council of Chiefs (not to be confused with the House of Chiefs, a legislative body). It is made up of between two and four of the Executive Council Chiefs, with four others from the House of Chiefs and the Premier: the Governor presides. It deals with 'the appointment, recognition, grading and deposition' of all Chiefs in the Region and takes a great responsibility on its communal shoulders from those of the Governor, who in the past carried this sometimes embarrassing duty personally. This Council has proved its worth on a number of occasions since its inauguration.

It was agreed that when the North came to self-government we would follow the same pattern as the East and West—that is, the Governor would become purely constitutional and act only on the advice of his Ministers; he would no longer preside over the Executive Council, nor over a legislative body.

There were a number of changes in the Federation—the most important of these was the creation of the post of Prime Minister (the title Premier is constitutionally restricted to the Regions) and the disappearance of the three British officers from the Council of Ministers. And, further, a Senate was to be set up based on equal numbers from each Region. This was supposed, in some way, to counteract the heavy weight of Northern members in the House of Representatives: in practice it has little effect in this direction since it can only delay legislation for six months: it can, of course, initiate Bills on its own (just as the House of Chiefs can here) so long as they have nothing to do with 'money'.

The number of members of the Representatives was increased to 320, or one for each 100,000 of total population: this played into our hands, though we did not initiate the proposal, but it also made a new problem—how to find this large number of people from our limited resources.

The argumentative points were: the police, Lagos, the minorities, and finance. The difficulty about the police was who should control this vital organisation, the Federation or the Region? It was agreed by all that for the police to come under the control of any one political party would be a disaster, and indeed for the other parties it might be even more serious than a disaster. A Police Service Commission was to be set up to deal with all police appointments, etc. It was agreed that there must be a Federal Force capable of intervention anywhere, since the Federation had a final and overall responsibility for law and order.

We thought that in the end some kind of Regional forces might also be established but that for the present things should go on as they were, giving the Regional Government an important say in the handling of the police stationed in each Region.

As for Lagos, we were determined that the Federal Capital should not return to the Western Region, as it had done at one time: it must be independent territory. The Action Group were very upset at our stand, in which we were strongly backed by the NCNC and some of the smaller groups. However, this time they did not walk out.

We were not satisfied then—and the position has not materially changed since then—about the amount of time and money assigned to Lagos affairs by the Federal Government, amounts quite out of proportion to the rest of the Federal Government's commitments. For example, we found that much of the schooling in Lagos was paid for by the Federal Government, so were the hospitals and dispensaries—there were more doctors and sisters in Lagos at that time than in any one of the Regions—and, of course, a large police force and fire brigade. In fact, the Lagos Town Council, owing to its continuously inadequate finances, seemed to evade very successfully most of the liabilities that fall on normal town councils.

More time was spent and more paper was pushed at us about the so-called minorities question than on any other individual item on the agenda. In the end it was handed to a Special Commission, which I will mention later on.

Finance was dealt with in the same way—another commission was asked for and came out later in the year. This is naturally the hardest of the problems to solve and, whatever answer may be produced, there are bound to be plenty of people who will disagree with its proposals. As they say, a man's tenderest spot is his pocket, and for active and determined governments any attempt to reduce the amount which they think they should be entitled to receive can only expect the treatment it will undoubtedly get. Both these Commissions implied the need for a resumed Conference some time fairly early in 1958.

There were a number of minor matters, detailed and technical, which took time but did not provoke much discussion, but the question of the date for the Independence of Nigeria could not be classed in this category.

At the very beginning of the Conference we put in an agreed memorandum asking for Independence in 1959—that is to say, two years after the date of the meeting. The Secretary of State was in a strong position here and he made the most of it. The East and West were only just getting self-government and the North did not want it at the moment, so would it not be better to wait and see how this first stage worked before turning to the future of the whole country? We pressed for a date.

There was a further statement in which Mr Lennox-Boyd thought that early in 1960 a newly elected legislature might pass a resolution asking for self-government and that this would be considered by Her Majesty's Government. By that time the reports of the Commissions should have been considered and the effectiveness of Regional self-government would have made itself apparent (or not). And there would then be nothing to stop Her Majesty's Government coming to a proper conclusion. We were very disappointed in this reply and the more so since it was produced at the very end of the rather protracted Conference; there was not sufficient time for us to work out and submit a reasoned answer or hold a full discussion. We were booked to leave the following day and bookings for so many people cannot lightly be altered at the last moment—and they certainly should not be altered. Much of the amiable feeling engendered by the Conference was dissipated. We did not blame Mr Lennox-Boyd in this matter: we felt that his Office had been unwise enough to 'hang back' on a matter of vital importance to us.

However, in the end, as everyone knows, the British Government fulfilled its half-promise and we did get Independence in 1960, though rather late in the year. You will scarcely avoid a slight smile if you now turn back to the Lagos crisis of 1953, where so much was said to so little effect.

Shortly after we got back to Kaduna, I had the pleasure of opening the new Kaduna Bridge, linking the northern and southern banks of the river at the capital. Until this moment all road traffic between the two areas had to use the railway bridge; naturally this bridge belonged to the railway and so, equally naturally, trains had the first priority. This was all very well, but there was no alternative, and people and cars were often held up waiting for a train that was still some distance away: it was nothing to be kept waiting for half an hour and, with the growing commercial and industrial centre on the south bank, delays of this kind could only involve great inconvenience.

It was interesting to note, as I said at the time, that the first letter of complaint about this bridge had been received in 1921, but nothing had been done about it: the traffic was for many years comparatively light and there was no through road out of Kaduna to the south as there is now. The matter was finally pressed in the House of Assembly, moved, oddly enough, by a member who was really not personally concerned at all. The bridge cost £125,000 and is nearly 700 feet long.

We were delighted when the Governor-General appointed Alhaji (now Sir) Abubakar Tafawa Balewa to be the first Prime Minister of Nigeria. Some people think that it is odd that I retained the leadership of the Party and did not hand it to him on this occasion: they do not understand that the Premier of any Region is not in any way subordinate to the Prime Minister: our paths are, in fact, quite separate and our functions do not overlap: in the Regions the Prime Minister is only concerned with his Federal matters and not with Regional affairs. He is, of course, a welcome and an honoured guest.

Some say that I control the Federal Government from Kaduna: how would I do that? How can I control the opinions of the Federal Cabinet, made up as it is of men of varying outlooks and background? Obviously I can have no say in day-to-day matters.

The Government which he chose in Lagos was a 'national' Government and was made up of members of the three major parties: this lasted until the new General Election under the revised Constitution increasing the number of seats in the House (see above) in 1960.

At last we were empowered to open up into a proper Ministerial system. As you have seen, we had been working on a virtually skeleton cabinet, with members doubling offices, so that the whole thing was most unrealistic. We now expanded to twelve Ministers from the Assembly and four from the Chiefs, a pattern which has only changed slightly since then. They were as follows:

Premier	Alhaji Ahmadu, Sardauna of Sokoto
Finance	Alhaji Aliyu, Makama of Bida
Education	Alhaji Isa Kaita, Madawaki of Katsina
Local Government	M. Abdullahi Maikano Dutse
Health	Alhaji Ahman, Galadima of Pategi
Works	Mr George Uru Ohikere
Trade & Industry	Abba Muhammed Habib
Agriculture	M. Mustafa Monguno
Animal Health & Forestry	M. Abdullahi Danburam Jada
Land & Survey	M. Ibrahim Musa Gashash
Social Welfare	Mr Michael Audu Buba
Internal Affairs	M. Shehu Usman
Without Portfolio	Sir Abubakar, Sultan of Sokoto
,, ,,	Alhaji Muhammadu Sanusi, Emir of Kano
,, ,,	Alhaji Usman Nagogo, Emir of Katsina
,, ,,	Atoshi Agbumanu II, Aku Uka.

With these came another great change for, in the middle of September, Sir Bryan Sharwood-Smith left us on retirement, at the end of his five years in Government House and of thirty-six years in Nigeria. As you have seen I had known him for many years, but to many of my colleagues he was quite unknown. He had been brought up in the 'hard school' in Sokoto, though his first seven years were in what was, until recently, the Southern Cameroons. I believe that his heart was in Sokoto, as was the case with many British officers, and though he served in Niger, Zaria, and Kano, his real interests to the end were in Sokoto.

We felt, as I said in a speech in Executive Council at the time, 'sincere gratitude for guiding us through the early stages of the Ministerial system—the views expressed have by no means been unanimous, but Your Excellency has succeeded in leading us through our differences to an agreeable solution—Your Excellency has been a living and steadfast symbol of unity in this Region.'

Sir Bryan's energy and determination were startling at times, but he had to be supreme and could not efface himself. This was perhaps due, I think, to his deep (but unwarranted) suspicions of everyone, black or white, and the belief that he was best fitted to arrange or organise or deal with whatever might crop up. In fact, he was reluctant to delegate. Because of this, I think he found difficulty in working under the changing constitutions, each change giving us more rein and reducing the power of the Governor and his officers. Though he was a man of the old school, he was sufficiently intelligent to know that these changes must come and, though they could be slowed down (to some extent), they could not be diverted, let alone stopped: I realise that these constitutional advances were often against the grain and it is to his credit that he went as far as he did.

There were times when he almost pushed us to extremes, but we could not deny that he 'filled the bill' as Governor and that he carried his difficult job with dignity and without stinting himself. He was really born out of time, for he would have made a good Governor of the old type, the kind who was constitutionally responsible for all acts of his Government: the impact of parliamentary government was always taking him by surprise, or so it seemed to us. He was at his happiest on tour, shooting or riding, and talking to the people he met, whatever their type or class.

We all saw him off at the railway station on a hot morning. The train pulled out of the station with nerve-racking slowness and we turned away into a new era: we regretted his departure as a man, but as we passed through the arch in the station buildings, we felt that we were facing a new dawn in the east.

State House, Kaduna

CHAPTER 18

THE GOAL

THREE months later we were welcoming our new Governor, who will probably be the last one to be appointed from outside Nigeria. Sir Gawain Bell came from the Sudan and the Persian Gulf with a good knowledge of Arabic and of Muhammadan people. He was almost in every respect the opposite of Sir Bryan; as within eighteen months he had to change into a constitutional Governor, this was perhaps just as well. He came to us knowing nothing more about the country than he had read in books and papers: he came with an open mind: all the country was the same to him; and that was exactly what we wanted.

At an impressive ceremony at Lugard Hall he took his oath as Governor and promised to study all our problems with an impartial mind and to advise us with only the best for this country in view; this he has faithfully carried out to our considerable advantage. In my address I said:

... Your Excellency is new to us; we welcome the new counsel and advice that Your Excellency will bring to us.

In times when rapid changes are taking place in a country, affecting so vitally the economic, social and political life of the people, it is right and most acceptable to us that someone with the wide experience of Your Excellency should be appointed to the high office of Governor of this Region.

We respect and treasure all that is best in our ancient customs and traditions. We have a deep-rooted respect for our elders and our leaders. And we are a peace-loving people who seek unity, but not uniformity. We are convinced that in these guiding principles lies the whole future happiness and prosperity of the peoples of the Region.

Your Excellency's arrival falls at a most critical time in our lives. We are about to open a new chapter in our constitutional history.

It is difficult to forecast accurately the pattern that this chapter will take. So many factors are involved, both inside and outside the Region. We know, however, that we can rely on the good sense of the people to preserve the social and economic stability in the Region in which we take great pride and on which alone, we know, can progress with peace be achieved. We know too, Sir, that with your understanding and experience of problems of constitutional development and administration in other countries of the world, we can rely on a sympathetic understanding and continuous help from you in consolidating and furthering the progress which we have made to date.

It is necessary here, Sir, to make mention of one great factor on which our future so vitally depends. In our policy of Northernisation lies the only solution to the long-term problems of staffing and maintaining our government services. This Government has not discriminated, and will not discriminate, against any public servant because of his race, creed or place of origin. We insist, however, that the whole force of our government system is directed with the utmost vigour towards training men and women of Northern Nigeria origin to take their place in the permanent establishment of the Public Service of the Region. . . .

Between the two Governors we enjoyed a visit from the Princess Royal: she opened our new Queen Elizabeth College at Ilorin—a fine girls' secondary school—and was to have opened the new textile factory at Kaduna South but was unfortunately indisposed that afternoon and was unable to carry out this task in person. This was the first of our big industrial schemes. The factory then opened covered over six acres under one roof and was easily the biggest building in Nigeria at that time: its purpose was to spin and weave Nigerian cotton into baft. It has since then proved so successful that it has been nearly doubled in size and extra processes have been added to the original weaving. If justification for the Kaduna River Bridge were needed, here it was.

Politically at this time our biggest venture was the 'integration' of ministries. This rather peculiar phrase means the physical combination of the former government departments with the ministries. Thus the Ministers took complete charge of the departments through their Permanent Secretaries and the heads of departments became technical advisers. Before this time the latter had continued to run their own shows and post their own staffs, under the general policy control only of the Minister. This was perhaps not entirely unfortunate, since it formed a convenient pause in the movement towards self-government: swifter changes might have been detrimental. There was a good deal of 'muttering' in certain quarters: some of the Permanent Secretaries were not as tactful as they might have been during this change-over and some of the Ministers did not appreciate the human factors involved in so sweeping a dissolution of departmental authority. Fortunately, our only serious loss was that of the Director of Medical Services who, though an excellent man and one widely respected, could not stomach this change in status.

We took a good deal of credit in this matter, for we were hereby well ahead of the other Regions of the Federation, who had not thought of it, and of Ghana, where the departments continued as such for some time. Though the change pinched some people sharply, I am sure now that we were right to take the plunge when we did. To have delayed would have been of little advantage and would in fact have been of real disadvantage in training the Ministers and the Permanent Secretaries.

Three Commissions made their way across our view. The Fiscal one made a fresh attempt at dividing up our national revenue so that each Region would get a proper share. I could write a good deal about this, but it is highly technical and this is really no place for it. I cannot leave it, however, without saying that, much as we appreciated the difficulties confronting the Commission, we do not think that the answers provided were the most satisfactory possible: the Federation gets far too much of the cake. After all, the Regions are responsible for most of the development of the country and for the subsequent maintenance of the institutions and schemes so started, and that cannot be met from loans but must come from Revenue.

The Federal Delimitation Commission carried out its task of dividing the country into single-member constituencies, to agree with the new number of members agreed for the House of

Representatives, in a very reasonable way. There were, as was to be expected, some anomalies: some areas had too many people and some had much too few, but, bound as they were to follow administrative boundaries, this could not be helped. We were glad to see as a member, Farley Smith, who had retired from us as a Resident.

The most embarrassing Commission was the one on the Minorities. This wandered round the country listening patiently to scores upon scores of people who thought, for one reason or another, that their area should be carved out of the Region in which it then lay, claiming that they did not get a fair deal from the party in power in the Region.

There were three groups which made the most noise: two of these were in the other Regions and need not concern us, but the third was the group advocating the so-called 'Middle Belt' —a long slice of country running along both sides of the Rivers Niger and Benue, with an extension to cover the Plateau and southern Zaria. Apart from the fact that it would be physically difficult, if not impossible, to administer such a peculiarly shaped area, there was nothing to show that the various people making up this group would, in fact, agree amongst each other, if they found themselves involved in a new Region: it would be only too likely that further fragmentation would ensue fairly soon after such an arrangement had been made.

Further, we felt that, far from being neglected, the people of this area had much greater advantages than the people of the four extreme Northern Provinces: in schools, in hospitals, in roads, and other amenities the river people were well ahead of the semi-desert people and, a point which is often overlooked, having the greater proportion of educated people, the numbers of their men and women who are in Government service now is greatly in excess of those from other areas: this means that in a few years they will inevitably hold positions of seniority in this Region.

I have given this problem the closest consideration for years and am forced to the conclusion that there is nothing in it beyond the personal aggrandisement of its leaders and a desire to embarrass us. It is abundantly clear that the whole movement is inspired by our political opponents, who are doing their utmost to destroy the Northern Region and so reduce its membership in the House of Representatives. It must never be forgotten that almost the whole of the Region as it is today, and a great deal outside it, was ruled by my great-great-grandfather's family through their Lieutenants or by the great Shehus of Bornu: the only important exception is the Tiv area south of the Benue River. Curiously enough, their neighbours, the Jukons of Wukari, are so much part of the North that they, in a period of extraordinary activity, three times raided the far North and once captured the massive fortress of Kano itself and swept on and nearly took Katsina before their attack lost its impetus. If that does not imply close association with the rest of the Region, I do not know what does.

The Commission produced a very lengthy report, of which the Northern section occupied about one-third of its volume. They made some suggestions about the Eastern and Western Regions, which are only just being implemented, but agreed that the North should be left as it was. They did not accept the proposals put forward to constitute a Middle Belt Region and were against any interference with our boundaries. We therefore had no reason to complain of their findings. Since then the whole agitation has died away into a few infrequent rumblings on the horizons of the Tiv Division and the Birom country of the High Plateau.

The year 1958 is noteworthy in my mind for three things. Firstly, the Emir of Kano and I went at the request of the Federation to Khartoum and Jeddah to clear up Pilgrimage problems. We were pleased to find that there had been a great improvement in the past few years and that conditions for our people were much better. But there were outstanding points, of which our use of travel certificates instead of formal passports was the most important. We were well received in Jeddah and the King was most kind to us. In a very short time we had got what we wanted in every direction and were able to return to Nigeria with success.

Secondly, after our return we welcomed in Kaduna the Commission which we had set up to advise us on reform of our penal law and of the Courts. This Commission was quite novel. There were two eminent judges—the Chief Justice of the Sudan and a Judge of the Supreme Court of Pakistan—one British expert in Islamic Law, and three Nigerians from Bornu, Niger, and Kabba Provinces.

In the House I said:

... The Panel have been given wide terms of reference to examine the system of law at present in force in the North Region and to make recommendations as to how conflicts between those systems can be avoided. Further, the Panel have been asked to make any recommendations as to the reorganisation of the Courts and the judiciary in so far as this may be considered to be desirable. ...

Four months later I was able to present a White Paper to the Legislature giving the recommendations of this Panel. The matter is complex and elaborate, and I do not propose to go into details here but will content myself with some extracts from my speech on the motion moving the adoption of their report:

... Honourable Members will be aware that some of the features of the legal and judicial systems of the Region have provoked criticism not only in Nigeria, but in the United Kingdom and other parts of the world. It was borne in upon us that these legal and judicial reforms would have to be carried out if the self-governing Region was to fulfil its role in the Federation of Nigeria and command respect amongst the nations of the world.

The present legal system, instead of being a single one, is in fact three distinct systems operating side by side. There is Nigerian law, which is based upon the British model, there is Islamic law, and there is customary native law. A further complication consists in the fact that customary law is neither uniform nor codified.

I wish to impress upon the House the magnitude of the problem which we face. This Region comprises a great diversity of peoples having different customs and cultural backgrounds. In religion, about seven out of ten are Moslems. Among the non-Moslems, there are a substantial number of Christians and, in addition, there are many ethnic minorities who, rightly or wrongly, have felt apprehension lest, in the future, they should be overwhelmed by the Moslem majority. Finally, there are the commercial and industrial interests, mainly financed by capital brought into this country from abroad, which we are doing our best to encourage and foster.

There is nothing in the central recommendation of the Panel that a new Penal Code of criminal law should be introduced into the Region that is in any way contrary to the tenets of our religion. The new Code will be almost identical with those which have been in force for years in the Sudan and Pakistan and which have been proved perfectly acceptable to the millions of Moslems among the populations of those countries.

The introduction of a single criminal law, applicable all over the Region, will do more than anything else to reassure the non-Moslem minorities and to allay the apprehensions which they have felt in the past. . . .

Honourable Members will appreciate that our future prosperity as a Region will largely depend upon the confidence which the world at large places in the probity of our institutions and especially in the courts and the system of law which they administer. If there is any lack of confidence the result will inevitably be that we shall fail to obtain the foreign capital and investment which we need in order to expand our economy and develop our social services. . . .

I wish to say that the Government is in full agreement with the Panel in thinking that the complete regionalisation of the staff of native courts is premature. We consider that the measures now proposed, whereby provincial native courts will be established and will be staffed by servants of the Regional Government controlled by the Judicial Service Commission, represent an important but not an over-ambitious step forward. . . .

The nature of the law is a matter which affects every man, woman and child in this Region. Similarly, the structure of the courts and the quality of the men who sit in them are very closely bound up with the everyday lives of the people.

The systems then recommended have been introduced with great success: any doubts felt at the time in any quarter have been dispelled by the results of this initiative. It meant a great deal of work on the part of the Attorney-General, Hedley Marshall, and of his staff, and a massive quantity of printing in two languages: the training of the staff of the Courts and the enlightenment of the people on the matter demanded much time and energy and patience from many people.

The third matter was, naturally, even more important and far-reaching. This was the first steps to the attainment of our Regional self-government. During the short August Meeting of the Legislature we laid a White Paper on the Tables; this one gave a statement of the measures we required for the attainment of self-government. It followed in general the lines taken in the Eastern and Western Regions and set out in some detail the constitutional changes required to bring us to this desired state. It was necessary for this to be passed at that particular time, so that we could take the proposals with us to the next London Conference to be held at the end of September—yet another 'resumed' Conference.

It may be of interest to quote the words of the motion standing in my name:

Be it resolved that this House accepts the Government proposals contained in the Sessional Paper on self-government for the Northern Region and that a humble address be presented by the Government of the Region to Her Majesty praying that on March 15th, 1959, the Northern Region be granted self-government in respect of all the matters within the competence of the Regional Government.

In moving it I said:

I have often said, and often been criticised for saying, that we in the North would ask for self-government as soon as practicable. We now consider that self-government is practicable. We have made this decision in our own time and we are now ready to take on the grave and weighty responsibilities of self-government. We do so with joy in our hearts, and a determination to build a happier and more prosperous Region. . . .

The Public Service Commission remains independent of political or other influences. This will mean the Civil Service as a whole will remain free from political influence and that appointments and promotions will be based on the established Civil Service principles of merit and seniority. Members will note that there will be a local Civil Service which we hope will be staffed as soon as possible by our own trained Northerners. But we will still require, while our own Northerners are being educated and trained in sufficient numbers, expatriate civil servants. . . .

The section dealing with the Judiciary is of great importance; it is a well-tried tradition in most countries that the Judiciary should be independent of the Executive, but the history of many countries is full of records of clashes between the two; it is now generally recognised that the Judiciary must be free to interpret and apply the law with no interference from other sources. One thing stands out very clearly—that the Judiciary in these countries is protected from interference from political or other sources. I believe that the proposals in the Paper will go a long way towards maintaining the integrity and independence of our judges and magistrates. . . .

I do not need to stress the importance of the Audit Service; many Honourable Members will have met the Auditors in the course of their careers, and indeed have worked long hours answering their queries! Here again it is established practice in most countries that the Audit should be independent and free to ensure that public money is not being squandered or otherwise diverted to improper uses. . . .

The thought of self-government and its celebrations naturally fills our hearts and thoughts. We are rejoicing and we have every right to rejoice. But let no one think that after March 15th next year all our problems will disappear and that we shall have nothing to worry about. Such thoughts are false. Our problems and difficulties will still be with us. They will have to be solved and overcome, and it is we who will have to solve them.

I have heard that some people have a completely wrong idea of what self-government means. It does not mean that anyone may scramble for what he wants for himself. It does not mean that anyone will cast off all restraint and behave and speak in an irresponsible manner. It does not mean that those in authority need not be heeded. It does not mean that the laws need not be obeyed.

What does self-government mean then? It means that we must all work harder. We must all bear more responsibility.

Do not let anyone think that he will wake up on March 16th and find everything has changed overnight. It will not have changed. The Native Authorities will be there. The Civil Service will be there, containing, as now, both African and Expatriate civil servants who will, I hope, serve a self-governing Region as loyally in the future as they have served in the past.

I wish to address a special message to the Native Authorities; self-government is going to mean that Native Authorities will have to shoulder more and heavier responsibilities. It may be that some of them think they will be able to go their own way, ignoring the Regional Government. If this is so, I wish to dispel that illusion here and now. The Regional Government is in control and will remain in control; as I have said elsewhere, we wish each Native Authority to develop along its own lines and along the lines best suited to the people in its area, but it is the responsibility of Government to see that those lines are the right ones; the Government is responsible for law and order and for seeing that justice is administered, and the Government cannot, and will not, shelve this responsibility. . . .

Just before we went on our journey to London, the Prime Minister 'turned the first sod' of the great 400-mile railway extension to the northeast, to Bauchi, Gombe, and Maiduguri, a line which incidentally goes through his own home-town of Tafawa Balewa. This will cost at least £20m. and will take four or five years to complete. It will open up many thousands of square miles and will assist, we hope very greatly, in the economic development of the country. This is one of the big adventures that we have undertaken since we assumed any degree of responsibility; though it has been talked about and discussed since 1948, it was our Government which decided to go ahead with the scheme.

The London meeting I have mentioned followed the pattern of the others. There were very argumentative points and there were others, quite important ones, which slipped through with little comment. The most important matters for us were the grant of self-government to us as a Region and the grant of independence to Nigeria as a whole: for the first we had put forward the date of the 15th March, 1959, and for Independence we had all agreed on the 2nd April a year later, 1960. There were also a number of matters left over from the previous meetings which had to be cleared up, and the whole thing in the end kept us away from home for about six weeks.

Our own recommendations were accepted without much discussion, so was the Fiscal Commission's Report, but it was laid down clearly that the Lagos Town Council should take over certain obvious responsibilities from the Federal Government; this was a step in the right direction, but it did not go far enough.

We failed in our proposed date for Independence and in the end agreed with the British Government's suggestion of the 1st October, 1960: there were good reasons for this decision.

The report of the Minorities Commission took a whole week; the arguments were pressed with vigour; almost everyone had something to say about it and in the end the Commission's recommendations were accepted without any alteration! Our proposal to have Provincial Authorities of some kind, implying a degree of devolution of powers below the Regional level, together with the Eastern Region's scheme for Provincial Assemblies, helped to allay the fears of some of the groups.

The future of Lagos was raised again, but no alteration was accepted. On the other hand, we made some progress over the question of the police.

The real advance here was the creation of a Police Council made up of the Prime Minister and the Premiers, and the Chairman of the Police Service Commission, with the Inspector-General and Commissioners as advisers. To this Council was given authority over the provision, maintenance, and administration of the Police Force. As it was to be responsible for preparing the Estimates and any legislation, it had to be responsible for the adequacy of the Force and for its distribution and its reserves and training policy. But its tactical use, and operational powers over it, were restricted to the Inspector-General working under the direction of the Prime Minister.

Similarly the Regional Commissioners were to be responsible for all that went on in their Regional forces, subject to the Inspector-General, and in close liaison with the Regional Government. Thus the force belongs to all the four Governments, though it has an over-all Federal point of view and is paid for by the Federation.

Local Forces, whether Regional or Local Government, could be raised, but none should be in respect of an area larger than a Province. In addition to these points we agreed to the inclusion of sections on Human Rights in the next Constitution, to the methods to be followed on alteration of boundaries, and on amendments to the Constitution, to the organisation of the superior Courts, to the rules regarding Nigerian citizenship and other matters.

We had invited the Duke of Gloucester to come out for our own self-government celebrations in the following year, and now that we were certain of the dates we set to plan the arrangements. We chose the 15th March as it was the anniversary of the skirmish outside Sokoto between Lugard's troops and the Sultan's men. This, as you have seen, led to the overthrow of the Sokoto Empire and the true beginning of the British Protectorate in Northern Nigeria. Unfortunately, apt as this date was, it fell right in the middle of Ramadan and it would therefore be impossible, owing to the Fast, to hold any kind of festivities— quite apart from the heat, which would have been intense at that time of year.

We therefore decided to hold a brief formal handing-over ceremony on that date and concentrate our full festivities, in the Royal Presence, at a later date. This had to be either before or after the rains; after would, we thought, be too far away and so the only reasonable time, from the point of view of the weather and the temperature, would be in May. And that is when we held them.

On the 15th March, 1959, there was a brief ceremony on the balcony of Lugard Hall in which Sir Gawain Bell handed over the Government of the Northern Region to myself and my Ministers. There were two speeches and we dispersed. At that time we had no Regional Flag and there was no Nigerian Anthem, so we could give little outward or emotional display. Meetings were held in all Provincial centres and our speeches were read to the crowds that gathered at each place. We flew to Sokoto and held a brief ceremony on the outskirts of the town. There were fireworks everywhere in the evening.

On the other hand, we were determined to do all we could to make the May celebrations memorable in every way. We were determined that the world would have reason to take notice of this great event in our lives. We decided on a Durbar similar to that which greeted the Queen, but much larger and more impressive since it was greeting the newly emancipated Region: there was also a State meeting of the two Houses of the Legislature and we took advantage of the occasion to lay the foundation stone of the special Chamber for the House of Assembly and

223

to open our new Nurses' Preliminary Training School. To impress the day on the young we had a great pageant giving the history of education in Nigeria.

This was to be our party and we ran it entirely ourselves. Sir Gawain was most amiable and gave us helpful advice, but kept in the background. My Ministers and I had our proper place.

We sent out about two hundred invitations to heads and representatives of states associated with us and to officials who had served us well in the past. I must say here that throughout our self-government celebrations, both here in Kaduna and later in Lagos, we made a special point of including retired people who had helped us, and this was not confined to those of high rank; there was nothing vindictive or anti-anyone in our take-over of power. We were supremely happy and wanted those with whom we had been associated in the past, and who carried us so far along the path of self-government by their wise and appropriate guidance, to share our joy physically and on the spot.

For the Durbar we summoned 4,000 horses and 9,000 men as well as some thousands of children. The horsemen trekked in as they had done before and there were much the same arrangements for their welfare. Thirty thousand large grass mats (*zana*) and twenty thousand building poles were used for their camp. The children came by train and bus. There were no accidents and little illness and, as we have seen before, no crime. The security people had learnt their lesson from last time and the arrangements were much better than they had been then.

The large numbers involved in the march-past at the Durbar made it slower, and in the end it was half an hour behind schedule. The odd groups of entertainers—and almost every Province had something of the sort—tended to stay in front of the Royal dais and held up the steady march of the horsemen. But no one minded very much, as it was such a magnificent show and so spectacular.

The State dinner at Government House produced new problems of seating. In addition to their Royal Highnesses and

224

their staff, the guests included the Prime Minister, four Premiers (for Foncha was there too from the Southern Cameroons), the Secretary of State for the Colonies, the Governor-General, the Commander-in-Chief, the President of the House of Chiefs and the Speaker, the Chiefly Members of Executive Council and four Ministers of the Region; there might have been much confusion, but in fact everyone was satisfied and the dinner was excellent.

The Duke impressed us all with his dignity and consideration and the Duchess with her charm and kindness. The Duke felt the heat a good deal—though by our standards it was comparatively cool—but he was very good about it and seemed to enjoy the various displays and entertainments. One of the best of these was the Children's Pageant. This was carried out with great vigour and enthusiasm by children from schools all over the Region and gave the story of education from the arrival of the first missionaries on the banks of the Niger to the present day. Two episodes were presented as ballets and were brilliantly performed. The separate acts or scenes were all rehearsed in the various schools, hundreds of miles apart from each other, and were only 'brought together' two days before the show itself.

The great stands were half empty for the pageant: it seemed to me a pity that they were not full: many people, black and white, must have said to themselves, 'Oh, this is children's stuff: why bother to go?' They missed a very good and entertaining spectacle.

We had an exhibition at this time and it was the first time that anything on that scale had been attempted. We had had, of course, smaller efforts, but this was ambitious and covered not only a great deal of space but also a great many subjects. My only objection to exhibitions, and this applies to museums as well, is that they are very tiring to walk round and take a lot of time if one is going to understand and appreciate many of the exhibits.

Their Royal Highnesses left us, after a very successful visit, for Jos, where they had a short period of rest. The rest of their tour must have been very tiring, for they visited a good many places. We said goodbye to them a fortnight later in Kano, where hundreds of thousands turned out to honour our Royal guests. And so we celebrated our self-government and entered into our inheritance.

CHAPTER 19

THE CONCLUSION OF THE MATTER

I THINK that it is fitting to bring my narrative to an end with the grant to us of our long-sought self-government. It might be called the restoration of the pre-1900 era, modernised, polished, democratised, refined, but not out of recognition; reconstructed, but still within the same framework and on the same foundations; comprehensible by all and appreciated by all. The train, the car, the lorry, the aeroplane, the telephone, the hospital, the dispensary, the school, the college, the fertiliser, the hypodermic syringe have transformed Othman dan Fodio's world, but the basis is still there. The old loyalties, the old decencies, the old beliefs still hold the people of this varied Region together.

It is true, of course, that the Federation of Nigeria was not to receive complete and absolute independence for another eighteen months, but, though we formed part of the Federation, the latter had no control over our administration and internal affairs, and to the man in the street the Federation is a long way off and more than nebulous. Thus, what happened in Lagos was not of great consequence here in the North.

It was for this reason, and not to do her any despite, that the streets of Kaduna were not be-arched and be-flagged for the Princess Alexandra on her homeward visit from Lagos. We appreciated her visiting us and her consideration in doing so, but we wished to stress that this visit was incidental to her formal duties in Lagos, which she performed with such dignity.

This requires perhaps a little explanation, and there are other matters on which the reader may wish to have our general views: thus it seems to me that this is the place to do what I can to disentangle and remove any doubts that may still be lingering.

Some find our attitude to the Federation to be a little strange and to some it brings dismay and fear: maybe a disintegration of the Federation might arise from this state of mind? Earlier in this book you will have read of the 1953 crisis. From that you will realise that disintegration was a sharp possibility just then. Behind this there was a long story of bickering and dissatisfaction between the Provincial administrations (as the Regions were in the first place) and the Nigerian Government in Lagos. Both were artificial and foreign, until the last decade, and both were run and staffed by British officers.

This feeling (though foreign bred) naturally communicated itself to us, but I must say categorically that, once the train of constitutional government was set in motion, the British Administration did their best to promote good relations. It is quite untrue to say that it was their influence that has created the present rifts and disagreements. Nevertheless, we discovered that the old British bickerings were not without reason and that, unless you fought hard, the Regions would certainly be left out and the central government would get away with most of the cake.

That is why we are so keen on our Regional self-government. This is the only guarantee that the country will progress evenly all over, for *we* can spend the money we receive, and the money we raise, in the directions best suited to us. To show what I mean, you have only to consider the former backwardness of our educational and medical provision, compared with that of areas near Lagos. As I have suggested elsewhere, if it had not been for the Native Authorities the North would have been left completely standing in these and other important developments.

Eight years have passed from the last crisis and we see clearly now that Nigeria must stand as one and that, as things are, the existing external boundaries cannot readily be changed—nor can those of the Regions. But that does not necessarily bind us to the present *form* of Government at the Centre. Obviously we cannot be left with a vacuum there; for example, someone must look after foreign affairs, foreign trade, and defence, to name the more important: but who? As things are in the present constitution, the North has half the seats in the House of Representatives. My party might manage to capture these, but it is not very likely for the present to get any others: on the other hand, a sudden grouping of the Eastern and Western parties (with a few members from the North opposed to our party) might take power and so endanger the North.

This would, of course, be utterly disastrous. It might set back our programme of development ruinously: it would therefore force us to take measures to meet the need. What such measures would have to be is outside my reckoning at the moment, but God would provide a way. You can therefore see that the political future must rest on an agreeable give and take between the parties. So long as all respect the common purpose, all will be well.

And so, what about the future of the Emirs? You will have noticed in this book my insistence on the theme that the old Emirates were originally much more democratic than they were when the British left them, and that we have been doing our best since then to put things back; to ensure that the Chiefs are surrounded by a wide body of suitable councillors, mostly chosen by election, whose advice they *must* take.

We are also determined that they and their Administrations—and this, of course, applies also to the Conciliar Administrations —must accept the technical advice of the Regional Government and must at all times keep us in touch with the important events in their areas; that means especially anything likely to endanger the peace. Their areas must develop in step, each with each.

The immense prestige of their office is thus harnessed to the machine of modern progress and cannot, I am sure, fail to have a notable effect in bringing the country forward. To remove or endanger this prestige in *any way*, or even to remove any of their traditional trappings, would be to set the country back for years, and indeed, were such changes to be drastic, it might well need another Lugard to pull things together again. We must get away from the idea that they are effete, conservative, and diehard obstructionists: nothing could be farther from the truth. I agree that there are one or two very elderly chiefs who probably do not fully appreciate all that is being done for their territories, but even these have progressive councils and their successors will be men educated and brought up to modern ideas.

I have insisted throughout that we are working on the principles of democracy in this Region. I must here stress the word 'principles'. There are many Europeans who are strongly convinced that the only form of democracy which is democratic is that in use in their own country. We observe that these differ from each other: the USA form is utterly different from that found in Great Britain; the Italian is different from the French, and I understand that it differs within itself from decade to decade. But they all have a common denominator, the vote of the common man: what they vote for may vary from place to place, but in each country they have, from time to time, the (often abused) privilege of casting their vote in favour of a certain man or a certain policy.

We have now established the use throughout this country—so primitive in many ways—of the ballot box. In spite of anxious fears expressed in many quarters, its use has been successful (and in our own last election in this Region, overwhelmingly successful) and that will, I am sure, continue to be the case. The people so elected meet in open parliament and not only discuss the matters laid before them by the Government they have themselves chosen, but are at liberty to put forward their own motions and to raise their own questions, without fear or favour. The Government, on its side, is bound to make clear statements of its proposed policy and to be as convincing as is possible in debate. The opposition is at full liberty to say what it likes about these proposals or to produce alternatives.

The real control, however, over the Government, to my mind, comes from the 'tail' of the party. The Government must carry this tail with it or risk defeat. This is not a unique situation and obtains everywhere. In any group of people you are bound to have different opinions on the same subjects. And the more people you have, the more strongly will such differing opinions be held.

In the 1956 Assembly we had over one hundred members (and more later): their opinions were diverse on many matters, and the tail wagged tiresomely at times. There were two occasions on which the Government had to reconsider its proposals owing to opposition of this tail, strongly expressed on the floor of the House. It seems to me that even without an official Opposition at all, there would still be plenty of opposition within the party and more than enough to keep the Government on its toes.

There is a further point which is not everywhere appreciated. So far none of the 'political' parties have produced programmes markedly different from each other, in the sense that the British Conservative and Labour Parties have different policies. The reason is simple. In the old days, when the British were the 'government', all parties concentrated on demanding self-government to the exclusion of all else, and had no well-defined policy beyond a general desire for 'development'. Attacking the existing government was the main occupation, and it was not particularly difficult and did not demand any real thought. Naturally, when the British withdrew gradually, and the power passed, there was no one to attack and, as we had got self-government, there was nothing more to be said about it. So far no burning question has arisen on which we are likely to take sides strongly.

As things are there is no real reason to think that the Oppositions in the Regions are ever likely to be in a position, in the foreseeable future, to form a Government and this can only be irritating to them. So far there is nothing to indicate any likelihood of a 'landslide' in votes in favour of the Opposition parties, except possibly in the West. This produces, I think, a rather careless attitude of mind and a regrettable tendency to be unrealistic. This does not, of course, apply to the Federation where things are delicately balanced.

We already have a good deal of socialism and a degree of state-ownership—railways, telephones, radio and electricity, and so on—and hospitals and schools are mostly free or very cheap.

We might come to a showdown on nationalisation of mines (but the coal mines are already national property and always have been) or on the future of Chiefs. We would resist any interference with the tin mines, for it is a specialised trade and would be expensive for us to run; indeed, it is more than doubtful whether we would get as much profit from nationalised mines as we do, with no effort on our part, from royalties and fees of various kinds. But until something of the sort comes along, I don't think that there is much alternative to the present form of the parties. And so the possibilities of a real Opposition on the Westminster model are rather thin; as I have said, I do not think it matters very much.

We are often taken to task about votes for women. The Eastern and Western Regions have given their women the vote, and during the recent Cameroons plebiscite the United Nations insisted on them registering and voting. I agree that no particular harm has been done, though I must claim that no outstanding good has come of it. I daresay that we shall introduce it in the end here, but—and this is important—it is so contrary to the customs and feelings of the greater part of the men of this Region that I would be very loath to introduce it myself. The education of women must reach a far greater strength, and the numbers of properly educated women must be increased to many times the present, before the vote would be used to full advantage.

It would, of course, greatly strengthen our position as a party, for all the women would vote in the same direction as their menfolk and thus our support would be more than doubled by a stroke of the pen. But the unrest and trouble that would ensue would, I am convinced, be serious and widespread, and I would not like to have to deal with it in the present circumstances. Most of the men, and certainly all the older ones, would be quite incapable of understanding the need for such revolutionary change.

I understand that there are still countries in Europe in which the women have no vote and in which there is no intention of granting them one, so we are not alone in our attitude. Women have a great influence in this country and they will continue to use it for the right, and for stability and peace: to thrust them into the political arena at this stage in our development could only, I think, reduce this influence and would gain nothing for the public interest.

This point of view is not particularly due to prejudice nor to Islamic teaching, for there have been many important and influential women, as well as many highly educated and pious ones, in the history of Muhammadan countries. But we here simply have not reached the right stage for so great an innovation.

Another question which seems to worry people—but not me —is the possibility of a Republic being formed in Nigeria. There were a number of reasons which influenced us at the time of Independence to accept the idea of a 'Queen of Nigeria'. Firstly, we are used to Queens here: for example Daura, the oldest of the Hausa states, in ancient days had queens and, within comparatively recent times, Zaria had at least two: in fact the present town of Zaria was founded by one of them.

Secondly, kingship plays an important part in Islam. This is widely recognised here and it is on this basis that the Native Authorities hold their places in the minds of their people. Thirdly, were we to become a Republic, what sort of President would we have and who would he be?

On the other hand there is something fundamentally odd in still having the British Queen as our legal head: in the eyes of most Nigerians it made a mockery of Independence. Theoretically they were, of course, quite wrong, but from a practical point of view, both locally and in the eyes of the world, it seemed to us that a change should be made.

It must also be realised that not only was the Governor-General her representative, but the Regional Governors were also her direct representatives: they did not represent the Governor-General in the way that the old Lieutenant-Governors represented the Governor of Nigeria. We found too that, legally, important appointments, e.g., of Ambassadors, had to be referred direct to Her Majesty and so on. Further the Governor-General on state visits abroad was not a Head of State in the sense that our friend the President of Niger is a Head of State. By and large it seems best to fall in with the wishes of the majority and have a Republic. This will not diminish our respect and admiration for Queen Elizabeth as Head of the Commonwealth and she will always be a welcome guest.

The position of what form the Presidency would take and how the occupant is to be selected are paramount.

There are other matters of importance which are constantly being brought up and I cannot help feeling that their promoters are not entirely disinterested. For example, there is the matter of 'African unity'. While I agree that we should 'get together' with the other new African nations as much as we can, and on as many subjects as may be reasonable, I think that it is premature to plan any kind of 'unity' or 'united states'.

The main reasons in my opinion are that firstly, we, all of us, have far too much to do in our own countries, in the way of practical development and the advancement of the people, and have little time to spare to worry about what is going on elsewhere; secondly, few, if any, of us have enough staff for our own purposes and we have simply no staff available for any big inter-state organisation; and thirdly, any such organisation requires money: where would we get that from for such a purpose? But I am all for conferences and consultations and central organisations for research on the lines of our WAITR.[1] They are another matter and should be pursued with enthusiasm.

There is too the difficulty of language: Africa is roughly divided into those whose adopted language is English and those who use French. And in general the language of one is, so far, not taught in the schools of the others. Shortly perhaps it may be further confused, as we may have Portuguese territory and

[1] West African Institute for Trypanosomiasis Research, mostly paid for by Nigeria and Ghana.

some Spanish to make two other blocs and that will not make it any easier, small though they may be.

Further, their laws and customs and official habits and points of view are based on the same divergencies. It is, moreover, difficult at this stage to say how great are the differences between us in the West and the Africans of East Africa: there are obvious differences in background and political growth, but whether these differences go deeper, and whether we will be able to see eye to eye in practical matters with them, can only be solved through actual contact in the future.

Whatever may happen in the Pan-African field, I am convinced that our only sensible course is one of neutrality. You may ask how we can follow such a course and at the same time be the enthusiastic members of the Commonwealth that we are. The answer is that India manages to do it with considerable success and so can we. We must not find ourselves in such a position in international affairs that we should feel morally bound to support some policy which does not win our wholehearted or intellectual backing, or attract us by its obvious rightness.

The whole point of the Commonwealth is surely the flexibility of its organism and the independence of its members in arriving at their own conclusions, dictated as they must be by local conditions and the minds of the various electorates.

We must also make it clear that the word 'neutrality' means avoiding commitments in the sense in which we are using it. It does not have the special meaning, so often ascribed to it, of not taking part in hostilities. The line we would take, in the dreadful event of a general war breaking out, would be determined by the facts and incidents leading up to that war—that is, of course, if we had time to come to any conclusion before we were overwhelmed. It would be incorrect to assume that, as we are neutral in peace, we would also be neutral in war. Similarly, it would also be unwise to think that we would automatically follow the Commonwealth bloc into a war.

At this point I think I might properly mention the armed forces. The Nigeria Police comparatively are well below the establishments of European countries and we have fewer soldiers in proportion to population than most African states. It may be necessary before long to increase their numbers slightly, but the increase would not be large. We have no thoughts of aggression in any direction and there are no indications of any serious aggressive spirit on the part of our neighbours, so we have no need of large and powerful forces. We find the expense of maintaining the forces we have at present to be quite heavy enough as it is. Our revenue is not inexhaustible and we must give anxious thought to increases in recurrent commitments. Our social services must obviously have first call on what we have.

We are fully aware of the need for many years to come of skilled technical help in many directions of development in this country. For this help we will pay fair market prices and will give good conditions of service, of leave, and so on. But—and this is an essential point—any such help would be at our disposal and would carry out our wishes; while the experts can, and should, offer advice, they can in no sense control or direct, even by the subtle method of 'going slow'!

We have been under European direction for a long time and are under it no longer. We have had the greatest help from the British Administrative staff over the past years and we appreciate it profoundly, but the time for that has passed and we can no longer tolerate the admonitory finger of people we are paying: we will accept advice but not 'grave warnings' from anyone, including the representatives of the United Kingdom and of foreign powers. We notice a regrettable tendency in this direction in several quarters.

I am sure that such advice is actuated by pure motives, but I fear that even these are tinged with some self-interest, for can anyone carry out the simplest act which is not coloured by his own personal feelings? We are frequently warned about the dangers and horrors of Communism, of which we are fully aware and against which we are fully armed. Otherwise would not all the numerous people of ours who have been to Russia in recent years have embraced Communism? And that has not been the case. When we get an active Soviet Consulate in Kaduna, I am sure that we shall be severely lectured on the grave risks, and possibly even horrors, of capitalism.

So far what we want of capitalism is to get some of the capital flowing our way. We have so much to do here and so little money to do it with. We welcome foreign capital, provided we have the say in how it is to be employed and also an eventual option to buy it out in due course. The days have passed when foreigners can come into the country and take out great profits, leaving behind nothing more valuable than a few rotting tin sheds.

Further we are determined to manufacture as much as we can in this country from our own primary products. What greater folly can be imagined than to export our excellent hides to Europe and re-import them as shoes, at whatever fancy prices may be fixed by the European manufacturers and the middle-men and merchants? The wages of the workers and the profits of the industry must be kept within our own boundaries, wherever it is possible to do so.

*   *   *

I have taken you through my life, from the little waterside village of Rabah to the office of Premier of the Northern Region. All my days I have worked hard and I expect, and have expected, those associated with me to work just as hard. There is so much to be done to develop this country that sometimes it leaves me quite dismayed.

As I drive along the roads and see the simple villagers in their farms, I see what a lot there is to be done to raise the standard of these good people to what it should be. I see the men working in their farms with the same kind of hoe that their fathers and their grandfathers used before them: they are bent double over their work in the blazing sunshine and their wives and children come and help them. What can we do to make things easier?

—quite a lot, but it costs money. I see sick people who are dying because they are too far from medical help: that we can and will deal with, but it will take time and money. I see, in the dry season, poor water supplies and people paying for the water drawn from the deep wells: we have spent millions on water supply but must go on with the work steadily and without distraction. And so on and so on.

When I fly over the country I see the villages far away from the roads: white threads of bush paths join them; great rivers flood and cut them off, sometimes for weeks at a time; steep mountains lie across their paths. They are many miles from what we call civilisation: they are many miles from succour, if anything goes wrong. All this can be dealt with, but, as I have said, it will take money and time and boundless effort: there is no room here for the idle and the lazy man, whether at the bottom of the ladder or at the top. They say that Africans are idle and lazy, but those who say so have never seen our people working on their own farms or doing their innumerable jobs, whether in groups with others, or on their own and unsupervised. They would talk differently if they had.

They say that I am proud and impatient. I am certainly proud, for I have much to be proud of, and not the least the trust that God has given me to lift up our people from their primitive conditions into the light of life and the happiness of contentment. But I am not proud in the arrogant sense, for I know that I am merely an instrument carrying out God's will and pleasure.

I am impatient, and who would not be, with all that lies before me and the responsibilities that have been placed upon me? I have a thousand causes for impatience, but I am not impatient for myself or my family. All my time I give to my work: my life has been in the service of the State even from the time that I went to school; for there I was learning for the future and that future has caught up with me. A new future lies ahead, into which I go, trusting in God's eternal mercy.

238

LINEAGE

This table shows my descent on two sides of my family thus[1]:

THE HOLY PROPHET

FADIMATU

HASSAN

Muhammadu	Shehu Nizami
Isa	Sanusi
Muhammadu	Yasi
Taminu	Musa Jokolo
Ahmadu	Akabu
Baddalu	Iliyasu
Wardi	Abdussidayiwu
Yusha'u	Abdussamadu
Kusaiyu	Masirano
Khatimu	Haruna
Hurmuzu	Ayuba
Abdul Jabbari	Salihu
Abdullahi	Usumanu
Abi Hassan Shazali	Muh. Fodio
Ahmadu	SHEHU USUMAN DAN FODIO
Mubaraku	
Salihu	
Abdul Razzaki	
Alu Yanbu'u	
Muh. dan Sharif	
Muhammadu	
Hawa'u	
SHEHU USUMAN DAN FODIO	

[1] I have used the Hausa form of these names as it will thereby be the clearer to my readers in West Africa.

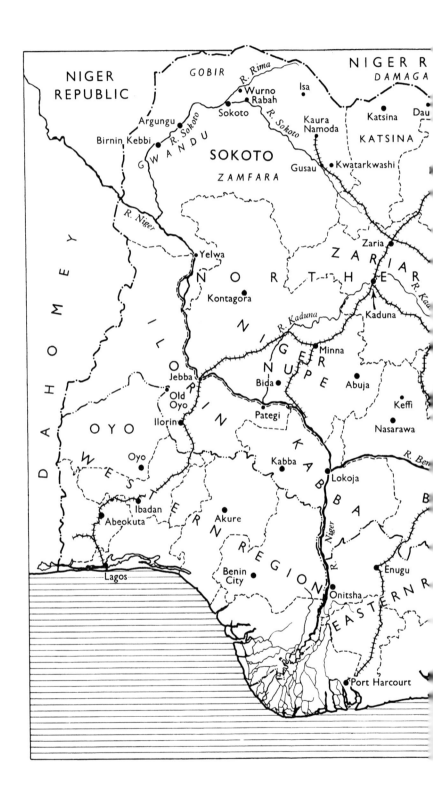

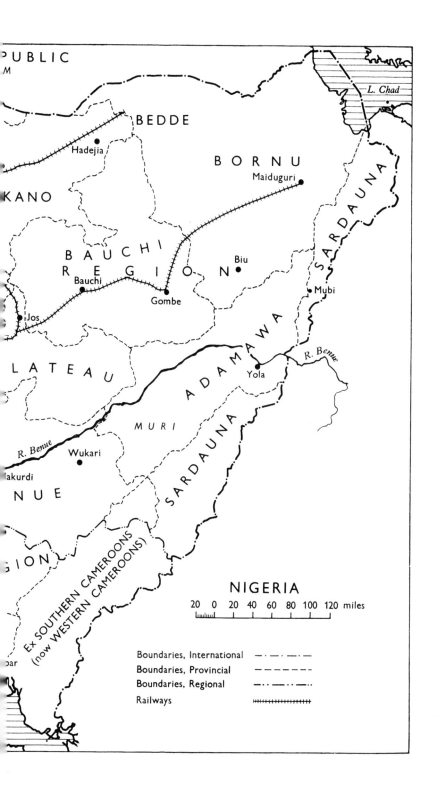

PUBLIC
M

L. Chad

BEDDE

Hadejia

KANO

BORNU

Maiduguri

BAUCHI

REGION

Bauchi

Biu

Gombe

Mubi

Jos

SARDAUNA

ADAMAWA

PLATEAU

R. Benue

Yola

MURI

R. Benue

Wukari

SARDAUNA

akurdi

NUE

GION

Ex SOUTHERN CAMEROONS
(now WESTERN CAMEROONS)

NIGERIA

20 0 20 40 60 80 100 120 miles

ar

Boundaries, International   — · — · — · —
Boundaries, Provincial   — — — — — —
Boundaries, Regional   — · · — · · — · ·
Railways   ++++++++++++++

INDEX

245

CPSIA information can be obtained at www.ICGtesting.com
Printed in the USA
BVOW05s1614200416

444940BV00001B/32/P

9 780521 092685